Demos Assembled

Demos Assembled

Democracy and the International Origins
of the Modern State, 1840–1880

STEPHEN W. SAWYER

The University of Chicago Press
Chicago and London

The University of Chicago Press, Chicago 60637
The University of Chicago Press, Ltd., London
© 2018 by The University of Chicago
Published 2018
Printed in the United States of America

27 26 25 24 23 22 21 20 19 18   1 2 3 4 5

ISBN-13: 978-0-226-54446-5 (cloth)
ISBN-13: 978-0-226-54463-2 (e-book)
DOI: https://doi.org/10.7208/chicago/9780226544632.001.0001

Library of Congress Cataloging-in-Publication Data

Names: Sawyer, Stephen W., 1974–author.
Title: Demos assembled : democracy and the international origins of the modern
    state, 1840–1880 / Stephen W. Sawyer.
Description: Chicago ; London : The University of Chicago Press, 2018. |
    Includes bibliographical references and index.
Identifiers: LCCN 2017033932 | ISBN 9780226544465 (cloth : alk. paper) |
    ISBN 9780226544632 (e-book)
Subjects: LCSH: State, The. | Democracy—United States. | Democracy—France.
Classification: LCC JC201 .S388 2018 | DDC 320.94409/034—dc23
LC record available at https://lccn.loc.gov/2017033932

♾ This paper meets the requirements of ANSI/NISO Z39.48–1992 (Permanence of Paper).

Contents

Acknowledgments

A history, like democracy, is a process. It is therefore as much a point of departure as an end. As we look around the world at the state of our contemporary democracies, as we search for perspective on our current political, social, and economic state, finding resources for coming to grips with our democratic condition seems as urgent as ever. This book seeks to contribute to this ongoing, indeed permanent, interrogation by exploring a period in the mid-nineteenth century, following the wave of revolutions in the late 1840s, when democracy was similarly triumphant and troubled.

This book has emerged through a practice of discussing, reading, researching, and writing in these unsettled times. While the past provides no answers for our current condition, the ideas in this book have formed in debate of the present and the historical through assembly and conference. Constructive exchange and the formation of judgments thus requires institutions as well as individuals.

In this regard, I must thank the American University of Paris for its support of academic research and dedication to an unprecedented and vital form of international teaching. A year as fellow with the Neubauer Collegium at the University of Chicago and a semester at the Institute for Historical Studies at the University of Texas–Austin also afforded me the time to complete an early version of this manuscript.

It would of course be impossible to thank all of the individuals who have engaged, contradicted, and encouraged the ideas in these pages, those who have bridged the gap between the formulations of the problem of our current crisis and the historical assembling of the democratic. But since writing is acting, just as thinking is representing, a thanks to my interlocutors is as essential as the commitment to uncovering the voices of the nineteenth century. Long discussions within our group on the transnational history of the nineteenth century including Nicolas Delalande, David Todd, François Jarrige, Blaise Wilfert, Rahul Markovits, Anne-Sophie Bruno, Manuel Covo, Jean-Numa Ducange, Pierre Singaravélou, and in particular Quentin Deluermoz, whose insightful comments on earlier drafts of chapters were invaluable, have been central to my thinking about how to approach nineteenth-century French history. The entire editorial team of the *Annales: Histoire, Sciences Sociales*, and in particular Etienne Anheim, Anne Simonin, Antoine Lilti, Jean-Yves Grenier, Romain Bertrand, Nicolas Barreyre, Laurent Thévenot, Camille Lefebvre, Guillaume Calafat, Vanessa Carn, Michael Werner, Antonella Romano, André Burgière, and Jacques Revel have provided an extraordinary set of interlocutors. The board of the *Tocqueville Review*, and in particular Françoise Melonio, Arthur Goldhammer, Olivier Zunz, Jennifer Merchant, Michel Forsé, Catherine Audard, and Laurence Duboys-Fresney, have been central to my rethinking of Tocqueville. Without Tim Mennel at the University of Chicago Press, Jo Ann Kiser's expert editing, and the anonymous reviewers of the manuscript, this book would not have been possible.

Regular discussions with Elisabeth Clemens and Gary Gerstle have given me deep new insights into the history and sociology of the state. I thank Jan Goldstein for her encouragement to pursue this project and her tremendous contributions to its development as editor of *JMH*. Pierre Rosanvallon has offered a consistent model of academic rigor and political engagement. I thank Stéphane Van Damme who has provided key insights into historical methodology and been a consistent source of support. I am also grateful to William Sewell, Claire Lemercier, Steve Pincus, Alexia Yates, Pauline Peretz, Aaron Hill, Olivier Cayla, Bernard Harcourt, Sung-eun Choi, Paul Godt, Serge Hurtig, Serge Audier, Daniel Steinmetz-Jenkins, and Iain Stewart. I offer a special thanks to my colleagues at AUP. Celeste Schenck's support has been invaluable. I thank Oliver Feltham, Peter Haegel, Jayson Harsin, Albert Wu, Michelle Kuo, Geoff Gilbert, and Miranda Spieler and the administrative staff, in particular Scott Sprenger, Christine Tomasek, and Brenda Torney, for their camaraderie and intellectual stimulation throughout the writing of this book.

Careful and thoughtful readers are as hard to find as they are invaluable. In this regard, I thank Michael Behrent and George Shulman, who gave me cherished comments in the last stages of the manuscript. Steven Englund provided precious insights to early versions of some of these chapters. Andrew Jainchill's comments on this manuscript were a model of insight and *justesse* that informed many of my ideas at every stage as the book took shape. I have cherished my discussions with Vincent Duclert, who is exemplary in his intellectual vitality and generosity. And I have had the great fortune of benefiting from Alain Chatriot's unrivaled precision, acumen, and friendship throughout this endeavor.

There are those whose impact runs so deep that one finds camaraderie and stimulation even in attempting to give expression to the most inextricable thought. More than books, such interlocutors give birth to projects. They sustain a life of engagement, interrogation, and fellowship. I have had the extraordinary opportunity to find two such colleagues and friends in Bill Novak and Jim Sparrow.

Nor does the democratic always respect a neat separation between public and the private. I thank the Wright family, William H. Sawyer, and my mother, Carol R. Dunn, who inspired my love of France and made it possible for me to become a historian just as she remains a constant source of encouragement. And stories can begin at unexpected times and in improbable places: Le Roc, with Genevieve, Jean-Pierre, and Claire, is the most solid ground one could imagine.

This book is dedicated to my wife, Cécile.

Problems of the Democratic State

The difficulty was in posing the terms of the problem in the way that they did, not re-solving it.
ALEXIS DE TOCQUEVILLE, *Rapport sur le livre de Macarel*[2]

The hypothesis presented makes possible a consistently empirical or *historical* treatment of the changes in political forms and arrangements, free from any overriding conceptual domination such as is inevitable when a "true" state is postulated.
JOHN DEWEY, *The Public and Its Problems*[3]

The escalation of an economic and depoliticized neoliberalism in the early twenty-first century introduced a paradox into our perceptions of the state in democracy. We witnessed a frightening expansion of state capacity in populist commitments to security, surveillance, militarized police forces, and mass imprisonment, as well as shadow and open military conflict across the world. At the same time, neoliberalism increasingly pinned the state into a corner, making it less responsive to the variety of forms of popular engagement it was supposed to serve. This book attempts to provide perspective on this tension through the historical investigation of an earlier, vital moment in the construction of modern democracy. It considers how from 1840 to 1880 the transition came about from a postrevolutionary political conception that was suspicious of the passions unleashed by democratic engagement and saw in the state the constant threat of tyranny—either absolutist or terrorist—to a new conception that embraced democracy as a positive means of building a collective order. In this sense, the book looks backward to look forward by focusing on a period when the democratization of postrevolutionary politics transformed state power. It was during this period, I argue, that key problems inherent in the modern democratic state became apparent.

An intense engagement with the democratic during this period brought forward a series of problems in which the power of the political community over itself—as described initially by early modern political thinkers—received one of its first systematic and lasting responses. Furthermore, these problems were posed in terms that remain compelling today and may best be grasped by the titles of the chapters of this book—*inequality, equality, emergency, necessity, exclusion,* and *terror*. Attempts to reckon with these problems revealed the extraordinary capacity and challenges of organizing society and the polity democratically, especially as they emerged at the crossroads of new possibilities for popular participation *and* the realities of brutal imperial practice, new modes of government oppression legitimized by emergency circumstances and necessity, gender and racial exclusion, and massive socioeconomic inequality. Thus, democracy in this period emerged not as a solution that would overcome all injustices if finally realized in its fullness. It provided a means of solving problems with all the profound failings such solutions could and did in some cases entail. Democracy became the very process of its self-institution through the constant danger that it could decompose into something else. In short, democracy emerged as a historical practice.

While we have learned a great deal about how the modern state slowly emerged from the early Renaissance through the seventeenth century, we still know relatively little about the next great act in the history of the concept: the birth and transformation of the modern *democratic state*. The door to a history of the democratic state has certainly not been entirely closed.[4] In his account of the emergence of the state from the late medieval through the early modern period, Quentin Skinner offered a glance when he explained that it was not "*our*" state to the extent that "they lacked the post-Enlightenment conception of the relationship between the nation and the State."[5] In spite of its extraordinary complexity, Skinner's avowal suggests one of the key traits of this new concept of the political order: it implied a new "relationship between the people, the ruler and the State." This new relationship was not without its own theorists in the early modern period. Given its first expression in the seventeenth century,[6] the notion received increasing attention during the Enlightenment, perhaps acquiring its canonical modern definition in Montesquieu, who noted, "When, in a republic, the people as a body have sovereign power, it is a *democracy*." In France, Jaucourt synthesized Montesquieu's position in the *Encyclopédie*: "Democracy is one of the basic forms of government in which the people as a body are sovereign." And Rousseau, for all of his importance in republican discourse, revealed himself to be one of the greatest students of democracy in the eighteenth century when he characterized it in the following terms: "The Sovereign may commit the charge of the government to the whole people or to the majority of the people, so that more citizens are magistrates than are mere private individuals. This form of government is called democracy."[7] These conceptions reveal a relatively clear—albeit very general—notion of the democratic in the eighteenth century. In its most basic form, democracy was a regime in which the people held sovereign power.

Since the eighteenth century, understanding exactly what this means has been a central feature of our political modernity. It was precisely this problem that gained steam in the 1840s and then came crashing in on post-1848 Europe as "democracy rose out of the audience, and quickly came to occupy center stage."[8] Pierre Rosanvallon has noted this moment as a key turning point in the longer history of modern democracy. "Semantic analysis, philosophical reflection, and political life," Rosanvallon argues about the period following 1848, "would henceforth delimit a single field—that of democracy understood as comprising both inquiry and experience." So as democracy became a structural current of modern politics, it was no longer just a question of creating a regime in which "the people" were sovereign. It also came to stand for a new method that challenged, as Rosanvallon concludes, "the division between the classical categories of understanding and action."[9]

Political idioms that took form during the early modern period were devilishly diverse, and conceptions of the democratic that followed were perhaps even more so. As a result, no more than classical republicanism or liberalism, modern democracy may not be told as the emergence of a single coherent discourse or line of reasoning. The lines above suggest, however, that the modern notion of the democratic state could be captured by the way it defined the origins of political power: as opposed to the monarchic or the aristocratic, the democratic reversed the origins of power from the prince or an elite few to the entirety (or some self-designated majority) of the political community. As a modern concern with democracy took hold across the second half of the nineteenth century, the complexities of such a notion came to the fore: democracy increasingly came to stand for a transformation in the relationship between the sources of power, modes of participation, and the institutions best able to channel them. The democratic came to be defined by the emergence of a social and political condition rooted in the self-government of an autonomous society. Democracy therefore emerged in this period as both social and political practice.

While few would contest that the political transformations in the Atlantic world from the late eighteenth through the nineteenth century were in some broad sense "democratic," political historiography of the late eighteenth and nineteenth centuries in recent decades has tended to focus on other, perhaps less murky terms to structure their analyses. Principal among the preferred frames of political analysis have been liberalism and republicanism. Indeed, it is striking how within the triptych of republicanism, liberalism, and democracy that shaped the birth of the state in the modern era, so much of the literature in political history and theory has focused on the battle between liberalism and republicanism. This is not to say that the notion of democracy has been ignored. To the contrary, the term is omnipresent. But such ubiquity is all the more troubling to the extent that it has been largely taken for granted and thus few have explicitly framed their studies as a "history of democracy."[10]

In France, the history of democracy has been overwhelmingly bound to the history of the Republic as well as the "failures" of French liberalism, and in many cases the tensions between them. The challenge with such conceptions is not so much that they are incorrect as that both approaches tend to exceptionalize the French case. This book turns in a different direction. Instead of looking to liberalism to save democracy from itself or reducing the history of democracy in France to its relationship to French republicanism, this approach seeks to recount the history of democracy from within the broader history of an international democratic turn. Indeed, between 1840 and 1880, there was an extraordinary recognition throughout western Europe and the Americas that democracy would play some role in organizing the social and political future of the modern state.[11] At the same time there emerged an extraordinary confusion over exactly what this tectonic shift toward the democratic actually meant. While this movement was deeply international, it was widely recognized both domestically and internationally that France had a particularly important role to play in its fashioning due to its past as an epicenter of the Enlightenment and popular revolution. The figures treated in this book participated in this discussion. They attempted to determine what the emergence of a modern democracy meant for France and beyond, even as they remained very critical of some of the forms democracy had and was currently taking.

What follows therefore explores the complexity of this democratic moment by pursuing a *critical democratic history*, in which the democratic question emerged by critiquing democracies that existed historically in the name of democracies alternatively defined.[12] To be clear, in this view criticizing historical forms of the democratic neither was, nor is, a critique of democracy as an *ideal*. Indeed, the approach outlined here suggests that for as little as we may ever know about a perfect democracy, there has been a tremendous amount of experience available for thinking about the very real historical forms democracy has taken in thought and practice. If democracy emerged during these years as a reflexive process of thinking about the plurality of democratic possibilities, then a thorough and realist understanding of the democratic also requires that it be studied from a pragmatic point of view, which necessarily entails a self-reflexive understanding of how democracy historically provided the grounds for a critique of itself. The figures discussed in this book pursued this path in the mid-nineteenth century by understanding political, social, and economic problems of their day to be the product of a specific and historically contingent experience of democratization, which also required a democratic response. And it is because these figures of the mid-nineteenth century elaborated and attacked these problems in this way that their work remains significant.

The Myth of French Statism

Since the postrevolutionary period, liberalism has posed a powerful paradigm for critiquing the democratic state in France and situating it within the history of political modernity. Collective authority in France and the European continent has been systematically opposed to the distinctive habits and methods of the British and US governments.[13] Building on a tradition of Anglo-American liberalism, we have been told, the United States and Britain constructed a regime committed to divided government, an independent civil society, and checked state power. The French, however, were the great supporters of a centralized state, born in the old regime and consolidated by a democratic revolution that rejected the limitations imposed by liberalism. Caught between the North Atlantic and its continental past and present, France's overbearing tradition of state was then a product of its innately conflictual relationship to liberalism, which gave free reign to a monistic vision of popular sovereignty and crippled the independence of civil society. Without the correctives of a legal, constitutional, and ethical liberal frame to soften the edges of popular rule, the state, even when it was democratic, tended necessarily toward absolutism, opening the door to an elephantine "strong" state running from the old regime to the present-day republic.[14] According to this line of reasoning, the liberal institutions of the United States and Britain in the nineteenth century effectively cut short the possibility of an inflated and invasive concept of sovereignty and power such as animated the continental European state.[15]

This opposition was perhaps most clearly articulated in Larry Siedentop's classic essay, "Two Liberal Traditions." Revising the notion that the French were bereft of a liberal tradition, he insisted upon a French liberalism that was at once more statist and more sociological than its Anglo-American counterpart. French liberals thus diverged from the ethical and legal liberalism of the Anglo-American tradition.[16] The idea of a distinct liberal tradition in France, which was somehow isolated from other liberal traditions in the nineteenth century and therefore opened the door to a more robust central state, has been a central pillar of European political thought up to the present.[17] And yet, the problem with reading the political history of France through the lens of a distinct French liberal tradition, as this book suggests, is that when many French liberals and committed republicans theorized the role of democracy in conceiving the state during the mid-nineteenth century, they did not merely turn back to a tradition of French liberal statism but also beyond their borders toward other democratizing polities like the United States and Britain. In other words, when posed as a problem of defining the specific relationship between the state and society, and ways of deploying democratic power, the idea of an exceptional "French" statist model—rooted in an exceptional liberal tradition—lacks explanatory power. Moreover, the opposition between the model of a "strong" French state, on the one hand, and Anglo-American weak states, on the other, in which liberalism was a means of limiting the power of an impersonal state apparatus "distinct from both ruler and ruled," appears similarly problematic.[18]

The insufficiency of these models has been at the center of historical work on the state over the last two decades.[19] Recent work has largely challenged the idea that France was somehow bereft of a liberal tradition or even that it was necessarily distinct from Anglo-American forms.[20] Indeed, the epiphanous and exceptional narrative of French liberalism has become increasingly problematic. It is insufficiently attentive to the depth of liberalism's historical roots in France and the Continent, its political heterogeneity, its relationships with contemporaneous liberalisms internationally, and, most importantly for this book, its structural engagement with the democratic.[21]

Central to uncovering the limits of these models has been a vast new revisionist history of the state and democracy in the United States and Britain.[22] We have, in recent decades, discovered the British state's "sinews of power" and its eighteenth-century "developmentalism," as well as an American "revolution in favor of government." We are also now familiar with an American "well-regulated society" and its "flexible capacity," which has thrown off the laissez-faire myth in favor of a history of America's "resilient" nineteenth-century state. We have also learned of how the British state waged such an effective battle against contagion in the nineteenth century and of the birth of US "warfare state" of the mid-twentieth century. Indeed, the history of American and British state-building has broken free of old oppositions between stateless and even anti-statist liberalism and a Weberian bureaucratic strong state model.[23] Moreover, in many cases, these histories have convincingly revised our traditional conceptions of effective and strong Continental states versus their weak Anglo-American liberal counterparts.

What merits attention then is that when we shift focus from the peculiarities of French liberalism or the exceptional features of French Republicanism to the problems confronted within the process of modern democracy, a new transnational history of the state emerges. Such a history pushes far beyond the narrow confines of French exceptionalism. Most importantly, we see that the middle decades of the nineteenth century discussed in this book have been portrayed as a watershed. In the United States, Max Edling has noted that the Civil War generated both a new role for the American state, making it possibly " 'the greatest military and naval Power in the world,' "[24] at the same time that "European observers were well aware that the war between the Union and the Confederacy would determine the future course of the North American continent."[25] This revolution of state power was not just legal, fiscal, and military but also intellectual. George Fredrickson's classic study of the United States during the Civil War has pointed to precisely such a transformation, noting that thought in this period inaugurated the shift away from "small producers to the organized, bureaucratized, and 'corporate' America," and concluding that there was "an elective affinity between certain modernizing attitudes encouraged by the social and economic developments of the mid-to-late nineteenth century and modes of thought directly inspired by the opportunities and necessities of the conflict."[26] What resulted, William Novak has noted, is that "the period from 1866 to 1932 was not just an 'age of reform' or a 'response to industrialism' or a 'search for order;' rather it was an era marked by the specific and unambiguous emergence of a new regime of American governance—a modern democratic state."[27]

This sea-change has also been identified in the British context. Recent work has highlighted the powerful role of a new democratic idiom in the Chartist movements of the 1830s and 1840s.[28] Joanna Innes and Mark Philp have similarly concluded that while in Britain "democracy was substantially discredited by the unfolding of the French Revolution," it was "reimagined entirely, from the 1820s through the 1840s, to make possible the shift that crystallized during the revolutionary wave of 1848."[29] This transformation had direct impact in thinking about the state, paradigmatically captured by the shift in J. S. Mill's thought. The transformative effects of industrialization, colonization, and racial violence as well as the women's movement all contributed to a transition in his thinking toward a new consideration of the powerful role of the state in democracy.[30] Mill's thinking on the state and democracy was influential enough that when Louis Blanc arrived in England in the wake of the 1848 Revolution, it was precisely in Mill's reconsideration of democracy and public power that he found the resources for reconsidering the democratic state: "The great thinker and honest man by the name of John Stuart Mill," wrote Blanc, provided him with the key to understanding "the question of *state intervention*, which is rightly of such great interest to us."[31]

Building on these new perspectives on the history of the nineteenth-century state in the United States and Britain, I seek to focus on a transformative moment in modern democracy. This moment took shape in the Enlightenment and found early expression in late eighteenth-century and nineteenth-century revolutions. It then underwent a sustained reflection across a wide range of the political spectrum in the middle decades of the nineteenth century, especially following 1848. This crucial change toward the idea of a democratic state deeply challenged the state's autonomy by rooting it in popular power and making it responsible for maintaining the conditions through which such popular power could be exercised. This transition profoundly transformed previously dominant modes of thinking civic life and popular participation in the polity, especially the classical republican paradigm inherited from the Renaissance and the liberalism inherited from the seventeenth and eighteenth centuries. It also however generated a new series of problems that needed to be rethought in a new democratic age. By the end of the nineteenth century, this democratic revolution of state introduced an extremely novel approach to questions new and old, marking a revolution in the history of modern society and politics.

Liberalism and the Problem of Democracy

For all of the theoretical interest in democracy during the Enlightenment, the tumult of the Atlantic revolutions of the late eighteenth and early nineteenth centuries unleashed a ravaging critique of democracy's supposed dangers. This was true to such an extent that "democracy" survived this revolutionary age as a dangerous challenge to civil government.[32] The response to the perils of the democratic was complex to say the least. Nonetheless, an overarching theme has emerged in studies of the eighteenth and early nineteenth centuries around the dangerous and liberticide power of absolutism on the one hand and the democratic excesses of the revolutionary state on the other. Among the central responses to this tradition was a renewed investment in liberalism which, we have learned, combatted the absolutist/terrorist tradition from a variety of perspectives. There were liberals who turned their backs on the state while remaining suspicious of democracy. Such a "liberalism against the state" focused on the individual subject as the primary source of political legitimacy in the modern age.[33] There was also an aristocratic liberalism informed simultaneously by a critique of absolutism and egalitarian democracy that focused on the "checking of central power."[34] A religiously informed liberalism (both Catholic and Protestant) took shape as well, seeking refuge in the collective power of the church instead of an ostensibly dangerous state.[35] And there were those who attempted a doctrinaire rationalism that adjoined liberalism and the state. They too did so, however, at the expense of democracy, outlining a parliamentary, undemocratic liberalism in which sovereignty was rooted in social reason captured by elites instead of popular will.[36] Finally, France also witnessed the birth of a liberal authoritarianism, which drew legitimacy "through restoring order on republican terms, though without abandoning constitutionalism all together."[37]

Even amidst this suspicion of the state and democracy, the liberal tradition did not remain entirely isolated from the dominant modes of thinking civic life inherited from the Renaissance and the Enlightenment. Building on the rich tradition of civic republicanism, some of the most important liberal thinkers of the early nineteenth century, including Madame de Staël, Benjamin Constant, and even Alexis de Tocqueville, infused their liberalism with an emphasis on politics while remaining extremely suspicious of notions of a democratic sovereignty. These "liberal republicans," as they have been called, tried to enrich the liberal emphasis on individual liberty and private life against the state through the political impulses of classical republicanism.[38]

Within this complex landscape, democracy nonetheless slowly reemerged as a means of conceptualizing a peculiarly modern form of power. In the 1820s and 1830s, the rise of a "Democratic" Party in the United States, the Reform Bill debates in Britain in 1831–32, and the ascent of a strong republican left after the 1830 Revolution in France gave new life to the idea of a modern democracy as it regained a positive—though still radical—valence.[39] In the years that followed, the idea of a modern "democratic" government picked up steam with the Chartists in Britain and the Republicans in France before exploding onto the European scene in 1848. Throughout the spring of 1848, cries for a democratic and socialist republic rang out next to Lamartine's democratic lyricism.

Of course, after 1848, the democratization of the state remained problematic, but the grounds on which the problem was posed began to shift.[40] During this period, a new form of liberal authoritarianism, or "democratic illiberalism," took root in France in the Second Empire, which turned its back almost entirely on former modes of political liberalism.[41] Once again, France seemed to be the avant-garde. This new regime creatively combined the techniques of the security state ("based on administrative surveillance and coercive policing")[42] used during the First Empire, as well as (though to a lesser degree) during the constitutional monarchies, a "modern" conception of democracy, and a more robust conception of the popular foundations of the state in which the emperor was an unmediated embodiment of popular sovereignty.

The fact that even a despotic regime like the Second Empire rooted its legitimacy in the democratic indicated the radical shift that 1848 introduced into the history of democracy. The period following the 1848 revolutions across Europe, the United States and beyond, toward the whole of the Americas, launched a transnational engagement and investigation of the meaning and forms that a modern democracy might take. Etienne Vacherot, professor for many of the brightest French minds in the years surrounding the Revolution of 1848, captured the spirit of the age in his book *Democracy* in 1860: "My country is not the only one gravitating toward democracy," he wrote; "this movement will be complete because it is the aim of modern civilization and the great revolution that is at work in all societies of the nineteenth century."[43] Indeed, from the postbellum-US, Latin American, and Mexican (often short-lived) experiments with liberal democracy, post–Reform Act Britain, Republican experiments in Spain, the new constitutionalism of Austria Hungary, and the unification of Italy and Germany, a new—if extremely diverse—wave of democratization came into view. There is no simple or straightforward way to characterize this widely varied (and of course, in many ways deeply problematic) engagement with democracy. For better and for worse, it was, however, rooted largely in a consideration of universal manhood suffrage and some form of parliamentary representative government—and, more importantly for this study, a growing sense that political authority, liberal or not, would be rooted in some form of popular approval.

In France, after the "democratic despotism" of the Second Empire, the Third Republic was endowed with a democratized liberal state that would preserve it for seventy years. The success of this liberal democratic state in France has been attributed to a synthesis between the latent influence of Orleanist doctrinaire rationalism—and thus the closing of the door on the tradition of liberal individualism of such figures as Tocqueville, Laboulaye, and Prévost-Paradol—and a new republicanism that shed its hardest Jacobin edges. That is, it was made possible through a return to a previous French form of liberalism of state and an amended republicanism.[44] And yet, an exploration of the intellectual and practical push beyond the somewhat claustrophobic walls of French borders opens new perspectives. The fact is that liberals such as Tocqueville, Laboulaye, Prévost-Paradol, and Thiers as well as a socialist democrat such as Louis Blanc and a radical democrat such as Jenny d'Héricourt elaborated new conceptions of the democratic by reconsidering the liberal suspicion of democracy and the state, challenging some of the basic tenets of classical republicanism to accommodate a modern democracy, or offering a radical theory of agonistic democracy and looking beyond the Hexagon.[45] Far from a marginal concern, democracy became an integral and fundamental part of building political modernity and was one of the most common elements animating international political thought and action. From across the political spectrum, the figures presented here participated in this international conversation on the foundations of a modern democratic polity by building on the French past as well as looking beyond the borders of the nation.[46] What came forward in response was a renewed investigation of the contours, legitimacy, and ambitions of modern democracy.

Such a vast transformation in modern western politics certainly did not go unnoticed in the years that followed. Writing just a few years later, in the heart of the Third Republic, historian Gabriel Hanotaux pondered the importance of this generation. Observing their originality, he suggested that the suspicion of democracy among liberals of the first half of the nineteenth century had been understandable in the wake of absolutism and the French Revolution, but that such distrust was left behind from the 1860s onward. Liberals of the 1860s, he insisted, embraced the positive possibilities of institutionalized forms of democratic life as "a new liberalism was born, at once democratic and parliamentary which attempted to realize the obscure ambitions of the country and its century."[47]

Hanotaux's contemporary, the philosopher Henry Michel, also embraced this silent revolution when he insisted that the terms of eighteenth-century individualism had "shifted gradually toward a meaning that was very different from its original understanding." This early idea, he argued, only found itself forced to formulate an opposition between the individual and the state by the circumstances of latent absolutism. "The error of our present," Michel insisted, "would be to continue this formula beyond the circumstances that forced its inception."[48] Indeed, for Michel individualism had not by nature been opposed to the state. It was the eighteenth-century reaction to the administrative monarchy and the Terror that had forced this opposition. But the generation of the 1850s and 1860s had revealed that individualism and the state were no longer opposed. "The high doctrine of the eighteenth century declined oddly enough across the nineteenth century, the question of the relationship between the individual and the state took on a new and preponderant importance."[49]

Just a few years later, on the other side of the Channel, L. T. Hobhouse demonstrated a startling awareness of the profound transformation of the modern state from an early modern to a modern form, highlighting a new integration of democracy and acceptance of the state across the mid-nineteenth century: "The modern State accordingly starts from the basis of an authoritarian order, and the protest against that order, a protest religious, political,

economic, social, and ethical, is the historic beginning of Liberalism. Thus
Liberalism appears at first as a criticism, sometimes even as a destructive and
revolutionary criticism." But, he argued, liberalism properly understood, or a
"new liberalism," had emerged that shifted this relationship profoundly: "The
modern State, as I shall show, goes far towards incorporating the elements of
Liberal principle."[50] This transformation, he insisted, "has its roots deep in the
necessities of Democracy."[51]

But it was perhaps the American John Dewey, writing just a few years later
in the interwar period, who provided one of the most compelling arguments
on the mid-nineteenth-century transformation of liberalism in his work *Liberalism and Social Action*. Pinpointing a dramatic international transformation in the 1850s–60s, he argued that a new liberalism had emerged, one that
recognized the need to transform radically conceptions of political and social
organization to meet the same ends liberalism had set for itself in the late
eighteenth and early nineteenth century. "Gradually, a change came over the
spirit and meaning of liberalism," Dewey argued, as it came "to be associated
with the use of governmental action." This new liberalism born of the 1860s
gained steam across the late nineteenth century, giving birth to the more robust liberalism of his generation. According to Dewey, this new liberalism
was so radically distinct from the liberalism of the late eighteenth and first
half of the nineteenth century that "the ends can now be achieved only by
reversal of the means to which early liberalism was committed."[52]

But while the pivotal role of this generation was widely recognized across
the North Atlantic and beyond well into the twentieth century, it was challenged amidst the cataclysm of totalitarianism and total war. Writing in the
same years as Dewey, in the midst of the mid-twentieth-century European
collapse, Friedrich Hayek recognized this transition; but instead of celebrating it, as Hanotaux, Michel, Hobhouse, Dewey, and many others had done, he
condemned it. Helping initiate the slow burial of this moment from historiographical and theoretical view, he called for the de-democratization of liberalism. This process, he opined, was the only logical response to the dangerous
primacy of the democratic through the state, which inevitably generated totalitarianism. Hayek therefore celebrated that European liberalism "is gradually being separated from the elements of French intellectualist democracy
which had overlaid many of its most valuable features." And this thanks to
the fact that "the totalitarian propensities of that French tradition come to be
more and more clearly seen."[53] Calling for a return to early nineteenth-century
liberalism to resurrect a strict opposition between individual liberty and
the state, he enlisted a rediscovered Tocqueville in his post-war neo-liberal
project. Tocqueville, in this context, as Carl Friedrich pointed out, became

"a patron saint of neoliberalism"[54]; under Hayek's pen, Tocqueville was being transformed from a thinker who had opened the door toward democratization of the state to a theorist who had foreseen the dangers of a political and economic serfdom that would surface if individual freedom were not preserved *against* the state encroachment inevitable in an untrammeled democracy.[55] By turning their backs on Tocqueville's *true* project, Hayek insisted, the generation under examination in this book had opened the road to serfdom, overturning the natural opposition between state, individual, and civil society.[56]

Hayek's, and many others', postwar liberal project in the twentieth century therefore cultivated an overwhelming emphasis on a specific reading of early nineteenth-century liberal skepticism of democracy. They emphasized the liberal reaction to the "excesses" of the post-Enlightenment modern democratic project, most notably de Staël, Constant, Guizot, and a certain reading of Tocqueville, among others.[57] Ira Katznelson highlighted precisely this point when he described the core group of postwar intellectuals who collectively "faced a task not unlike the one articulated by Madame de Staël after the Terror."[58] Liberal thinkers writing in the aftermath of the French Revolution and especially of the Terror offered a powerful resource in the mid-twentieth century for those who sought a new liberal response in the wake of a totalitarian *déroute* in Europe and the Soviet Union.[59] From this perspective, a return to postrevolutionary liberalism in the second half of the twentieth century was driven, at least in part, by a renewed suspicion of democracy and by positing a formal opposition between society and the state.

A shift in focus from the postrevolutionary generation of liberals to those of the period surrounding the 1860s is therefore emblematic of a shift within the history of the political itself—from a refutation of the revolutionary tradition to a reinvestigation of its democratic potential and power;[60] from a strict state/society divide to an informal and pragmatic democratic art of government that refused to cordon off the social from the political;[61] from a postrevolutionary liberal critique of democracy to a new investment in the power and shape of the modern demos.

The Political as Problem Solving

Recent decades have witnessed the emergence of a new historical interest in the possibilities of modern democracy. Since the late 1960s, a reinvented antitotalitarianism has helped push beyond a postwar Manichaeism between liberalism and socialism to reinvest the terrain of the democratic.[62] While the richness of this first-wave revival of interest in democracy precludes any facile summary, two overarching concerns may be noted: the dangerous and liberticide threat of totalitarianism and a stark suspicion of the bureaucratic as an institutionalized form of public power. One of the most important contributions of the new democratic conceptions during this period was therefore an insistence on the autonomy of the political and a critical approach to the state and its authoritarian potential.[63]

Though these works have been central to a "democratic renaissance" since the 1970s, they have overwhelmingly tended to look outside or beyond the state in their efforts to reassemble the demos. To this extent, they share a common trait with another—though otherwise very different—school of post-Marxist antitotalitarian historians. While these thinkers contributed to elaborating a philosophically informed history of the political, the central place of liberalism in these histories of democracy was patent. No doubt, some—like François Furet—used liberalism to cultivate a deep ambivalence about the democratic, almost systematically juxtaposing the liberal histories of the United States and Britain to the antiliberal democratic passions of France.[64] But at the same time, others have opened up the possibility of a history that places the complexities and possibilities of democracy and the state at its center.[65]

Within these approaches, the work of Pierre Rosanvallon has offered a promising point of departure for a democratic history of the political. Arguing for the structural role of conceptual aporias within democracy's history, he highlights the foundational character of its indeterminacy. "Far from corresponding," Rosanvallon argues, "to a simple practical uncertainty as to how to bring it about, democracy's unmoored meaning is due quite fundamentally to its essence."[66] In such a context, democratic politics becomes "the place where society works upon itself."[67] Rosanvallon has certainly not been entirely estranged from an interest in liberalism and its critique of the modern state. Indeed, two competing conceptions of the reflexive foundations of democratic indeterminacy may be found in Rosanvallon's work: one is indebted to his early interest in "auto-gestion" and a critique of centralized administrative authority. While it of course was not limited to liberalism, this critique of a "state-centered society" shared with the rediscovery of liberalism more broadly during this period an investment in the idea of liberating society against the state. Coming to terms with the implications of this liberal critique of the administrative state has been at the heart of much controversy amidst the rise of neoliberalism and the broader dismantling of a redistributive public power.

At the same time, however, there is another conception of democratic indeterminacy within Rosanvallon's work, one that is more indebted to his reading of Claude Lefort and a history of democracy.[68] This approach couples the redefinition of democratic sovereignty, marked by the disappearance of a personal power, with the positive construction of a state authority. "What I have referred to as the operation of negativity," Lefort argues, "is just as constitutive of a democratic space as the process that builds the state in the form of a custodial power." Thus, Lefort insists, just as democracy is rooted in the impossibility of entirely incarnating social power—that is a process of negativity—it necessarily engages in the positive construction of state as a form of "symbolic externality."[69] The two tendencies then have developed hand in hand. Rosanvallon's work on the history of democracy has consistently explored the tension generated by the "negative" evacuation of a personal power and the need to actively construct a new form of public authority within this democratic context.[70]

From this perspective, what is needed is a historical exploration of how democracy has been pursued as a social and political project through the state. This book attempts such an investigation by exploring a critical moment in the second half of the nineteenth century. It seeks to do so less by uncovering an ideological context or exploring the history of the democratic state as a symbolic order than as a practice of problem solving.[71] Assembling the demos thus refers to a specific (and therefore necessarily incomplete) historical moment when democracy came to be perceived as both the origin and solution to social and political problems of the day. In this sense, democracy during this period was far more than a fugitive moment, since its legacy far outstripped the mere compromises of institutional settlement.[72] Rather than a principle of legitimacy or set of institutions, the ubiquity of democratic discourse and practice by the mid-nineteenth century shifted democracy to a sustained engagement with a host of practical issues relating to the tasks and functioning of a modern state. Pushing far beyond the notion of a regime or constitution, democracy emerged as a range of problems with which modern polities must still grapple. It is because of the consistent challenge posed by the democratic that the state continuously reemerges as a central feature of democratic life.

To the extent that this book focuses on a historical process of democratic questioning, these chapters do not posit a reigning ideological context within which the ideas of these actors developed. To the contrary, it would be quite impossible to determine any singular context, any one problem, and any finite set of solutions that could have determined the problems inherent in the democratic. In this sense, it builds on Michel Foucault's methodological suggestion "that a given problematization is not an effect or consequence of a historical context or situation, but is an answer given by definite individuals."[73] By specifying the formulation of problems by specific individuals my aim is obviously not to offer a simple statement of caution or a call for a more sophisticated sociology of intellectual production, however helpful that may be. It is more generally an invitation to develop a method that is in keeping with the subject under study. In response, the democratic process of investigation discussed here is pragmatically defined. Such an approach reverses the methodological proposition inherent in the notion of "ideological context" by arguing (and perhaps at first counter-intuitively) that for the figures discussed here, the context emerged from the problem, not the reverse. In this sense, it expressly makes its own Lucien Febvre's outline of a history of problems—*l'histoire-problème*—and his observation that "no historian could ever adhere to a method" in which "political ideas were compartmentalized with the blow of a sharp knife severing the arteries and the nerves that gave them life."[74] Building on this proposition, I suggest that the formulation of specific problems in political and social organization contributed to positing this period as a new democratic moment.

Moreover, I have not chosen these problems, posed by these people at this time, because they exhaust the full set of possibilities of thinking about democracy or even because they are in any way entirely "representative" of the overarching problems of the period. From the perspective of this study, there would be something decidedly contradictory, or at the very least ironic, in trying to organize all of the voices discussed in this book into an overarching narrative about the "nature" of democracy in France or beyond. The ambition is at once humbler and, perhaps, more radical: I have assembled these problems and these attempts at solutions because they provide an inherently pluralist, and even conflictual, interpretation of what they—and we—have identified as the democratic. When I say "we," I am invoking both a temporal and an analytical position. Temporally, a historical pragmatism rooted in "our" concerns is of the present, if not presentist in the sense that Marc Bloch proposed understanding the past through the present.[75] The men and women discussed in this book speak to us because we have lived amidst the complexities, promises, and disappointments of the democratic. And in this sense, a reference to "our" understanding also analytically introduces, or at the very least recognizes, a certain freedom in the choice of the people, problems, and solutions studied.

I therefore attempt to trace this democratic moment through a *pragmatic history of the political*. While this is not the place for discussing all the methodological implications of such an approach, a brief summary of its broader contributions may be helpful for understanding the aims of this book. Such an approach does not look to isolate a reigning symbolic imagination or to explicitly define the political labels of "liberal," "socialist," "democrat," "republican," much less split any of these into distinct or stable subgroups. Symbolic architecture and semantic categorization are not a concern of this book or approach. Rather, such an approach examines the ways specific individuals attempted to manage particular problems in what they came to define as a new democratic age.[76]

Such a history necessarily recognizes that aporias may structure democratic life. But it attempts to restore the agency, the specificity, and the power (and therefore limitations) of the particular problem-solutions brought to bear. The political, in such an account, therefore does not transcend politics.[77] Rather, the distinction between the political and politics collapses because the problems and figures studied here show that uses of the political only emerge as forms of practice.[78] As a version of the political, democracy was not episodic; it was neither a passing thing nor a symbolic order distinct from practices, actors, or events.[79] The path back and forth between politics and the political remained (and remains) open, rooted in the situations, sources, and effects of any given enunciation, from its being employed (accurately or not) in a constitutional debate, stranded on a bookshelf, or discovered by a historian on the other side of the ocean more than one hundred years later.[80] Like the ideas presented here, such practices or enunciations may have been immediately forgotten, helped one solve a nagging immediate problem in the white heat of a revolutionary moment, swayed one's position on a given policy, or served later as a grocery list—the relationship between practices and the political, I suggest, may not be determined.

To this extent, there was not one scale, one way of shaping the relationship between ideas and practices, or one type of intellectual formation used to respond to these problems. The scale, ideas, practices, and variety of tools brought to bear on any of these problems were each unique to the extent that they were largely determined by the problem itself and how it was posed in the first place. For this reason, responses to these problems may not be isolated from the particular material, institutional, moral, or emotional concerns that generated them. In other words, "reality and its conscious treatment," as Reinhart Kosseleck has suggested, "are always related and mutually determined by one another without being entirely derivable from each other."[81] The problems of *inequality, equality, emergency, necessity, exclusion,* and *terror* were everyday experiences and therefore did not "exist" as discrete scientific or intellectual objects outside of the nagging persistence of problems that required a response. These individuals wrote histories, pamphlets, and newspaper articles, and spoke in legislative bodies, lecture halls, and private homes in order to constitute and respond to what they perceived to be the challenges and promises of a new democracy. More than paradigms, this exploration of the democratic engaged the political as problem solving.

Such a method is particularly useful for a history of democracy since the history of assembling the demos is necessarily a history of its undoing. A pragmatic history of democracy is by definition suspicious of establishing any determined formal relationship between ideas and facts, ideology and context, the symbolic and the real, or the political and politics since even the very nature of these relationships is matter for constant debate. As a social and political project, democracy remains profoundly undetermined even as it seeks solutions to the problems generated within it. To this extent, democracy is rooted not in a transcendent set of questions and potential answers but as a persistent set of untidy problems and partial solutions; that is, its history.

*

In what follows, I argue that Tocqueville set the stage for what it meant to place democracy at the center of the modern polity as early as the 1830s. The importance of Tocqueville has certainly not gone unnoticed. In historical and political thought, a dominantly liberal interpretation of Tocqueville has contributed to a number of recurrent features of contemporary political history. To name but a few, it has cemented American and French exceptionalisms, provided an unrivaled critique of the modern administrative state, and contributed to a historiographical and political interest in opposing civil society to the state. Thus any attempt to displace an exceptionalist history of the liberal critique of the state in favor of the possibilities of the democratic in modern political history necessarily passes through Tocqueville, which is where this book begins.

I argue that Tocqueville's liberal critique of the state in fact led him to an impasse as he recognized the necessity of a modern state power in a democratic age. The problem revealed itself as he confronted the fundamental issue of *inequality* in democracy. Indeed, this problem forced him to adjust a consistent undercurrent in his thought—which has dominated his reception since the 1950s—the tension between democratic equality as a social condition and individual liberty. Since alleviating socioeconomic inequality required political intervention, it challenged the passion for democratic equality within modern society at the same time that it introduced the idea that the state was, in some cases, essential for ensuring liberty. The idea that the state could ensure liberty contradicted, however, key tenets of his liberalism. Thus Tocqueville turned to democracy to investigate a positive administrative power, one rooted in a revised notion of the police powers and administrative law. It was through the rediscovery of these almost unlimited democratic administrative powers that Tocqueville was able to elaborate his concept of liberty at home and imperial domination in North Africa.

Tocqueville's concept of a democratic state gave him leverage in solving what he recognized as the need for a modern custodial power. Just as it simultaneously introduced a new set of questions, which remained those of his contemporaries and (to some extent, though on different terms) ours today. If democracy was not just a social condition of equality, but also an administrative one; that is, if modern equality also required administrative intervention to offset the dangers of a new "industrial aristocracy" then the question of the political foundations of the community of equals was posed anew. It required rethinking the nature of *equality* by moving beyond a theory of natural right and toward the question of how to determine in specifically political terms who was "equal" and who was not.[82] This question became particularly pressing on the scale of an empire governed by a "democratizing" metropole. Thus the problem of the democratic state raised the more fundamental question of where and on what grounds political equality started and stopped.

Tocqueville's positing of a democratic state power thus brought forward a broader question that troubled many of his contemporaries: the problem of how to set limits on the exceptional—in many ways unlimited—power that a people bound democratically brought to bear. Indeed, as they attempted to craft a democratic state, these figures consistently ran into the basic problematic that democracy does not require formal limits on what the number can and cannot do since it is, at least in principle, doing these things "to itself." As a result, the question of exception is a recurrent theme throughout this book.[83] To be sure, this problem did not exist outside of the precise forms it took in particular situations for particular individuals. Rather, it manifested itself pragmatically and therefore materialized as specific individuals posed the problem of the boundaries of the democratic state through the modes and extent of popular participation, the scope and range of activities it comprised, and the institutional and material means for effectively deploying such democratic power.

One of the most pervasive responses was to reconsider the legacy of liberal limits to state power first elaborated in the early modern period and then reinvented in the postrevolutionary era. Here Edouard Laboulaye (*emergency* powers) and Adolphe Thiers (*necessity*) both expounded the new capacities that a democratic state afforded them in special circumstances, while remaining trapped within a relatively thin conception of institutionalized popular political power. Once again, such a conception was particularly helpful in negotiating the complex relationship between nation and empire and went a long way in overcoming a liberal resistance to building a more robust and interventionist state. At the same time, however, this recognition of the power of democratic organization to bring order, coupled with a relatively thin conception of democratic institutions, has contributed to an ambiguous legacy through the twentieth century and up to the present day.

There was a more robust means of coming to terms with the exceptional powers of the democratic state: rethinking the very relationship between the individual and the collective. If the individual was not an abstract entity, but as some concluded, a fundamentally social being, then building a state in the service of the collective no longer emerged as a threat to liberty. To the contrary, it was the condition for the individual's liberation. Dedicating her book to her "friends" and "adversaries," Jenny d'Héricourt explored this approach through her adversarial conception of the political. Her emphasis on agonism however did not focus on establishing unity or homogeneity among friends within the polity but instead on the problem of individual distinction within society. Through her gender critique, she politicized what were perceived as even the most natural distinctions to develop a theory of the social individual. This individual was not bound to the political community through its homogeneity, but rather found in the state one means of cultivating a practice of individual distinction in society. From this perspective, the threat of *exclusion* was a threat to the state because it denied individual participation in the agonistic foundation of the political.

Finally, any attempt to define a robust democratic concept of the political confronted—then as now—the prodigious threat of the *Terror*, which is where the book ends. Looming since the Revolution, the Terror has raised the ultimate question of what unleashed democratic energies would or could do in the name of the people. The stakes of the challenge of the Terror and its ostensibly totalitarian potential to destroy the polity that created it has risen and fallen in step with the history of democracy itself, perhaps reaching its zenith in three key moments: the early years of the postrevolutionary period, the Second Empire, and then once again rising to new heights among anti-totalitarian thinkers of the postwar twentieth century. The discussion of the Terror presented here uncovers a perspective which very much differs from these critiques of democracy. I explore a history of thinking about the Terror within more robust conceptions of democracy and the state that emerged in the mid-nineteenth century. This tradition refused the idea of a "neutral" liberal state that has so saturated notions of what is possible within democratic rule and that has thrived in arguments on the Terror as a profoundly totalitarian expression. In particular, the chapter focuses on a conversation that has thus far remained buried between Louis Blanc, John Stuart Mill, Ralph Waldo Emerson, and Thomas Carlyle on the Terror and the nature of popular rule in a moment of institutional suspension. I suggest that a more robust history of democracy rooted in the social individual outlined the possibility of a regime that outstripped the mere realm of elections and an anemic view of institutions and formal constitutionalism. Instead it provided a concept of the political that preserved a commitment to democratic norms at the same time that it maintained the full potential of everyday governance in a democracy, including every citizen's decision to go along or contest, to comply or resist.

Together this long generation contributed to assembling the demos into a new collective order. Through them, and many others, liberalism was democratized in the 1850s and 1860s as it came to be associated with more robust governmental action. In the French case, this transformation was largely responsible for the creation of a liberal democratic (and imperial) state in the Third Republic, just as it paved the way for similarly democratized states in the US, Britain, and beyond. This democratization was profoundly international, but it took place in myriad ways through attempts by individuals to solve specific problems. Thus this story also breaks with any overarching or triumphalist narrative of democracy. In the case of Tocqueville and Prévost-Paradol, specific formulations of the problems of inequality and equality were both major steps to greater political liberty for some while they reinforced the possiblity of imperial violence for others. For Laboulaye and Thiers, democratizing liberalism through the problems of emergency and necessity proved essential to building a more robust state while introducing the dangerous problem of how and when executive power and government needed to desist. D'Héricourt and Blanc no doubt chose the most progressive and robust means of democratizing the state through the social individual. At the same time, their legacy was not always recognized and many of their goals were only very partially realized.

These earlier engagements may prove valuable for how they posed the question of the democratic state. At the same time, what follows reveals how their conceptions of the democratic provided tools that, in some cases, actually reinforced economic and gender inequality, racism, and imperialism. The organization of the book is designed to capture and contemplate this conflicted, critical legacy. The thinkers present here make clear that there are no straightforward answers in democracy's past for our present or future. What they do offer, however, is the means for understanding democracy as a historical practice. In this, they gesture toward the full complexity of posing the question of the democratic state, and therefore of problematizing the articulation between democracy and power. And from this perspective, recovering their history is meaningful as much for its profound insufficiencies as for its achievements.

1

INEQUALITY:
Alexis de Tocqueville and the Democratic
Foundations of a Modern Administrative Power

Throughout Europe . . . we will witness the birth of something that resembles our administrative law; for this law is no less than one of the new forms of the State in the
world. . . . It is the modern system.

ALEXIS DE TOCQUEVILLE, *Rapport sur Macarel*[1]

Perhaps no one in Europe or the Americas did more to push the democratic
question to the center of politics during this period than Alexis de Tocqueville.
John Stuart Mill captured his significance when he unabashedly stated that
Tocqueville's *Democracy in America* was "the first philosophical book ever
written on Democracy, as it manifests itself in modern society."[2] More than
a century and a half later at the outset of the twenty-first century, political
philosopher Sheldon Wolin opened his vast exploration of Tocqueville's work
stating that "*Democracy in America* represents the moment when democracy
first came into focus as the central subject of a political theory." Precocious
and genuinely international in its focus, Tocqueville's work convinced many
that democracy was the inevitable path of political modernity. The political
thought and practice of the decades that followed the publication of this work
shared in the attempt to work through the implications and contradictions
inherent in the democratic problem as presented by Tocqueville.[3] Thus, any
attempt to place democracy at the center of an international political history
of the state in the second half of the nineteenth century starts there.

Tocqueville's prominence for thinking the democratic reached new
heights in the second half of the twentieth century. Since his postwar rediscovery, his history and theory of democracy as a "social condition" has provided the foundations for one of the most long-standing and powerful liberal
critiques of modern democratic life. In particular, Tocqueville's account of
the inevitable push toward a democratic "equality of condition" within political modernity, we have learned, rendered state administrative institutions a
constant danger. From his celebration of an American weak state and vibrant
civil society in his *Democracy in America* to his critique of an overbearing

French statism in the *Old Regime and the French Revolution*, Tocqueville's account prophetically warned of the perils of a centralized administration in the modern world. He understood, we are told, that isolated individuals were produced by—and proportionately ill-equipped to resist—the omnipresent threat of a modern bureaucratic despotism designed to look after their every need. For Tocqueville, the democratic equality necessary for distant administrative institutions to govern threatened liberty, which therefore could only be ensured by vibrant civic associations opposed to the state. To be preserved in this age of mounting equality, the story thus concludes, liberty required a relentless critique of administrative power.

There is no doubt that this interpretation captures an essential, perhaps even one of *the* essential, lines of reasoning in Tocqueville's thought. Tocqueville did negotiate the tension between liberty and equality through a critique of state power. He did posit equality as a social condition. And he did think that liberty required an uncompromising recognition of the dangers of a centralized administration for modern liberty. Our awareness of these central strands of Tocqueville's thought reach far back into the politics of Tocqueville's rediscovery in the twentieth century, especially in the context of antitotalitarianism, the threat of communist socialism and liberal critiques of the welfare state.[4] Raymond Aron laid the cornerstone of Tocqueville's rediscovery when he explained "Tocqueville means by the term democracy, a social state and not a form of government."[5] Following in this tradition, François Furet similarly noted that this emphasis on democracy as a social form blinded him to the positive potential of the state: "He [Tocqueville] accumulated the political inconveniences of statification [*étatisation*], without yet presenting any of its practical advantages."[6] And Wolin's commanding intellectual biography states straightforwardly that for Tocqueville "the democratic state is a contradiction in terms."[7] Indeed, it is precisely as a liberal critic of democratic society—as opposed to a theorist or historian of democracy as a form of state—that Tocqueville's work has been so generative for more than a half century.[8]

And yet, there are some deep historical difficulties with such a reading of Tocqueville.

For one thing, it has entirely evacuated a positive conception of administrative power found throughout Tocqueville's work.[9] Of course, like his liberal contemporaries and predecessors, Tocqueville shared a suspicion of the absolutist and terrorist state. And yet, the state sat at the center of his preoccupations. As we know, on a personal level, Tocqueville spent the better part of the July Monarchy and the Second Republic in the state's service, not to mention his off-and-on lifetime engagement with local government in Normandy.

Tocqueville only turned his back on public service at the same time that many of his colleagues, like Thiers or Louis Blanc, did, as Louis-Napoleon consolidated power. Tocqueville spent the central years of his life as a "statesman." This alone might raise doubts about a profound antistatism in his work.

Beyond the personal, however, such an approach imposes a relatively limited conception of the state—largely borrowed from twentieth-century European social theory and sociology—back onto Tocqueville.[10] Of course Tocqueville conceived of the modern state as a bureaucratic hegemon invented by absolutism and then realized through the despotic tendency within postrevolutionary French political culture. However, alongside this institutional account, Tocqueville also told a history of different ways of deploying power, a diversity of technologies and objects around and through which regulatory capacities and administration were constituted. For Tocqueville, administrative power was not a thing nor some singular mechanism that operated in the same way in all times and all places. It did not have normative or monopolistic properties which lorded over all societies across time and space. Rather, administrative power contracted, expanded, structured, invented, and interacted with a variety of other governmental and social practices over the *longue durée*. In short, the state was a historical process.

There are, of course, some readings of Tocqueville that have signaled beyond a liberal critique of democracy and toward a history of the democratic state in his work. Writing at the turn of the twentieth century, Henry Michel's towering history of *The Idea of the State* in France placed Tocqueville squarely within the "Democratic School." Michel offered Tocqueville a privileged position within his history of the democratic state explaining that in opposition to the individualism inherited from eighteenth-century liberalism, Tocqueville provided a theory of "power that was designed precisely to give birth and maintain the solidarity between citizens."[11] A few decades later in the interwar period, Guido de Ruggiero also placed Tocqueville in the democratic camp, arguing that he had been an essential force in democratizing early nineteenth-century liberalism: "Tocqueville dispelled a nightmare by showing that the democratic idea, far from being a revolutionary aberration, stood upon the highway of French history."[12] Ruggiero concluded insisting that in Tocqueville's work "liberalism and the new form of democracy come to coincide in their formal conception of the State."[13]

What follows brings this line of thought under new light to understand how Tocqueville's work contributes to a history of the democratic state. The approach shifts from the overwhelming emphasis in Tocqueville's thought on the tendency toward democratic equality to an investigation of his perspective on the problem of inequality in democracy. Instead of the dominant harmonic line of equality, an investigation of the counterpoint of inequality reveals a profoundly revised vision of the relationship between democracy and the administrative state. In sum, while Tocqueville certainly elaborated a complex and devastating critique of certain modes of centralized administrative power in democracy, when his work is examined through the lens of inequality what appears is a consistent critique *and* recognition of the importance of administrative power and law in modern democratic regimes. In other words, Tocqueville cultivated an ambivalence toward public administration that at once recognized its potential dangers while maintaining the imperative of governing in a modern democratic regime.

What follows then does not so much seek to deny Tocqueville's usefulness as a critic of modern administration as to recover another central stream in his work which highlights his positive conception of administrative power. Indeed, across his oeuvre Tocqueville posed the question of how to cultivate an administration and public law that provided public services in the interest of the citizens within a democracy. From *Democracy in America* through *Old Regime and the French Revolution*, and especially in his lesser-known texts on administrative law, he widely recognized that public administration was necessary in modern democracy. Tocqueville therefore did elaborate a positive theory of the state that went beyond prophetic foreboding: one that could develop the infrastructural power and mechanisms necessary for the provision of services and goods in the public interest. He theorized a state in society: a state that did not so much dominate society as emanate from it. In so doing, he established a foundation upon which an entire generation of democratic thinkers would begin to reconsider the state.

The Problem of Democratic Inequality

For all of Tocqueville's exploration of the problem of democratic equality, he also showed a profound interest in new forms of economic and social inequality within modern democracy and industrial capitalism. Analyses of the problem of inequality can be found in many of Tocqueville's texts, large and small, as well as suggestions that this topic was of central importance to him and his conception of democracy. Reflecting upon his chapter on democracy's impact on salaries in *Democracy in America*, he revealed that "this chapter has the inconvenience of presenting on the most important questions of our time."[14] Later, noting the absolute centrality of inequality in one of his most important texts on the question, *Memorandum on Pauperism*, he explained: " 'I confess to you in all frankness that . . . this small piece of writing . . . touches on one of the most important questions in the modern world or even the most important."[15]

While Tocqueville remained convinced of the structural tendency toward equality as a social condition within modern democratic society, he was also convinced that, if left unchecked, modern capitalism in a democratic society would generate what he called "a new aristocracy." In *Memorandum on Pauperism*, written following his visit to England in the 1830s, Tocqueville clearly admitted that "industry has preserved a form of aristocracy in modern nations, just as all the institutions and mores to which aristocracy gave birth are disappearing."[16] Tocqueville's political economy was in effect pulled in two directions at once—toward an equality of condition on the one hand and a new form of modern inequality on the other.[17] Or as he stated in his discussion of the industrial proletariat in Volume II of his *Democracy in America*: "This state of dependence and misery in which one finds a portion of the industrial population is in fact exceptional and contrary to all that surrounds it."[18] This tension between a generalized tendency toward equality and the rise of sharper modes of inequality led him to investigate what may be titled *the problem of democratic inequality*.

In his discussion of salaries in the United States, Tocqueville insisted that rise in salary pay would continue the general trend toward equality in democracy: "As conditions become increasingly equal, salaries rise and as salaries rise, conditions become more equal." On the other hand, he pointed out, when observed from the perspective of inequality, "today a great and unfortunate exception can be seen." Recognizing the obvious asymmetry between owners and workers in industrial capitalism, Tocqueville noted, "The number of those who become entrepreneurs is very small. Being rare, they can easily join together and fix the wage that they like. . . . If they refuse work out of a common agreement: the master, who is wealthy, can easily wait without going into ruin until necessity forces them to return." As a result, the very structural tendencies that encouraged social equality simultaneously produced the possibility of meaner and more sinister forms of inequality.

While there had always been inequalities, the situation of the new industrial proletariat was very different from the poor farmers of the past, Tocqueville argued: "There is this great distinction between the rural and industrial proletariat, which is that the latter, independent of the usual miseries that may be brought on by a lack of foresight may also be endlessly exposed to the accidental woes that could not be anticipated and that do not threaten the former. And his chances are infinitely greater in industry as such than in agriculture because industry, as we shall see, is subject to crises that agriculture does not face. These unanticipated woes are born of commercial crises."[19] So there were both structural and contingent reasons for the rise of inequalities in modern democratic society. The problem was compounded, moreover, by the fact that intervention by a centralized administrative state was poorly placed to overcome the new kinds of inequality that emerged within it.

Indeed, according to Tocqueville, an administrative revolution, which had introduced a new technology of government since the seventeenth century was more suited to isolating individuals than actually helping them. In his sketch for Chapter XI in *Old Regime and the French Revolution*, "The Growing Inequality in Institutions and Mores Even While They Decline in Fact,"[20] Tocqueville clearly stated the paradoxical nature of modern inequality. "This idea seems paradoxical at first," he remarked. "If we go back multiple centuries . . . one finds what we called inequality to be far greater." But, he continued, "we see that the isolation of distinct classes that characterized the eighteenth century, did not yet exist." "In a word," Tocqueville continued, "while inequality existed, isolation did not."[21] It was the modern administrative state that was responsible for this new condition: it had at once generated a growing equality of condition and new levels of isolation, which made the forms of inequality of the modern era more difficult to manage and accept.

For Tocqueville, then, centralized state power was less a potential solution than a danger in such a context. Speaking of the role of tax collection in the attempt to reduce inequality, Tocqueville argued, "Taxes ceased to be shared in common and were focused exclusively at first and then principally on the person and the property of the *roturiers*, and while this inequality was ultimately smaller than it would be when the common taxes were later created by Louis XIV for the two classes, it still generated an indissoluble barrier, creating more marked and perceived differences between the two classes, and a more thorough isolation than had ever previously existed."[22] Instead of reducing inequality, Tocqueville argued, taxes had in fact exacerbated inequalities by reinforcing social barriers and isolation through increased dependence on administrative authority.[23] Similarly, the degradation of the condition of the French peasants and the greater inequality that befell them, for example, had only been increased by the reform of the *corvée* into a local tax. Tocqueville discusses the startling information, uncovered in the intendants' correspondence, that it became widely accepted that the roads would be paid for by the poorest, who used them the least.[24] From a historical perspective, the administrative state of the old regime had been at best ineffective and at worst responsible for generating the conditions for an irremediable inequality that marked the modern condition.

Hardly a linear process, the absolutist administrative state had generated the new social and political structures that simultaneously ensured a rise in equality of condition while also creating the possibilities for a new, more insidious form of inequality. In the realm of the administrative state, this paradox raised the problem of how to solve modern social and political problems like inequality democratically without reinforcing the state's nefarious tendencies to isolate and disempower individuals. The administrative state was ineffective, because it was responsible for cultivating individual and class isolation. Any remedy, in effect, ostensibly worsened the disease. The problem of democratic inequality then could be stated in the following terms: How could public authority respond to the tendency toward inequality without worsening the social atomization structurally produced by a central administrative power?

Histories of Administration

As many of Tocqueville's critics have pointed out, Tocqueville's critique of the administrative state seems entirely compatible with a classical liberal critique of social regulation.[25] "Any attempt to establish legal forms of charity on a permanent basis and give it an administrative form," Tocqueville notes, "creates a weak and lazy class."[26] This is of course not the only occasion when Tocqueville critiqued an administrative guarantee of socioeconomic equality. His positions in 1848, for example, when he showed a strong aversion to public welfare and the experience of the national workshops, have confirmed a general sense that Tocqueville's critique of a modern administrative state extends into all forms of modern social and economic welfare.

But much less noted have been claims Tocqueville makes in a very different, indeed opposite, direction. For example, in his *Memorandum on Pauperism*, he writes: "It is still possible to improve the comfort of those classes and render their individual woes less cruel and rarer. It is the duty of government and all good people to work toward this aim."[27] There are other places where he posits similar arguments. "There is a point at which so many faults and miseries of individuals compromise universal well-being and preventing the ruin of a private individual becomes at times a public affair."[28] Similarly, in his discussion of administration in New England he made a case for the importance of public authority: "All societies, in order to survive, are necessarily subject to some form of authority without which they fall into anarchy."[29]

Tocqueville developed this theme in his correspondence with John Stuart Mill just after the publication of the first volume of *Democracy in America* in 1835: "I do not know of one friend of democracy that has attempted to explain in such clear language the essential distinction between delegation and representation, nor one who has elaborated the political meaning of these two words. . . . For partisans of democracy, it is far less important to find the means for governing the people than choosing those most capable of governing and giving them a wide enough empire to guide their conduct as a whole and not the details of their acts nor the means of execution."[30] This comment provides a particularly important insight into Tocqueville's thinking on democratic power. Democratic thinkers, he argued, had focused overwhelmingly on the process of choosing representatives, emphasizing suffrage as the key component of democratic life, instead of on the kinds of powers to be delegated. Tocqueville considered this insufficient. He wanted to focus on elaborating the kinds of powers necessary and, thus, on giving the means to effectively govern in a democracy. For Tocqueville, the question of a democratic art of government had simply been ignored.

So, Tocqueville, it would appear, was convinced that public administration could only combat modern inequality at the expense of social freedom and, at the same time, he considered it the public authority's responsibility and called for a democratic art government. Tocqueville, it would seem, conceived administration as both the source of the malady *and* its potential cure. Was he simply contradicting himself?

No.

To come to terms with this ostensibly contradictory position, it is necessary to grasp a distinction within Tocqueville's history of democracy. Tocqueville insists that his critique of modern democracy is historical: "To develop my ideas, I must find a solid and continuous factual basis. I can only find that in writing history."[31] Only a historical understanding, he suggested, could provide a sufficiently robust portrait of democracy. Tocqueville recounted democracy's past as a distinction between a "social state" and a "political constitution."[32] A "social state" denotes the sociological and historical form of democratic modernity in which equality sweeps everything into its path. A "political constitution," however, makes reference to the history of political forms through which this "social state" may come into being. The "political constitution" does not merely develop over time; it is the historical and political conditions that contribute to making an "equality of condition" possible. For example, without the creation of the "*contrôleur général*" during the old regime, the local nobility would not have been reduced to a historical artifact and social equality would not have been consolidated.

It is in this way that the historical "political constitution" laid the groundwork for the modern democratic condition. New administrative processes were being put into place which pushed the bourgeoisie and peasants toward a "social state" of democratic equality—the situation was of course somewhat different in Tocqueville's account of the United States, where there was no aristocracy or peasantry to speak of and therefore the democratic condition of equality was achieved more fully. The changing political circumstances therefore established the groundwork for a movement toward democratic equality of condition: "The democratic revolution, which destroyed so many old-regime institutions, thus had to consolidate this one, and centralization took its place so naturally in the society which the democratic revolution formed, that we have easily been able to think it one of the new society's own works."[33]

Obviously the historical interpretation presented by the Revolution of itself—that it was a complete break with the past—was insufficient from this perspective. The emergence of equality (and inequality) could therefore only be understood by uncovering the history of political constructions that ensured democratic forms of social equality, even if they were not themselves democratic. Reading democracy critically—that is reading it against itself—was then a precondition for its sociological and political understanding. Only a history of this sort, Tocqueville argued, could explain how a democratic revolution emerged out of an absolutist administration. Tocqueville provides us then with a perspective from which we may read the history of democracy. "One sees that history is an art gallery where there are few originals and many copies."[34] The past deceives; history uncovers.

In a letter to Gustav de Beaumont dated December 26, 1851, as he began preparations for the *Old Regime and the French Revolution*, Tocqueville referred to the history he hoped to write in the following terms: "It must be contemporary and provide me with the means to mix facts and ideas, the philosophy of history and history itself [*l'histoire même*]. For me, these are the conditions of the problem."[35] Solving contemporary problems historically, then, requires mixing "facts" and "ideas," which he also presents as "a philosophy of history" and "history itself." Tocqueville accepts, in other words, that the history of democracy is at once the history of an idea and the history of facts; that there is a philosophy which pertains to certain "institutions" or "political constitutions" and interacts with, to the point of becoming one with, the actual facts or "history itself."

The examples of "history itself" are numerous. In the old regime they are the innovations of public administration, the central strut of political modernity without which equality of condition and its attendant forms of isolation cannot be grasped. Tocqueville portrays this administration as a "hidden illness" "that is common to all, whatever the form of their constitution; whether it was aristocratic or democratic."[36] It was precisely this illness that prepared the path for postrevolutionary democracy: "In the eighteenth century," Tocqueville explains, "public administration was already, as we shall see in this book, very centralized, very powerful and prodigiously active." And it is here, Tocqueville describes, that "everywhere I found the roots of present society deeply implanted in the past. The closer I got to 1789, the more I saw the spirit which made the Revolution sprout and grow."[37] Up to this point, we are following a Tocquevillian story that sounds very familiar—the modern administrative state opened the door to a new kind of despotism which rendered the people unimaginative, lazy, and jealous.

And yet, it would seem that there is another side to the administrative story in Tocqueville's work. On a number of occasions, Tocqueville discusses a very different administrative form, which still existed at the moment of the Revolution in spite of almost two centuries of absolutist administrative innovation: "When the Revolution took place, almost none of the old administrative edifice of France had been destroyed; another one had, so to speak, been built within it [en sous-œuvre]."[38] Throughout the Old Regime and the French Revolution, Tocqueville describes the displacement of this previous mode of administration, what he refers to as the "debris of old powers."[39] There were then two modes of administrative power—one that was almost defeated and another growing in strength—existing side by side on the eve of the revolution.

The history of administrative power in Tocqueville's work is characterized by the coexistence of these two historical forms of administrative power. "Under the old monarchy, there were only ever two ways of administrating," Tocqueville argues, pointing toward administration through assemblies or by a single appointed official. The former was traditionally used to govern cities, and, as Tocqueville points out, "the assembly not only governed and oversaw the administration, but administrated as well."[40] Tocqueville discusses these two kinds of administration and their histories throughout the old regime, without ever clearly giving them distinct names. He does however provide the means for identifying them; let us refer to these two modes of administrative power under the titles *local police regulation* and *central state administration*. Local police regulation was the earlier form of governing power, inherited from the medieval period, which was slowly being displaced by the new absolutist administrative apparatus that prepared the revolution designed to "abolish the political institutions that had, for many centuries, reigned without rival." Local police regulation, however, had not entirely disappeared: "In France, even in the eighteenth century, there are still a few vestiges," he writes.[41] Indeed, in some places he suggests that the competition—and incompatibility—between these two administrative forms contributed to the Revolution.[42]

Of course, as we know, absolutist central administration introduced a form of equality that would ultimately prepare the foundation for the democratic revolution. But, surprisingly, Tocqueville also suggests that earlier forms of local police regulation contained a democratic mode of governance. "Louis XI restrained municipal liberties because their democratic nature frightened him; Louis XIV destroyed them without fear."[43] Tocqueville makes this point on a number of occasions: "During the middle ages," he explains, "inhabitants administered themselves democratically . . . even in eighteenth-century France one could still find traces."[44] Hints of this previous democratic administration could be found everywhere: "Up through the end of the seventeenth century one can still find [cities] that continue to form little democratic republics." And in some cases, it continued even up to 1789: "Until the Revolution, rural parishes in France conserved within their government something of this democratic nature." This previous democratic tendency of local police regulation, however, was distinct from the modern democratic equality of condition being prepared by the central administration, since its power had been largely dismantled by the new central administration: "The democratic assembly could easily express its wishes but it could no longer enact its will." Tocqueville's history of administration and its relationship to democracy is, in fact, double.

What was this older regulatory power, this old administrative edifice, that Tocqueville introduces into the historical picture of democracy? Tocqueville provided a fairly clear analysis of his conception of this form of public authority. He defined the possibility for effective public intervention along three essential lines. First, as he insisted on numerous occasions, this public authority was not an autonomous territorial administrative apparatus; for, in keeping with the chiastic nature of modern democratic inequality, the construction of any permanent large-scale administrative structure would necessarily increase equality, but with it servitude and atomization and therefore create a class of poor that were without social resources and unable to respond to periodic crises of industrial capitalism that increased inequality. But while it was necessary to avoid the construction of a habitual administrative apparatus, it was still necessary to have a public authority that *intervened regularly* into the daily lives of citizens, even down to the minutest detail.

The notes to his chapter on New England administration in *Democracy in America* reveal a kind of fascination with the effective regulation of daily life in New England. "Observe the Town Officer," remarked Tocqueville, adding the extraordinary display of administrators in the smallest county, "Select men, Assessors, Collectors, Schools, Surveyors of highways." Amidst this list of administrators, what struck Tocqueville was not their incapacity to act, but their extraordinary penetration: "Law descends into the minutest details," noted Tocqueville. "It determines both the principles and the means of their application; it encloses the secondary bodies and their administrators in a multitude of obligations tightly and rigorously defined."[45] He then provided a series of examples: "The State forbids traveling on Sundays without motive . . . the selectmen authorize the construction of sewers, designate places for building slaughterhouses, and where it is acceptable to build certain types of commerce that may be harmful for the neighborhood."[46]

So, as central as Tocqueville's critique of administration was, it did not, by any stretch, lead to a condemnation of intervention on behalf of public authority as a whole. Tocqueville's argument was as far as one could imagine from a laissez-faire liberal critique of all public authority—it was a recognition of the capacity for regular public action in a potentially thriving democratic regime.

Second, this intervention of public authority was driven by necessity. That is, it needed to be able to intervene in moments of emergency or crisis in the public interest. This was particularly the case in the context of pauperism: "I recognize not only the utility, but the necessity of public charity applied to inevitable dangers . . . ; I further insist on its momentary utility in times of public calamity." And then, highlighting the importance of state intervention in these cases, he writes: "The alms of the State are in such cases as instantaneous, unpredictable and passing as the harm itself."[47] The ambition of public authority could not be to prevent the possibility of poverty, but to act effectively and immediately when necessity called. Finally, central to Tocqueville's conception of the public authority in the 1830s was that it could not operate according to the logic of creating a sustained system of poor relief. Instead, this model of public intervention had a larger, more ephemeral goal—it helped maintain and regulate public welfare. "This simple exposé speaks for itself," noted Tocqueville in his essay on pauperism; it is "in the interest of order and public morals."

So how might one explain the apparent paradox between Tocqueville's critique of administrative intervention, on the one hand, and his interest in this capacious mode of public interference into the most everyday and exceptional features of modern democratic life, on the other? Indeed, this power that descended into the minutest details of the everyday, managed necessity and crisis, and regulated public morality without constructing a modern administrative apparatus formed a central strut of administrative history reaching back into the Middle Ages, the police powers.

Tocqueville and the Police Powers

In recent decades, we have learned a great deal about the importance of the police powers in early modern and modern governance.[48] And yet few, if any, analyses of Tocqueville have focused on his conception of this capacious administrative technology. The overwhelming tendency among those who have characterized Tocqueville as a liberal critic of democracy and the state has been to suggest that his interest in older forms of municipal governance was part of a broader critique of administrative centralization. It was therefore, we have learned, a call for decentralization. While there is no doubt that Tocqueville was also a proponent of decentralization, and that the police powers as they developed in the medieval and early modern period largely operated on the local scale, the problem with understanding this approach merely as a call for decentralization is that it denies that the police powers, in general, and specifically in the work of Tocqueville, were not merely about giving less power to the center. The regulatory police powers and centralized administration are distinct technologies of governance.

Tocqueville's histories of local regulatory powers and centralized administration provide an account of the interaction between these two technologies of power. For Tocqueville, local regulatory police powers were a distinct technique for solving public problems—such as inequality—as opposed to creating an overarching state apparatus—that generated an equality of condition to more effectively govern. They also each had their own distinct histories. The police emerged out of the late medieval conception of "community or association that is governed by a public authority." Centralized administration, however, was a technology that emerged during the seventeenth century to preserve the interest of the state both within and with regards to its neighbors.[49] The police powers then did not simply evolve into a centralized administration, in Tocqueville's account. Rather, local regulatory police was a distinct mode of governance that differed fundamentally from the territorial generalized administrative apparatus born by absolutism.[50]

Throughout the early modern period and up to the final years of the old regime, police and central administration confronted one another without ever fully merging. "The bodies of justice conserved the right to establish police regulations [règlements de police] and often used this right; but these regulations were only applicable on one portion of the territory, and, most often, only in one place. The [king's] council could always break them, and did so consistently. . . . The number of regulations, or as was said at that time edicts [arrêts] of the council, was immense and it grew incessantly as they approached the Revolution."[51] So while the police powers continued to provide a potentially effective means of solving public problems, their effectiveness was limited because they remained local. The police powers treated specific problems and situations without any capacity or intention of being scaled up to the territorial level at the same time that the king's council and the centralized administration "made general regulations for the entire kingdom every day."[52]

The technology of the police powers differed from centralized administration not simply in its scale, but also in the way it constructed the object to be administered. It was a means of solving specific problems as they presented themselves instead of attempting to create a general structure imposed from above.[53] Capturing the full powers of the "police" in a democratic context, Etienne Vacherot,[54] contemporary of Tocqueville, influential philosopher and an intellectual founder of the Third Republic, wrote in his *Democracy* (1860) just a few years after the publication of Tocqueville's *Old Regime*:

> The police, in its specific meaning, covers simply the general security services. In its grand and ancient conception, it includes all administration included today under the minister of the interior. The police must be understood according to this definition, the administration that oversees the execution of laws, either by control exerted over all public services, or by supporting the law, everywhere where the need is felt. Everything relating to the execution of laws, and regulations that are attached to it, come under its jurisdiction. In this way, everything is within its domain, justice, public schooling, finance, commerce, industry and the army.[55]

A contemporary of Tocqueville, Maurice Block published his *Dictionnaire de l'administration française* the same year that the *Old Regime and the French Revolution* appeared, in 1856. Block also provided an elaborate explanation of the authority and object of the police powers "with a much wider meaning in science than in everyday language . . . following Macarel, administrative science has granted it the title of human providence. We will see that this is not an exaggeration."[56] Attempting to dissect the complexity of these powers and their delegation, Block wrote: "In the presence of the infinite variety of circumstances in which the police is called to exert its action, the legislator has wisely abstained from entering into very precise detail."[57] Block then went on to list the extraordinary powers and almost total "freedom of action" under the heading of police: "the acts pertaining to the police powers are not in any way definitive or irrevocable with regards to themselves; a measure taken on one day can be replaced the next day by one that is different or even contrary as long as its raison d'être is in the public interest."[58] In short, the police powers were so capacious precisely because they were pragmatically, instead of normatively, defined.

Considering his emphasis on the police power, and the importance of Macarel for Tocqueville's thinking on administration, as we shall see, the capacious definition Block and Vacherot give to the police is hardly banal.

Tocqueville made specific reference to these extraordinary capacities of the police power throughout his work. In Book II, chapter 1, of the *Old Regime*, "Why Feudalism Was Hated by the People in France More than Anywhere Else" and his discussion of Frederick the Great's legal code in his notes to this chapter, he investigates a specific moment in the history of the police powers. Institutions from the Middle Ages still governed throughout Germany in the late eighteenth century, Tocqueville argues. Thus the German example provided an ideal counter-factual to the French case because the "tremendous work" of Frederick's legal code, which to Tocqueville's great dismay had been all but forgotten by jurists and historians, had proposed a modernization of this medieval administration without revolution.

In Tocqueville's view, French and German administrative history had taken two very different paths. On the one side, in France the previous modes of administrative police rooted in feudalism had been destroyed by a new absolutist administration. On the other side, Germany attempted to modernize the medieval police powers that France had replaced through centralized absolutist administration. "All the civil servants of the parish were under the government or under the control of the central power." "Nowhere," Tocqueville argued, "did the nobility administer either together or individually; this was peculiar to France."[59] Ironically, Tocqueville argued, it was precisely the creation of this new administrative revolution in France that prepared the path for a new democracy after the Revolution, not the tremendous weight of medieval feudal traditions in Germany.

Tocqueville took a great interest in Frederick's legal code, describing the powers it laid out in detail and then reserving an extensive note of multiple pages to highlight its importance. Notably, Tocqueville observed powers that he had emphasized in his study of New England, such as being "subject to Sunday laws that oversaw private life and punished intemperance and laziness."[60] As in his account of New England administration, he explains how these powers were to be delegated and deployed and myriad responsibilities adjoined to them. The difference with New England (and medieval France), however, was that in Frederick's code, all of these powers were placed into the hands of a single prince, as "only he could give laws and make general police regulations."[61]

Of particular importance for Tocqueville's histories of administration, however, is the continuity he establishes between the police powers enumerated in Frederick's code and the early documents of the French Revolution. For Tocqueville, Frederick's work was far more than a legal code. "This code is a veritable constitution," he writes. "It not only has the aim of regulating the relationship between citizens, but also the relationship between citizens and the State."[62] Here Tocqueville provides a profoundly original argument about the early documents of the French Revolution. Hardly considering them a declaration of natural rights, he sees in the *Declaration of the Rights of Man and Citizen* and the Constitution of 1791 principles similar to those underlying Frederick's "constitution." "It rests or at least appears to rest on a number of general principles expressed in very philosophical and abstract form, which resemble in many ways those that guided the *Declaration of the Rights of Man* and the Constitution of 1791." Listing their shared principles, he wrote, "The good of the state and its inhabitants is the purpose of society and the limit of the law; that laws may not limit the freedom and rights of citizens except in the pursuit of the common good; that every member of the state ought to work for the general good in accordance with his position and his fortune; that the rights of individuals must be ceded to the general good." "Nowhere is there any question," Tocqueville insists, "of individual rights which would be separate from the rights of the state." The discussion of the general rights of man, then, is "founded on the natural liberty of pursuing one's own good provided it does not interfere with other's rights. . . . Every inhabitant of the state may demand from the state the defense of his person and property, and has the right to defend himself by force if the state does not come to his aid." These common principles of a modernized police power therefore provided the foundation for both Frederick's code *and* the most important documents of the early revolution. In short, the *Declaration of the Rights of Man and Citizen* and the Constitution of 1791 defined a positive political liberty.

So where did these early documents of the Revolution and Frederick's legal code differ? According to Tocqueville, the real difference was in the way the Constitution of 1791 asserted "popular sovereignty" and "the organization of popular government in a free society." The early Revolution, he suggests, offered the possibility of a modern democratic government. But this short window was ultimately shut down by the Terror and then given its fatal blow by the Empire. Though it was animated by the same principles, Frederick's legal code had gone in an entirely different direction. His code introduced a new form of modern despotism, one which Tocqueville uses as a veiled critique of the Bonapartist tradition. He accuses Frederick of pursuing the dangerous, "equally democratic but illiberal" model which made "the prince the sole representative of the state."[63] Frederick's code then could be best understood through the image of a "an entirely modern head" placed upon "an entirely gothic body": "On the one hand, the great principle of modern society, that everyone ought to be equally subject to taxation, is proclaimed;

on the other hand, provincial laws which claim exceptions to this rule are allowed to persist."⁶⁴ Through this awkward mix of medieval and modern, Frederick had stumbled upon one of the most liberticidal forms of modern government, illiberal democracy.

Amidst this complex administrative landscape remained one of the most important questions for modernizing the police powers, one that dated back to the Middle Ages: poor relief. Since the Middle Ages, providing relief especially in cases of extreme occasional want, fell necessarily under the responsibility of the local authorities' police powers. Tocqueville discussed this function within Frederick's legal code of modernized police powers: "Throughout this work—half-borrowed from the middle ages—appear tendencies toward an extreme centralization, bordering on socialism. Thus it declares that it is the State's responsibility to provide food, employment and a salary for all those who cannot support themselves and who do not have a right to help of their lord or their municipality: they must be guaranteed work in conformity with their strength and capacity. The State must create establishments through which the poor citizenry can receive aid."⁶⁵ This long explanation, in which Tocqueville recounts its "theoretical audacity and originality," offers perspective into Tocqueville's conception of what a modern police power might have been able to achieve—one that had not been destroyed by centralized administration while remaining democratic. According to these rules, "The lord must ensure that the poor peasants receive an education. He must, as far as possible, procure the means to life for those of his vassals that do not have land. If someone falls into indigence, he must come to their aid." Borrowed from the Middle Ages—and bordering on socialism, he argued—it was designed to tackle the fundamental problem of poverty with almost no limits to what the state could do to make this possible, from providing employment to ensuring food and a salary in times of necessity.

It was of course this capacity that had been destroyed by centralized administration. In the wake of absolutism, "No such law had existed in France for some time," since "the central government boldly undertook to look after their needs all by itself." Tocqueville thus concluded that any attempt to provide poor relief through an elaborate central administration was problematic. "It is easy to believe that charity pursued at such a distance remains blind and capricious and will always be insufficient."⁶⁶

Was it possible then to craft a modernized police power without falling into an ineffective or illiberal democracy? While the early documents of the Revolution had provided only a small window into what a modernized democratic police power might look like, Tocqueville ultimately found the sustained remnants of a modernized medieval and democratic police power in the United

States. Here, Tocqueville hardly shunned the administrative and interventionist capacities of the New England townships. Instead, he was fascinated by their capacity to respond to an almost endless list of social and political needs through the local regulatory police powers. Recent work has revealed the extent to which the antebellum United States, New England in particular, was governed through law and the police powers. As William Novak has noted in his discussion of Tocqueville's nineteenth-century United States: "Police power was the ability of a state or locality to enact and enforce public laws regulating or even destroying private right, interest, liberty, or property for the common good (i.e. for the public safety, comfort, welfare, morals, or health)." Novak then concludes, "Such broad compass has led some to conclude that state police power was the essence of governance, the hallmark of sovereignty and statecraft."[67] Tocqueville's *Democracy in America* captured the importance of this technology when he argued: "One sees them at each instant giving demonstrations of sovereignty; they appoint their magistrates, make war and peace, establish police regulations [*règlements de police*], and supply their laws as if they descended directly from God himself."[68]

Indeed, Tocqueville was particularly sensitive to the capacities of this form of administrative power. Explaining the nature of public authority in New England, Tocqueville wrote: "The fate of the poor is ensured from the outset; severe measures are taken to maintain the roads, they name civil servants to oversee them; the communes have public registers where they inscribe the results of all general deliberations, deaths, marriages, the birth of citizens; clerks are designated to keep these registers; officers are charged with administrating all wills without designated heirs [*les successions vacantes*], others oversee the inheritance [*la borne des héritages*]; many have the principal function of maintaining the public peace in the commune. Law enters into the minutest details to avoid and manage a mountain of social needs [*une foule de besoins sociaux*]."[69]

So what struck Tocqueville in democratic New England was not the lack of administrative capacity, or its unwillingness to take on problems such as poverty, road maintenance, or the management of the public peace. In fact, it was just the opposite; he celebrated the extraordinary capacity of New England administration to solve public problems, and inequality chiefly among them. What marked this administrative capacity was its proximity to social needs. Tocqueville maintained his concern that an autonomous centralized administrative apparatus would destroy the social fabric of a democratic polity. But, and this was an essential contribution, this did not mean turning one's back on administration *tout court*; it meant democratizing it through a modernization of police powers.

In New England, he therefore celebrated the fact that this public authority had the tremendous advantage of being largely accomplished by locally
elected officials. These officials were in constant contact with the population,
and most importantly, could be revoked. Of course, the fact that this took
place on a local level was important, but again it is important not to fit this
entirely back into a debate on the decentralization of administrative power.
In Tocqueville's view, what made the administrative power so effective in the
counties of New England in the 1830s was only very partially about decentralization. It was also about managing "a mountain of social needs," as he put it,
in a democratic fashion that did not separate the social and the administrative and that provided means for the public to regulate the private and satisfy
social needs. It was therefore a question of how to manage particular problems by delegating the authority of the police powers effectively.

A couple of decades later, in his *Old Regime and the French Revolution*,
Tocqueville acknowledged his mistaken assumption that such police powers
were solely found in the townships of New England. In a moment of scientific
confession, he explains: "When I began researching for the first time in the
archives of the intendance to find out exactly what a parish of the old regime
looked like, I was surprised to discover in this community that was so poor
and so enslaved, many of the traits that struck me in the rural communes of
America, that I had previously, and wrongly, judged to be exclusive to the
new world." Medieval French parishes and the New England townships had
at least two characteristics in common: "Both were administered by civil servants that acted on their own, under the direction of the entire community."
He then concluded: "The rural parish of the middle ages became the town-
ship of New England."[70] New England had modernized the medieval police
powers while France had let them wither on the vine only to be briefly re-
kindled in the early years of the Revolution and then absorbed once again by
the Empire's despotism.

So, there was a history of administrative governance that was distinct
from the absolutist administration of the seventeenth and eighteenth centuries. Seeing it as inherited from medieval Europe, Tocqueville had located a
revolutionized police power historically in a number of places: the aborted
project of Frederick's legal code, the early documents of the French Revolution, and the administration of the New England townships. Far from a
monochromatic critique of administrative power which paved the way for
a democratic equality of condition, Tocqueville recounted the complex and
variable histories of administration and their relationships to democracy.

At the center of Tocqueville's interest in the police power was an attempt
to come to terms with how to solve key public problems democratically; it

was about functions like public service, rather than political structure; it was a matter of uncovering technologies of public action in a larger social-state context of democratic policymaking; it was about building substantive policy and public service as opposed to a mere formal matter of governmental organization. As the examples he explored reveal, however, the problem was reintroducing such an administration on modern terms without falling into the Prussian/Bonapartist trap. And it was precisely in considering this problem that Tocqueville took a special interest in the nascent world of administrative law.

Toward the Legal Foundations of a Democratic Administrative State

From the earliest phases of his trip to the United States, Tocqueville cultivated a curiosity concerning administrative law. While it is largely recognized that Tocqueville originally traveled to the United States to study the penitentiary system, few if any have recognized that this necessarily pushed Tocqueville onto the terrain of administrative law. And yet, writing to a friend, Vicomte de Blosseville, in 1831 from New York, after he had already embarked on his voyage with Beaumont, he explicitly stated the fundamental importance of this question. "I must count on your kindness, sir, to request a favor." "This is what it entails," he continued; "everything that is related to judicial institutions here provokes in us a particular interest. After having examined the ordinary courts [*tribunaux ordinaires*], we began investigating the exceptional courts [*tribunaux d'exception*]; nowhere thus far have we found even the slightest trace of administrative judges that resemble the councils of the prefecture or the State Council [*les conseils de préfecture, le conseil d'Etat*]." This lack of a clear system of administrative justice or administrative judges was problematic for Tocqueville, especially since "there are administrative matters." "By whom are they judged?" he wondered. "How do they do without administrative courts? What are the political consequences of this situation?"

Equally problematic for Tocqueville was his relative ignorance about the French system of administrative law.[71] He therefore also turned to his friend and colleague de Blosseville in search of some basic information on the French and American systems of administrative law. "Would it not be too indiscreet to ask you to trace quickly the constitution of administrative courts in our country and the principal rules of their competence."[72] Similarly, a decade and a half later in 1846, a few years after he had completed his second volume on American democracy, Tocqueville revealed how important this question remained for him in a report given to the *Académie des sciences morales et politiques*. Regretting once again how little was still actually known about the subject, he noted: "Our administrative law has generated intelligent and useful commentaries; but it has not been studied or judged as a whole by a great public thinker [*publiciste*]." This situation was particularly regrettable, Tocqueville argued, because "there is perhaps no other subject in our times that merits more attention by our philosophers and statesmen. Not only is it a question of new principles and institutions, but also principles which will be adopted and institutions that will slowly be imitated throughout Europe."[73] For Tocqueville, the question of administrative law sat at the center of modern governance.

Historians have broadly considered administrative law to be the inheritor of the police powers of the old regime and Tocqueville of course did not deny this heritage. At the same time, however, his account introduces an important and overlooked complexity to this story. In keeping with his broader oeuvre, he examined how administrative law and modern regulatory powers emerged out of the two competing forms of administrative power during the old regime.

According to Tocqueville, the legal faculties of the police powers had always been largely ill-defined. "When we take a look at the old administration of the kingdom, we observe what would appear to be a great diversity of rules, authorities, and overlapping of powers. Courts took part directly in the legislative power; they had the capacity to establish obligatory administrative regulations within the limits of their powers."[74] The police powers of the old regime were at once administrative and juridical since much of the regulation took place through legal decisions by local judges. As a result, "Mere judges declared police ordinances [*ordonnances de police*] in the cities and towns where they resided."[75] The old legal technology of the police powers was a relatively informal blend between regulation, public administration, and legal decision, so the courts had important legislative and regulatory powers, including "the right to have judges who decide certain cases in their own name, and from time to time establish exercised regulatory police within the limits of the *seigneurie*."[76] It was not the inability to intervene in public or private affairs that characterized these ancient modes of public authority, but rather how they intervened through a multivalent, case by case capacity.[77]

As Tocqueville tells the story, this fluid blend of juridical power that allowed for the regular intervention into daily life also provided a means to resist the absolutist administration that was emerging above and around it. "Sometimes they resisted the official administration, boldly criticizing the measures and decrees of its agents."[78] In his notes on the *cahiers* of the nobility, he remarked how the nobility wanted "reform of the regulatory police and that the police be completely in the hands of judges, even in the case of a riot."[79] The legal police powers—or what was left of them—became one of the sites from where the displaced holders of the police power were able to resist the new absolutist administration that was being put into place. These figures used their residual legal powers to protect themselves from the absolutist administration. "The magistrates often crudely referred to the government procedures as despotic and arbitrary acts."[80]

In Tocqueville's reading, then, the old social and political practices of the local regulatory police dating back to the Middle Ages were defined by their nebulous nature: a mixture of legislative lawmaking, regulation, and justice; an ability to intervene in the daily lives of their communities; and the capacity of resistance that this ambiguity and intervention provided. It was, in short, an alternative model for delegating a positive administrative authority on a casuistic basis. An instrument of power, legal practice did not guarantee liberty from; it provided a mechanism to administrate for.

Thus what demarcated it from centralized absolutist administration was clearly not its capacity for intervention of public authority into an otherwise socially autonomous self-regulating sphere. The social and political organization dating back to the Middle Ages was deeply interventionist. Rather, it was a distinction in *how* law was being used to intervene. On the one hand there were the highly informal police powers that regulated local polities and resisted centralized administration. On the other were the administrative technologies of an absolutist centralization that undermined the fluidity and pragmatic legal foundations of these powers, rendering administrative justice, in Tocqueville's view, more arbitrary, on the one hand, and the old capacity to regulate through law superfluous, on the other.

The central administration's arbitrary aspiration to judge and manage all administrative issues was therefore rooted in the absolutist desire to disrobe the juridical ambiguity that gave the police powers their efficacy. "It is true that the royal power succeeded in disrobing the ordinary courts of any knowledge of almost every issue that could have been of interest to public authorities."[81] The absolutist administration slowly removed the powers of local justice and the administrative capacities that went with it: "Royal power gradually reduced, limited and subordinated seigneurial justice."[82]

More dangerous still, in the eyes of Tocqueville, the absolutist administration created a separate, exceptional juridical sphere for which it alone was responsible, removing all regulatory powers of public interest from local judges. Prior to the emergence of a centralized administration, the local judges had managed both ordinary civil cases and extraordinary cases on issues of public utility. However, "from this period forward, most litigious issues with regards to taxes became the exclusive jurisdiction of the intendant. The same happened for the police." The issues under the control of the old police powers were slowly being pushed into a distinct legal system that fell solely under the control of the central administration. This was true to such an extent that "in general all trials dealing with public authorities were heard before administrative tribunals. The intendants worked hard to ensure that this exceptional jurisdiction consistently expanded."[83] For Tocqueville, the problem was neither administration nor the necessity of exceptional powers per se, but rather the attempt to withdraw them into a distinct sphere and make them the exclusive domain of the central administration.

Finally, Tocqueville was deeply critical of the justification for this separate juridical sphere: "The reason given by one of the magistrates for obtaining these judgments merits mention: 'Ordinary judges,' he writes, 'are subject to fixed rules that force the judge to decide against any unlawful act; but the council can breach the general rules in the name of utility [*but utile*].' According to this principle, one often sees the intendant or the council bringing trials under their control that pertain to public administration only by an invisible thread, or not at all."[84] Tocqueville's observation merits special attention because it may appear counter-intuitive at first glance. For Tocqueville, it was clearly not the ability to derogate from the rule of law in the interest of public utility that was problematic. He recognized that such interventions could and even should take place in some cases. What was problematic was removing these powers from the hands of "ordinary judges." What was dangerous, therefore, was that the intendant or the king's council were accumulating the powers to decide all cases regarding problems of public authority, even issues that they were incompetent to judge.

For Tocqueville, it was precisely the ability of ordinary judges to decide ordinary *and* exceptional cases that made it possible to intervene in the name of public utility without creating a potential despotism. The democratic power of these local judges came from the source of their power—the community— but it also came from *how* they exercised their power: in the words of Tocqueville cited at the beginning of this chapter, it was not just a question of *representation*, it was also a question of *delegation*. As long as the ordinary and extraordinary interpenetrated informally, the democratic foundations of local police regulation could be preserved. To the contrary, the centralized and administrative attempt to formally isolate these two realms from one another laid the foundations for absolutist or democratic despotism. "Little by little," Tocqueville argued, "the exception became the rule, facts were transformed into theory."[85] It was precisely the formalization, the shift into the pure realm of theory, of a central bureaucratic legal approach that made exceptional legislation dangerous.

Thus, far from condemning administrative intervention in general, Tocqueville dreaded the idea that all administrative decisions would be cut off from the immediate circumstances and practices that generated them. Instead of local judges operating fluidly between law and regulation, nonadministrative and administrative affairs, absolutist administration cornered them into a realm where they only managed ordinary nonadministrative affairs. "In legal matters or those managed by ancient custom," Tocqueville argued, "the council intervenes regularly through its judgments removed from the hands of ordinary judges." While the police powers of the local judges had operated in a fluid space between ordinary and extraordinary administrative justice, the slow colonization of all administrative affairs by the king's council, in Tocqueville's reading, resulted in a hardened distinction between ordinary justice and administrative justice. "They were established not only in law, but also in the spirit of those that applied to them as a maxim of the State, that all trials with a relationship to the public interest or that are born of the interpretation of an administrative act, are not the responsibility of ordinary judges whose only role is to judge between particular interests." This distinction, Tocqueville concluded, provided the origins of modern administrative law: "In this realm, we have simply found the formula, the idea belonged to the old regime."[86]

But if the old regime prepared the foundations for administrative law, the Revolution posed the problem of the relationship between law and administration in a new way.[87] A new specific body of law, "administrative law," was fashioned during the postrevolutionary period.[88] While the old regime had been deeply marked by the interpenetration of older regulatory police powers and centralized administration, following the Revolution a new system was created which placed all administrative decisions "on the same level [*sur un même plan*]." This ambition to systematize the administrative competencies of public authorities confronted a central difficulty. The centralized administration had left some powers haphazardly distributed across the local regulatory police powers while creating general rules that applied to the entire kingdom. While the centralized administration was despotic and inefficient, the local regulatory police powers had been sapped of their power and operated intermittently on a local level. Creating a functional, democratic administration in a modern state that respected liberty, Tocqueville recognized, required finding a means of modernizing the police powers to provide a legitimate foundation for intervention on a national scale without creating administrative despotism. A modern public administration was needed to manage administrative business and transform the local regulatory capacities of the old regime into "the most natural and necessary guarantees." It was a question of modernizing the old police powers—which required a knowledge of "existing facts"[89]—while at the same time founding a system based on "a certain number of general principles." Or, as he had suggested of his own interest in history, of finding "the means to mix facts and ideas."

Administrative law, Tocqueville suggested, potentially provided such a framework. Here a new set of general principles could be combined with the facts of administrative life. In the 1840s in his report on Macarel's treatise on administrative law, Tocqueville therefore pondered: "What are the natural principles and necessary rules that emerge from the very depths of the needs and ideas of time that must be an immutable part of this new administrative law?"[90] Administrative law potentially provided an essential new framework for building a modern public administration. But, he insisted, this was only possible if it remained in the hands of ordinary judges, as had been the case under the local regulatory powers of yore.

He therefore deeply disagreed with contemporary jurists that administrative law was to be purely managed by the administration itself. Tocqueville elaborated this critique in the heart of his *Old Regime and the French Revolution*: "Modern jurists assure us that we have made great progress with respect to administrative justice since the Revolution," he argued. He then cited a fellow jurist: "'Formerly the judicial and administrative powers were confused,' they say: 'since then we have separated them and returned each to its place.'" Tocqueville, however, was not entirely convinced that such a system was a sign of "progress." "In order to really appreciate the progress of which we speak, one must never forget that if, on the one hand, judicial power under the old regime constantly extended itself beyond its natural sphere of authority, on the other hand, it also never completely filled it." As already pointed out, Tocqueville recognized that on certain occasions the local regulatory judicial powers of the old regime overstepped the limited realm of ordinary law. However, he insisted, even if they did so, they never entirely occupied the administrative realm. That is, they intervened, but their interventions were always relatively incomplete. Thus, "whoever looks at one of these two things without the other," Tocqueville continued, "has only a partial and incorrect idea of the subject. In some cases, the ordinary courts were allowed to make rules for public administration, which was manifestly outside their sphere; and in others they were forbidden to judge real trials, which meant excluding them from their own domain." In its attempt to separate out the judicial and the administrative, the new system of administrative law therefore had removed all administrative capacities from the judges, which he recognized could be at times outside of their specific capacities. But at the same time, they completely isolated them from judging any administrative cases, which meant that the administration had been pushed completely outside "ordinary" legal decision.

"We have, it is true," Tocqueville insisted, "eliminated the judiciary from the administrative sphere where the old regime had very wrongly introduced it; but at the same time, as we have seen, the government of the old regime constantly intruded into the judicial sphere, and we have left it there." For Tocqueville, it was not the judging of administrative cases and the regulatory powers that went with them that were problematic. Rather it was the attempt to completely separate the administrative realm from ordinary justice. Ordinary judicial power, in Tocqueville's view, could overstep into the regulatory sphere by managing administrative issues in the name of public utility. In such cases the worst that could happen would be inefficiency. But there was certainly no danger of despotism in this incomplete, intermittent intervention of local judges into regulation. "As if," he concluded this passage, "the confusion of powers were not as dangerous in one direction as the other, and even worse. Since the intervention of the judiciary in government only hurts efficiency, while the intervention of the government in the judiciary debases people and tends to make them simultaneously revolutionary and servile."[91] So removing any independent legal mediation between the administration and civil realm necessarily generated servitude. When administrators cannot be judged independently, despotism lies in waiting.[92]

The key argument that emerges in Tocqueville's discussion, then, is the following. By making ordinary judges responsible for administrative matters of public utility, it would appear that Tocqueville was falling back on an argument for rule of law protection from administrative intervention. But such an analysis misses the complexity of Tocqueville's argument. Tocqueville was not looking for legal protection from regulation; he was looking for a democratic and pragmatic means of intervening which remained accountable to its community. In this, he sought a way of updating regulatory powers and the ability to solve public problems by modernizing the tradition of the police powers that he had dated back to the Middle Ages.

Tocqueville of course recognized a central challenge in attempting to modernize this capacious technology for deploying law, administrative orders, and regulatory capacities: how to integrate general principles that made them effective on the scale of the entire territory without giving the capacities of the police over to a distant centralized administration. As suggested above in his discussion of Frederick's legal code, it would appear from Tocqueville's discussion of the *Declaration of the Rights of Man and Citizen* and the Constitution of 1791 that Tocqueville thought such a possibility briefly existed historically in the early years of the Revolution. He made similar comments in his discussion of administrative law in his report on Macarel: "Almost the entirety of our administrative organization is the work of the Constituent Assembly."[93] For Tocqueville, the Constituent Assembly had opened the door to a new set of principles that potentially administrated democratically: creating "executive councils," "elections," and judging them in ordinary tribunals. "As in the constitution of 1791" it put into place "a popular government in a free society." During these early years of the Revolution, one could catch a glimpse of what a modernized regulatory administration with democratic controls might look like. Unfortunately, it didn't last.

This brief experiment with democratic administration was quickly brought to an end, in Tocqueville's view, with Napoleon's rise: "Napoleon merely conserved while reinventing the system established by the Constituent Assembly. He improved it and completed it in certain areas, but above all he profoundly transformed its spirit." Instead of an executive council, he put in "one single agent who was only responsible to him"; instead of elections, "he gave the prerogative to the prince"; and "he made the smallest agent inviolable and forbid that he be judged before the courts." Through these measures, "Napoleon succeeded in appropriating this vast machine that had been conceived and crafted by liberty, for the purposes of an absolute power."[94] Tocqueville then concludes his thought on this tragic end: "Never forget that our administrative system was conceived by liberty and nourished by despotism."[95] The Revolution had opened the door to a modernized regulatory power with democratic controls. And this remained, for Tocqueville, the road not taken.

The Legacy of Tocqueville's Democratic State

Tocqueville's conception of a democratic administration reached back to his analysis of American democracy, through his investigations of the administrative law tradition, and into his critique in the *Old Regime and the French Revolution*. His attempt to move beyond the mere question of equality to solving the problem of modern inequality pushed him in two directions at once. On the one hand, he sought an understanding of how the equality of condition was created by, and even furthered, despotism. On the other hand, he grappled with the question of how a public administration might solve a specific problem in a modern state, while remaining democratic. This aspect of Tocqueville's work was hardly lost on some of his most influential contemporaries, even if it slowly faded from view in the following century.

Tocqueville's importance for understanding the organization of a modern democratic administrative power was perhaps most immediately recognized by John Stuart Mill. Mill's *Autobiography* insists that he had undergone a great transformation in his thought, from the utilitarianism of his father and Jeremy Bentham to what he called a conversion to "democracy" and even "a qualified socialism." He referred to this as "the only actual revolution which has ever taken place in my mode of thinking."[96] He then specified that this transformation "consisted, on one hand, in a greater approximation, so far as regards the ultimate prospects of humanity, to a qualified Socialism, and on the other, a shifting of my political ideal from pure democracy, as commonly understood by its partisans, to the modified form of it, which is set forth in my *Considerations on Representative Government*." Attributing the origins of this transformation, he wrote: "This last change, which took place very gradually, dates its commencement from my reading, or rather study, of M. de Tocqueville's *Democracy in America*, which fell into my hands immediately after its first appearance." He then concluded, "the consequent modifications in my practical political creed were spread over many years, as would be shown by comparing my first review of *Democracy in America*, written and published in 1835, with the one in 1840 (reprinted in the *Dissertations*), and this last, with the *Considerations on Representative Government*."[97]

It was his reading of Tocqueville, Mill recollected, which had opened the path toward a new conception of democracy. Tocqueville's influence touched on many areas, but from the outset Mill emphasized the importance of the passages on the power of administration in New England that revealed Tocqueville's commitment to the importance of regulatory powers. After quoting Tocqueville's discussion of the "municipal officers [and] parish commissioners, who audit the expenses of public worship, different classes of inspectors, some of whom are to direct the efforts of the citizens in case of fire, tithingmen, listers, haywards, chimney-viewers, fence-viewers to maintain the bounds of property, timber-measurers, and inspectors of weights and measures," he concluded, insisting on the regulatory powers of this state: "this invaluable part of the American constitution seen only in creating, but at least equally so in regulating, the spirit of interference in public affairs."[98]

Mill returned to the importance of public administration in Tocqueville's work in his review of the second volume: "M. de Tocqueville sees the principal source and security of American freedom, not so much in the election of the President and Congress by popular suffrage, as in the administration of nearly all the business of society by the people themselves." What Mill had discovered in Tocqueville then was an attempt to sketch a democratic administration, public intervention, and regulation that was not autonomous, but rather what he referred to as of "the people." If properly conceived and pursued, this work would not threaten democracy but perfect it. Or as, Edouard

Laboulaye—inspired by Tocqueville—argued in these same years, "if we hope
to cultivate the deep roots of administration in this country, it is imperative,
as I already said, that its primary organization be democratic."[99] In this sense,
the best solution to the dangers of democracy was the creation of a democratic administration.

Moreover, Mill insisted that the ideals outlined by Tocqueville had found
their most thorough realization in the new poor laws in England. These laws
against inequality required the local administrative bodies in their management. But, he insisted, such a mission could not be entirely managed on a
local level. Like Tocqueville, he recognized that modern public administration needed some form of central agency—in other words, a central administration was also a necessity. "The existence of such a central agency allows
of intrusting to the people themselves, or to local bodies representative of
them, many things of too great national importance to be committed unre-
servedly to the localities; and completes the efficacy of local self-government
as a means of instruction, by accustoming the people not only to judge of
particular facts, but to understand, and apply, and feel practically the value
of, principles." He then concluded, ensuring that this was precisely the kind of
lesson that Tocqueville's work inspired: "the extension of a similar mixture of
central and local management to several other branches of administration,
thereby combining the best fruits of popular intervention with much of the
advantage of skilled supervision and traditional experience, would, we believe, be entitled to no mean rank in M. de Tocqueville's list of correctives to
the inconveniences of Democracy."[100]

Mill was certainly not alone in recognizing Tocqueville's contribution to
a history of democratic administration. Indeed it was precisely by posing the
Tocquevillian question anew that thinkers like Prévost-Paradol and Laboulaye
would reconsider the limits and possibilities of the government and the state
in democracy. As we shall see, both of these thinkers embraced and attempted
to come to terms with the problems posed by Tocqueville's work. Lucien-
Anatole Prévost-Paradol directly pursued the question of how to democratize
government while Edouard Laboulaye wrote one of his most important books
on the state, *The State and Its Limits*, attempting to theorize precisely where
these new administrative powers started and stopped within a liberal democratic constitutional context. Adolphe Thiers, a contemporary—and consistent thorn in Tocqueville's side—also recognized the positive governmental
powers inherent in the *Declaration of the Rights of Man and Citizen* just as
he adopted a language similar to the police powers—necessity and public
utility—in an increasingly democratic context. Jenny d'Hericourt also went
to the United States to look for answers on the future of democracy. And at

the same time, as we shall see, Louis Blanc would credit John Stuart Mill with providing him an adequate theory of a democratic state—the irony of course is that Mill, in turn, gave credit to Tocqueville for his own thinking on this question.

Later, as jurists of public and administrative law confronted the increasingly fundamental problems of modern industrial society, such as inequality, head-on, they too retheorized the notion of administration and specifically its relationship to law in positive terms. In spite of common arguments that the tradition of administrative law, which was partially responsible for the creation of this form of public service during the Third Republic, owed little to its predecessors, Tocqueville's legacy suggests that it was precisely out of these attempts from the 1850s to the 1880s to rethink the relationship between law, administration, and democracy that the possibilities of a modern state emerged.

2

EQUALITY:
Lucien-Anatole Prévost-Paradol and the Democratization of Government

The fact cannot be repeated enough: The French Revolution founded a society; it is still looking for its government.[1]

Democracy is imposed everywhere as an almost inevitable fact.[2]

In 1848, the opportunity to build a democratic authority erupted onto the European continent. Already an accomplished statesman and political thinker, Tocqueville was immediately called upon to participate in drafting a constitution in that year. A note within his papers during these discussions suggests how he understood the task before this constitutional committee: "What is a democratic government?" he asked. "It is a government that instead of reducing human liberty comes to its rescue in a thousand different ways, which instead of limiting it on all sides, opens all sorts of new perspectives."[3] For all the idealism and generality of the response, the problem of democratic government was posed.

The election of the first (and only) president of the Second Republic, Louis-Napoleon, however, offered little in the way of a resolution to this problem. As he consolidated his power in the years that followed, reducing the republic to a mere "experiment," Louis-Napoleon added yet another layer of complexity to what governing "democratically" could mean. Convinced that democracy was the order of the day, he claimed to be crafting a modern democracy that was far superior to those that preceded him. By the time he consolidated power in the Second Empire just four short years after the 1848 revolution, Napoleon III's empire emerged as a new modern—though liberticidal—democratic regime. Referred to alternatively as a "modern democracy," "a democratic despotism," or "illiberal democracy," there remained the consensus that his regime was, nonetheless, a democracy. The creation of a modern democratic dictatorship thus introduced the profound conundrum of formulating a critique of one democracy in the name of another. Or stated somewhat differently, in the case of Prévost-Paradol, it provoked what had hitherto been a tautological question: Is it possible to govern democratically in a democracy?

Prévost-Paradol tackled this problem by pursuing the path opened by Tocqueville.[4] A generation younger than Tocqueville, Prévost-Paradol was born in 1829 into an accomplished family of Parisian cultural and intellectual life.[5] From his birth, Prévost-Paradol was a brilliant, if disquieting force. Son of an extramarital affair between an actress at the Comédie Française, Anne Catherine Lucinde Prévost-Paradol, and the poet, historian, and playwright Léon Halévy, Lucien-Anatole made up for what he may have lacked in parental legitimacy with help from his family and friends (Thiers in particular), the ostensibly innate self-assurance of a Parisian bourgeois, and his pen. Entering the *École normale* the same year Tocqueville accepted the position of minister of foreign affairs in 1849, he quickly made a name for himself as one of the best of his class. In 1856, as the aging statesman Tocqueville completed his opus *Old Regime and the French Revolution*, the young Prévost-Paradol's stars began to align as he took over the opposition newspaper *Journal des Débats* and launched his brilliant career as a publicist. By the 1860s, after Tocqueville had died, liberal eyes turned to Prévost-Paradol's nervy, if thinly veiled, critiques of the Empire which came out in regular journalistic jabs. Ever brilliant, he was welcomed among the Académie française's immortals by his thirty-sixth birthday, expanding his intellectual legitimacy and his audience with it. From there, he quickly asserted himself with his most widely read work, *La France nouvelle* (1868), welcomed as a masterpiece of French political thought in its day in France and beyond.[6]

A rising star of French liberalism in the Second Empire, his contributions to the press and critiques of the Bonapartist regime made him one of the most prominent public voices on the democratic question in France.[7] Moreover, although he did not live to see the birth of the Third Republic, like many other figures discussed in this book, Paradol's conception of democracy had a direct impact on the institutional, political, and cultural foundations of the Third Republic. Prominent constitutionalists and historians of the Third Republic, such as Adhémar Esmein, emphasized his importance for the origins of the Third Republic. In particular, he was one of the central figures in preparing the institutional outlines of the regime's constitutional laws,[8] especially in defining the powers of the legislative branch and the creation of the Senate.[9] The jurist Joseph Barthélemy summed up Paradol's influence when he wrote: "The political education of the generation that realized the constitution of 1875 read a little Proudhon, a lot of *Democracy in America* by Tocqueville and above all the works of Broglie and Prévost-Paradol."[10]

Outside France, Walter Bagehot cited him as one of the few non-English to truly grasp the English constitution, while a generation later, Carl Schmitt chose him as the obvious bogeyman to represent the foolish optimism of those nineteenth-century thinkers who believed in the "value of parliamen-tarianism over the 'personal regime' of Napoléon III."[11] In the same years, his nephew Élie Halévy, inspired by his model, became one of the great French philosopher-historians of England and liberal democracy. And more recently, jurists and historians have affirmed this impact,[12] highlighting his influence in some of the most important laws of the early Third Republic.[13] So while Prévost-Paradol has largely disappeared as a key figure in the his-tory of democratic thought since the second half of the twentieth century, he was an inescapable fixture of liberal democratic thinking—and its critics—up through the interwar period.

Coming to terms with why Prévost-Paradol's work was so influential provides an important perspective into the problem of the construction of a democratic public authority. In posing the problem of political modernity as a challenge of democratic government, Prévost-Paradol's legacy was power-ful for two reasons. First, he built on Tocqueville's exploration of democracy to break with many of the liberal thinkers that had preceded him, especially those of the postrevolutionary period. Where they sought to offset the poten-tial risks of democracy by limiting the power of government, or cordoning it off as a sociological form, or reducing the state to the singular will of one leader, Paradol focused on the novel question of how to democratize govern-ment within a democracy.

Posing the problem in these terms, he insisted that democratic government was not a mere means of selection or of representation; it was also—and far more importantly—a means of managing the public interest. In other words, democracy was a way of exercising power. To be clear, many had already dis-cussed the notion of democracy and popular power, but these discussions had largely avoided the question of democratic government. As Richard Tuck notes, many of the most important theorists of democracy in the old regime from Hobbes to Rousseau to the Girondins had come to largely accept the idea of democratic sovereignty. At the same time however, the focus on democratic sovereignty came at the expense of a deep conviction about the importance of democratic government. The sovereign could remain democratic, even as it slept under the watchful eyes of its governors.[14] In the wake of 1789, and espe-cially in the years leading up to 1848, the emphasis changed, even as democratic government overwhelmingly came to be associated with universal suffrage and the importance of creating a more representative legislative power. Within these explorations, the question of what it meant to actually make decisions and execute them in a democratic way remained largely untouched. Posing the question of how to *exercise power democratically*—especially executive and administrative power—marked then a key turn in the history of democracy.[15]

Prévost-Paradol thus merits investigation for the importance of his legacy and for the novel way he posed the democratic problem.

To achieve this democratization of government, Paradol explored the French past and present, but he was particularly attentive to the liberal institutions of England. Adapting an analysis of the British system, Prévost-Paradol portrayed the democratization of liberal government as a positive and more robust political form than the illiberal democracy of Napoleon III. However, Paradol's interest in Britain did not stop with its parliamentary and executive institutions; he also envied their colonial model. It was here, on the colonial periphery, that Paradol uncovered a central problem of the democratic, the limits of political equality. In keeping with his interest in the democratic state, Paradol understood equality as a purely political project. By affirming the political autonomy of equality, he argued that equality was not the product of natural right but rather created by the demos to which such equal individuals belonged. He therefore defined equality within the boundaries of those who had fought for it—the metropole—as opposed to those who had not—such as the indigenous populations of the colonial periphery. Such a vision generated an inside and outside of the demos, and the indigenous populations of Algeria were clearly outside, even as they were ruled by the demos that built itself without them. Paradol was therefore able to construct a vision of the French democratic state in which assembling the demos at home would help consolidate a singular national interest in the colonies. This disquieting weave of democratic state power left an ambivalent legacy for the Republic.[16]

Democratic Dictatorship

Louis-Napoleon's successful coup in 1852 did not condemn democracy, but the republic. During the almost two decades that followed, the Second Empire tossed republicanism aside as an unstable and potentially dangerous regime just as it tossed out political liberalism as an illegitimate check on the emperor's authority. Rejecting the republic in the name of democracy could be achieved by claiming the legacy of the Revolution. Thus the first article of the constitution of 1852 declared: "The Constitution recognizes, confirms and guarantees the great principles proclaimed in 1789, which are also the foundations of French public law." Through the French Revolution, Napoleon III appropriated democracy at the republic's expense.

Key democratic ideas of the preceding decades formed the foundation of the new imperial regime. As one of the emperor's most ardent supporters, journalist and *publiciste* Granier de Cassagnac argued, this modern regime could boast itself democratic because it depended upon an unprecedented

participation of the people in public affairs. By maintaining the universal suffrage initiated in 1848 and consulting the "people" regularly through plebiscites, "it was impossible over the long run that popular ideas would not
penetrate into the most intimate elements of government."[17] Where previous
postrevolutionary regimes had radically reduced the number of voters, the
Empire embraced this modern form of participation. The minister of state,
Eugène Rouher, argued along precisely these lines: "What was constructed in
1852 . . . is a national and democratic monarchy which does not have the same
foundation as the electoral regimes of 1814 and 1830, consisting of 80,000 voters and then 200,000, but universal suffrage in its entirety . . . sincere, absolute,
incontestable and uncontested."[18]

Embracing universal suffrage, this new "democratic" regime rejected any
hint of pluralism. The people was considered a singular manifestation of popular sovereignty and its unified will entirely captured in the unique will of
the emperor. This one-to-one equation, supporters of the regime argued,
was ensured by an administrative apparatus that was singularly purposed to
serve the emperor and therefore to replace politics: "In a democratic state like
France, administrative organization has more importance than anywhere else;
for it dominates up to a certain point all political organization," Louis Napoleon himself had argued. In this administration of things—which came at the
expense of the troublesome democratic politics of individuals—questions of
government were entirely in the hands of the emperor himself: "In a government with a democratic foundation, only the head has governmental power;
moral force derives only from him; everything flows back up to him as well."
Since all authority came from the singular will of the people channeled through
the unified will of the emperor, this modern democratic ideal could only be
preserved through an administration that was efficient, autonomous, and hi-
erarchically organized: "Centralization must be stronger than in any other; for
the representatives of power only have the prestige that the power is willing to
give them. And for them to conserve their prestige, they must enjoy a great deal
of authority without ever losing an absolute dependence on the head, to ensure
that the most active surveillance will be exercised upon them."[19] This democracy therefore depended on the emperor's ability to govern in the name of the
people: "Only the head of the democratic government can establish unity and
orchestration in the direction of public affairs."[20]

Similarly, proponents of this democratic regime elaborated a discourse on
liberty, generating some of the more original illiberal conceptions of liberty
in the second half of the nineteenth century. A key theorist of Napoleon III's
democratic despotism, Édouard Boinvilliers, argued for example that there

were two forms of liberty: "political" and "effective." In the eyes of Boinvilliers, those blinded by their attachment to a democratic republic confused these two notions: "Liberty of the press is a political liberty; the liberty to make, to sell, to exchange one's products as one wishes is an effective liberty." He concluded that if political liberty was ultimately of small necessity, "France remained no doubt the country that was richest in effective or real liberties."[21] Among these "effective" liberties was a strong commitment to economic development and growth. Transforming long-held arguments by 1848 democratic socialists and republicans that liberty required some degree of economic equality, Boinvilliers traded one for the other as he claimed that "the worst servitude for the people is misery: the supreme liberty is well-being."[22] The commitment to comfort and wealth became the regime's credo.

The commitment to "effective" economic liberalism contributed to Napoleon III's decision to sign a free-trade agreement with England, the Cobden-Chevalier Treaty in 1860.[23] Orchestrator of the agreement and leading voice of free trade in France, Michel Chevalier, longtime Saint-Simonian and professor of political economy at the Collège de France, incarnated the kind of expert leadership that Napoleon III recruited to his imperial ends. He insisted that politics and parliamentary debate could only soften the resolve of the government and prevent such important reforms from being passed. He therefore stated outright that the agreement between France and Britain was only possible thanks to the emperor's ability to act unilaterally in the interest of the people: "I was convinced that we could not put in place the customs reform and push toward free trade without using the power, recognized in the Emperor, to make commercial treaties without the sanction of the legislative body."[24] The emperor's ability to channel the national interest and the will of the people prevented unnecessary resistance from undermining the "effective" liberties of the age.

So out of democracy's ostensible triumph and the joys afforded (to some) by economic liberalism emerged a great conundrum for political thinkers like Prévost-Paradol and those around him who were absorbed by the democratic question. In one sense, this was a strange moment to be building a political critique rooted in democracy, since from the perspective of many, liberty and democracy had triumphed in France, even as social equality had been set aside. For those who supported the regime, Napoleon III had brought prosperity and stability in the name of the people rooted in universal suffrage and built an increasingly efficient and autonomous administration while its continental neighbors supposedly hobbled along under antiquated monarchical regimes. In this context, formulating a new democracy required a critique of one democratic regime in the name of another.

What Is Democratic Government?

Prévost-Paradol's journalism, political thought, and final position as French ambassador to Washington were driven by two ambitions: an unrelenting critique of Napoleon III's democratic despotism and an effort to reconsider the contours of a democratic government in France. He pursued this critical democratic project to grapple with what he considered a blind spot in previous analyses of the democratic. While there had been many advocates of the democratic cause since the Revolution, the restrictions on universal suffrage had provided a relatively transparent goal which equated the achievement of universal suffrage with the realization of democracy. At the same time however, this vague ambition clouded the specifics of what democratic governance might actually entail once universal suffrage was finally achieved. This left in turn a tremendous confusion at precisely the moment that democracy had supposedly triumphed.

Observing the democratic dictatorship before him, Prévost-Paradol asked a question that marked his generation: How could the term "democracy" be applied to such very different regimes?[25] He framed this problem in the following terms: "We have come to understand under the name *democracy* political regimes that are extremely different. Though the word means, in the proper sense, power of the people or government of the people, it only applies to a particular political situation. We apply the term democracy indifferently to the United States, the French constitutional regime of 1830, Republican France of 1848 and imperial France of 1852. And yet what differences there are in the ways these regimes subsist and govern themselves."[26] Prévost-Paradol's formulation of this problem, which nagged at so many in the 1860s, is valuable for the way it presents democracy as a reflexive and historically plural regime. Refusing the idea that modern democracy had come forth in a singular historical unfolding, Paradol insists that the modern world witnessed very different types of regimes, all of which understood themselves to be democratic. The challenge for Paradol, then, was squaring any given regime's claim that it was democratic with the fact that other, very different types of regimes could make similar claims.

There were many ways out of this ostensible conundrum in the 1860s, but Prévost-Paradol elaborated a critical perspective on democracy by doubling the democratic problem. His approach elaborated a distinction "between the form and the foundation of political institutions."[27] In other words, a democratic social foundation could provide the grounds for any number of political institutional forms, even un-democratic ones; one could be living in a democratic society even though one was not "governed democratically." Modern societies throughout Europe, the Americas and into Australia, he argued, were all subject to the inevitable tendency toward a democratic society even as their regimes differed profoundly. But to claim to be a democracy a nation needed to be "served by a democratic government" or as he put it "constituted as a democracy."[28]

By posing the problem in this way, Paradol provided new perspective on the rise of democracy in Europe—a continent that found itself at the center of nineteenth-century democratization even as it preserved many of its oldest monarchies. Instead of placing an emphasis on coupling democracy to a specific regime—such as the republic—he founded it on a new principle: whether or not a democratic society was *governed* democratically. Refusing to favor any specific regime type, he argued that a society could be governed democratically in a republic, or with an aristocracy, or by maintaining a constitutional monarchy. It must be noted that this was not a classic early modern idea of the mixed regime. Though he was not against the idea of mixing democracy, monarchy, and aristocracy, he was suggesting a very different perspective from which to judge the quality of the regime. In his view, it was a question of aligning democratic social foundations and political institutions. He thus opened his book on *La France nouvelle* with a definition of democratic government: "Public power comes from all, and may be reclaimed by all at any moment, granted to a few by everyone, solely by means of persuasion, and concentrated for a time."[29] This definition, which emphasizes *public power*, *persuasion*, and *responsibility*, provides the best point of entry into Prévost-Paradol's attempt to solve the conundrum of democratic government.

POPULAR FOUNDATIONS OF PUBLIC POWER

While Prévost-Paradol places the public, or alternatively the people, at the foundation of representative government, he remains ambivalent about the notion of sovereignty and the sovereign. He employs the term "sovereignty" only a handful of times and in a variety of ways, and never as the founding and necessary principle of a democratic government. Instead of the language of sovereignty, he prefers to describe a democracy through such expressions as "the power of the people," "the people governing themselves," or "a government in the image of society." He uses the term "sovereign" far more often, but his refusal to favor constitutional monarchy or a republic left him open to the possibility that there would be a "constitutional sovereign" or a president, whose power would then be a delegation of popular sovereignty. So while he of course recognized and considered the importance of sovereignty, his openness to either form of government pushed him to look for other ways

of posing the foundation for democratic government.[30] He did so by refor-
mulating the notion of democratic society initiated under the constitutional
monarchies by the liberal doctrinaires.

The notion of democracy as a social form had been one of the great contributions of political thought of the 1820s–1830s, perhaps best captured in the
work of Pierre-Paul Royer-Collard. Writing amidst the Bourbon Restoration,
Royer-Collard favored the notion of democratic society over popular sovereignty. "The equality of rights (which is democracy's truth) has prevailed;
recognized, consecrated, and guaranteed by the Charter, it is today the universal form of society, and as such democracy is everywhere."[31] By defining
democracy as a social form, Royer-Collard, as well as others of the July Monarchy like François Guizot, provided the grounds for accepting the sociological consequences of 1789 while dismissing its political consequences. The 1789
Revolution had been, in their minds, a democratic social revolution. However, as a social condition it had not provided a sound political form or a type
of government. It was precisely because the leading actors of the Revolution
had misunderstood this fact that they had led France into the Terror. Building
on this idea, François Guizot even went so far as to justify limited suffrage by
claiming that representative government was not the result of representing
sovereign will, but social reason, in which case the small number of electors
was of little importance, and even an advantage. By defining democracy as a
sociological condition, doctrinaires defanged the demos.

We have already seen how Tocqueville offered a groundbreaking consideration of democratic administration even as he accepted the definition of
democracy as a social condition through his exploration of the modernization
of the police powers. Prévost-Paradol built directly on Tocqueville's proposition.[32] Writing under a caesarist empire, Prévost-Paradol also accepted the
doctrinaire notion of democracy as a social form. But the extraordinary infla-
tion of executive power and the almost complete servitude of representative
institutions required searching for the political requirements of democratic
government from within its sociological form: "A society that has become
democratic comes closer every day to a redoubtable question: it aspires
instinctively to establish a government in its image, to constitute itself as a
democracy," he explained.[33]

POWER OF PERSUASION

Prévost-Paradol's conception of representative government was rooted in what
he referred to on numerous occasions as the power of persuasion. Clarifying
his friend's views on the matter, Octave Gréard noted: "Paradol summarized

his elevated views when he called politics: 'the art of employing the least amount of force necessary for conducting human affairs and acting upon the will through authority of character and the power of persuasion.'"[34] Convinced that beholders of office could not incarnate the people, but could only hold their position through their ability to convince others, Paradol challenged any argument for total identification between the governed and the governing.

The argument for persuasion had a long history in democratic thought. In the case of Prévost-Paradol it was part of his attempt to reinvigorate the society-government relationship through the democratic. To do so, Prévost-Paradol, and his close friend Hyppolite Taine, turned back to Baruch Spinoza, as did so many political philosophers and historians of the following generation, including his nephew Élie Halévy.[35] Shedding—sometimes violently—the previous generation's fascination for Victor Cousin,[36] Prévost-Paradol's new democratic project looked to this philosopher who had been so central to spawning the democratic ambitions of the previous century.[37]

Prévost-Paradol insisted on a number of occasions that Spinoza's work was at the center of his political thought and practice. It was a common theme in his correspondence with Taine in his early years as a student, and later he insisted that it was thanks to Taine that he had come to see the genius of Spinoza's system.[38] There are traces of Spinoza's thought, heavily filtered through his mid-nineteenth-century concerns, across Prévost-Paradol's work. They appear perhaps most clearly in his attempt to realign democratic society with a democratized government. Paradol latches onto a specific interpretation of Spinoza, which was essential to his post-1848 conception of democracy, reading it as anti-utopian. For Paradol, Bonapartist despotism as well as the darkest moments of the Terror derived from the dangerous conviction that it was possible to recreate a society according to an idea or a transcendent symbolic order. According to his reading of Spinoza, society was not driven by ideas, nor did it have an ideal form. Instead, any given society was dominated by specific tendencies or social practices and the order of a given society was to be found within those practices.[39] Democratic institutions and governmental practices were therefore not to be grounded in utopian ideas—which would ultimately serve dictatorship—but to express the singular practices of a given society.

Because it was social, democracy could be neither achieved nor preserved through one person, one revolution, or one idea. It was a practice rooted in the peculiar sociological traits of any given nation. Here too Paradol drew on an interpretation of Spinoza—which he also shared with Taine—that no one individual could contain the truth or completely understand the significance of a given phenomenon. To claim to have an overarching, complete vision was, to Prévost-Paradol's mind, entirely irrational and ultimately dictatorial.

Instead it was necessary to embrace the particularity and extraordinarily partial view of any single perspective. In such a context, only persuasion afforded the foundations of properly democratic government, because there was no superior view from which one could understand all. Paradol used these ideas to trouble the Second Empire's, or any dictatorship's, democratic assertions, to argue that democratic government was the expression of a democratic society's peculiar habits and practice.

RESPONSIBILITY

In his ambition to define a specifically democratic mode of governance, Prévost-Paradol refused to overstate the dangers of internal revolt. While he openly recognized that the Revolution had generated the Terror, fear of this moment had been inflated and provided an overwhelming justification for the political abuses of the Second Empire. Instead of emphasizing the necessity of maintaining order and preventing the dangers of democracy, Prévost-Paradol focused much more on the problem of how to prevent abuses by political leaders and the emergence of too great a distance between public opinion and those who governed. Being governed democratically, therefore, required establishing a regular means of ensuring that the government was responding to opinion outside occasional elections.

In his discussion of the local departmental councils, Paradol argued that they "must be represented in between sessions by a permanent commission, elected from within for a limited amount of time, and charged with overseeing the loyal execution of . . . [their] resolutions."[40] Prévost-Paradol drew this idea from the abuse of elections under the Second Empire. In his view, mere election was insufficient to guarantee democratic governance. To govern democratically it was necessary to find mechanisms—like a permanent oversight committee within elected bodies—for ensuring that local officials were effectively following through on the decisions they had made. Here he was moving a step beyond calls for fairer elections or decentralization by proposing technologies for democratic governance to ensure active and regular responsibility.

Such ideas can be found throughout his work. For example, he showed a particular interest in the question of ministerial responsibility. Unlike England, France was bereft of a doctrine of ministerial responsibility in the first half of the nineteenth century.[41] Throughout the Bourbon Restoration and the July Monarchy ministers resigned, but not as a part of a formal legal or parliamentary mechanism. Generally, such resignations followed what was referred to as a "ministerial crisis" in which the ministerial cabinet was unable to collect sufficient votes for a given bill. Prévost-Paradol therefore looked to England to propose a form of ministerial responsibility. He posed four distinct possibilities of responsibility: the sovereign's accountability in a hereditary monarchy; a president's accountability in a republic, without ministerial accountability; presidential and ministerial accountability in a republic; or ministerial accountability along with a constitutional monarchy. He quickly dismissed the first, suggesting that it was impossible to imagine that a monarch could reasonably be held accountable for all the decisions made in domestic and foreign policy in the modern age. There were just too many issues to be handled. Furthermore, he suggested that it was unstable, because ultimately the case against Louis XVI had turned precisely around his total responsibility and Paradol could not imagine founding a system on this precedent. For the second system of presidential accountability, he looked to the impeachment procedures engaged against Andrew Johnson in the United States and suggested that this too was problematic. "We saw the congress hesitate for a time in 1867 between the grave inconvenience of unsettling the state if it applied full presidential accountability and the equally problematic inconvenience of enduring a President who was openly hostile to the Congress and in a declared struggle with the Assembly on the subject of executing the laws."[42] He therefore concluded that this was not an ideal system either.

Caught between the difficulties of the American and the French experiences, he turned to the British model. "Ministerial accountability under the constitutional monarchy, which is its primary resource, has become so familiar in our century," he argued, that it revealed "in Queen Victoria the image of an accomplished constitutional sovereign."[43] The advantages of this government were not that it was rendered so weak that it could not overstep its bounds. Rather, the creation of a head of government chosen by the legislative body, and "submitted for all the details of its conduct to the quotidian control of Parliament," would generate a "government that ensured respect of liberty for all."[44] This cabinet, he insisted, would be able to govern more effectively and with far greater force because it was responsible before the legislature and therefore, he suggested, the people. "This cabinet, supported by the parliamentary majority could do anything, except, according to the famous constitutional quip of our neighbors, change a man into a woman." This was precisely because "it would have as a constant and powerful brake, the entire exercise of parliamentary liberty and jealous surveillance of the party that it replaced and that hopes to replace it in turn."[45]

But who would be responsible for dissolving parliament and how and under what conditions could the legislative power be dissolved? The power of dissolution was fundamental for the maintenance of "a democratic state" according to Paradol. "Indeed, the greatest peril against liberty and, as a result, order in parliamentary government, is the existence of a discord between the public power and general opinion." Breaking with other nineteenth-century liberal concerns of the tyranny of the majority, Paradol considered to the contrary a legislative majority that ceased to agree with the majority of the citizens to be a "tyranny." "With the word tyranny, we do not hear the acts of violence or oppression, but simply the existence of a minister or an Assembly that conserves power legally, after having lost confidence or general approbation." "The institutions of the free and democratic state [*l'État démocratique et libre*] that we have sketched," he argued, were designed precisely to avoid this tyranny and ensure that the majority of the population was represented in parliament. In this context, dissolution was a necessity for maintaining the democratic foundations of the regime.

The problem was: Who was best entrusted with this power? Could it be effectively entrusted to an elected president? While he accepted the necessity of parties in the political process, he also recognized that they could have negative impact by forcing an elected official to serve his party before the people: "Will he send his friends and partisans back before the voters at the risk of destroying his own majority and party?"[46] He therefore suggested that the proper power for dissolution was a constitutional monarch who would not act out of party interest. This claim by Prévost-Paradol may be accredited to his Orleanism, but there is also something else at work. Exploring the possibility of ensuring democratic governance by the executive power had been one of the most difficult points of the democratic question since the Revolution: How to integrate an executive power into a democracy without falling prey to the whims of a given individual or party? The danger, it was argued, was that the election of the executive made the president a political figure, subject to his own will and that of his party. Here, however, instead of seeking an institutional mechanism to guarantee the executive's neutrality, Prévost-Paradol responded to this problem by substituting potential regulations on the head of state for a "kind" of head of state, who he considered was less likely to be subject to the abuses produced by a party system. Prévost-Paradol sought the means of depersonalizing the power of the executive thereby by removing individual ambition from the process of establishing political responsibility. But in his account, even in a democracy, a constitutional monarch was best suited for this role.

The Power of Democratic Government

Through the sociological foundations of democratic government Paradol provided a more robust and practical conception of state intervention than many of the liberals who preceded him. Providing, for example, a fresh critique of economic liberalism in the name of the democratic, he refused its techno-cratic emphasis of economic freedom over political procedure: "I criticize the Saint-Simonian school for their exclusive focus on the material well-being of people and a guilty indifference for liberty and political dignity: in a word, I see in them the principle of the sovereignty of ambition applied to the development of industry and well-being; and they show little concern as to whether or not the people govern themselves or are governed by a mas-ter."[47] Political liberty necessarily trumped the natural laws of commerce in Paradol's democratic vision. Economic liberals had revealed their true colors by accepting the passage of the free-trade agreement through authoritarian means. "Like everyone, I have projects of reform," he argued, "but I would use my life to defend them before seeing them put forth in any other way than through a free parliament and the national will."[48]

In turn, he argued for a public power, rooted in its social condition, with the capacity to intervene in public affairs. Examining the railroads, for example, Paradol insisted that proper regulation by a public power was a necessity in some cases. Though Paradol was an inveterate anglophile, on this particular point he argued that France had chosen the more productive path.[49] To his mind, a free market would not sufficiently build all necessary industries. The state was necessary to encourage "specific types of industry" in order to pre-vent the deleterious effects of competition and "the abuse of monopoly."[50] A democratic government had the right to intervene because it was invested with a particular form of power. Though designed to ensure liberty, a democratic government was not defined by its incapacity to coerce or act upon its popu-lation. "This force," he asked of democratic government, "is it condemned to an irremediable weakness?" No, he argued. He recalled that the French Rev-olution had revealed the power of a democratic government to mobilize its citizens. Napoleon III, he insisted, could never summon such support: "If the most concentrated government has great advantages at the beginning of a war, a prolonged struggle offers better chances to a government that is more free, for it finds in the moral strength of the nation and in the universal adhesion the means to suffer from a failure without being defeated."[51] A democratic re-gime could summon a moral strength, according to Paradol, that made it even more powerful than the highly coercive and concentrated regimes that claimed to have democracy in their favor.

The challenge then with a government that was not democratically consti-tuted was that "a government that is too concentrated does not have loyal citi-zens, for its liberty of action and its strength cannot inspire fear without at the same time soliciting mistrust."[52] Imperial regimes, monarchies or even republics that concentrated power in the hands of too few for too long, could not generate the confidence necessary to last and to ward off threats to the regime. Therefore, just as they would be incapable of defending themselves against a prolonged foreign enemy, they would necessarily face threats from within: "Excessive responsibility, unreasonable expectations, inevitable deceptions, these are the ordinary elements of our internal commotions; and it is in following this constant movement that we can explain the curious phenomenon: that the governments of France are in general weakened by their longevity, which should have consolidated them; in their duration they lose the driving force that created them and each day that goes by adds something to the increasingly heavy burden of responsibility."[53] By concentrating too much power in one point, such a regime offered an obvious target to be criticized or defended. The center of the system became so invested that it fell under the weight of its own responsibility. As a result, the longer they lasted, the weaker they became. This was not then a mere critique of the state or call for decentralization. It was rather a critique of a kind of state. A properly organized democratic state—a democratic society governed democratically—would maintain its strength over time. Thus, for Paradol, the socially constructed democratic government was both more powerful and endowed with a capacity for greater longevity.

At the center of this conception of the democratic state was also a critique of the bureaucratic autonomy that was a central pillar of the Second Empire. Of primary importance for Paradol was the dependence of civil servants on parliament. "In our centralized country, the elected Chamber is destined to control the administration and not be confounded with it," he argued. As a result, it was necessary to decrease the independence of civil servants by pushing their loyalties back toward elected officials instead of the administrative chain. "Civil servants who vote their own salary provide an unattractive spectacle which is poorly positioned to lift up the perception of national representation in public opinion." At the same time, he insisted, civil servants whose position depended on the executive should not be allowed to sit in the parliament. Here, he once again looked to England: "The only reason, or rather the only excuse, that we have ever been able to give for accepting civil servants in the Chamber is worthless. It is, we are told, to ensure that the Chamber has the aid of competent and enlightened people. Is the House of Commons in England an Assembly that lacks enlightened people?"[54]

Paradol therefore proposed a government in which the civil servants would be dependent not because they followed their superiors' orders directly, but because they faithfully served the parliament. He sought to achieve this by focusing on the possibility of career advancement:

It is necessary to make a simple calculation and ask ourselves what action the fear of dismissal has on the behavior of public civil servants. If one reflects for a moment, one will surely recognize that it is not the fear of dismissal (an exceptional accident which usually has merit) which keeps civil servant in a state of dependence with regards to the government. The guaranty of this necessary dependence, the stimulation of their zeal, is not the fear of the extremely rare dismissal, but it is the desire for advancement.[55]

For Paradol, England had been most successful in realizing this conception of state. Here, Laboulaye and Paradol formed an important pair for understanding international influences on reconceptualizing the French state in the years surrounding the foundation of the Third Republic. Indeed, Prévost-Paradol's fascination with the lessons of the English system for France matched, as we shall see, Laboulaye's interest in the American state. Both were founding figures of the Third Republic, though in very different ways, and both saw in their respective affinities for the United States and Britain a state model that could be imported back to France.

At the heart of Paradol's interest in the English model for France, then, was an attempt to import the basic structures that would ensure what he referred to as a democratic government. This democratic government was not marked by its incapacity to act or its weakness; it was instead defined by its capacity to govern more effectively by making it more accountable and more directly responsive to the people through the constant threat of an impartial dissolution. Summarizing the extraordinary powers of a system rooted in this organization, Paradol argued: "The freest people in the world, those who are furnished with local and individual liberties, that are represented correctly as so many interior fortresses against which all absolute power fails, this people has nonetheless judged that a sovereign authority can be usefully invested with the power to suspend or to reduce the most dear liberties; but this immense power has never been given to one man, it has been given exclusively to the jealous and all powerful guardianship of general liberty."[56] Even a democratic government could be invested with the power to suspend liberties—indeed, it was precisely because it was democratic that it was able to do so. But such power could never be given to just one person; it needed to be spread across the state, to its ministers and to parliament. The essence of good government then was the guardianship of general liberty—a liberty that could be ensured only by a state that could, on some occasions, reduce the very liberties it was designed to guarantee.

With Paradol's notion of divided government, we see a shift from an emphasis on the strong state that has dominated so much of our understanding of the French political past to what Michael Mann has called state "infrastructural power": the state's ability to coordinate social resources as opposed to its "despotic power"; that is, its ability to constrain and coerce.[57] No doubt, many of the previous nineteenth-century regimes, and especially the regime of Napoleon III, wielded more despotic power. But while Paradol's state model was less despotic, it also, far more importantly, distributed accountability across the bodies of the government and expanded its reach deeper into a French "democratic" society. Ira Katznelson has referred to precisely such a process in the American case as "a distinct form of statebuilding," one "that led to enhanced fiscal stability and capacity, augmented borrowing capabilities and an effective military."[58] In their respective works on the British state, Peter Baldwin and John Hobson have made similar claims on Britain's infrastructural capacity. "All states can be situated along a continuum," Hobson argues, "ranging from those polities that are 'embedded' within their societies at one end (Britain), to those which are 'isolated' from society at the other extreme (Russia)." Paradol's conception of democratic government shared this fundamental concern. In his view, the British state was able to ensure liberty and stability because it was "broadly embedded within society," as Hobson argues, or in the terms of Paradol, "a democratic society politically constituted as a democracy."[59] Paradol's ambition to democratize the French state was precisely an attempt to shift along this continuum from a less to more embedded government.

Equality and Colonization

Like many liberals of his day, Paradol's democratic conception was deeply committed to the question of liberty. However, his specific focus on the essential question of building a democratic government also pushed the question of equality to the fore. Here too, Paradol built on his liberal predecessors. Alluding directly to Tocqueville, Paradol noted: "One might believe that equality, upon which democratic despotism seems in part founded, and which it takes willingly as its flag, has nothing to fear; but is it not the idol for which everything else has been sacrificed?"[60] With this assessment, Paradol recited a common liberal critique of the first half of the century: an overemphasis on equality engendered despotism. In such a context, emphasis needed to be placed on liberty over political equality.

Paradol responded to this problem somewhat differently than others, however, arguing for a "democratic" practice of equality. From the perspective of actual practice, democratic despotism would ultimately betray the equality it claimed as its own: "democratic despotism will inevitably be reduced to fighting a war against equality."[61] He therefore sought to clarify modern democratic

equality by providing three essential conditions for its achievement: meritoc-
racy, equality before the law, and the refusal of nepotism. Democratic despo-
tisms would ultimately betray all of these modes of equality. They would hand
out favors to those who supported them most directly; they would apply the
law unevenly to the friends or the enemies of the regime; and, finally, all those
who betrayed the democratic ideal would necessarily seek to pass their power
on to their families and their children. In practice, democratic equality and
despotism would inevitably find themselves at odds.

But the political construction of equality also had other, less comforting
consequences. As stated above, Prévost-Paradol used his reading of Spinoza
to argue that a democratic government should be built on the peculiar social
conditions of a given nation. It is here that we encounter Prévost-Paradol's
nascent positivism. As in the works of others of his generation such as Ernest
Renan and Taine, social knowledge was the product of observation as opposed to the mapping of universal abstractions onto society. But this positivist approach had a surprising side-effect on Paradol's notion of equality.
If equality, from this perspective, was no longer an abstraction, then it was
properly conceived as a political construction that should animate a government rooted in the specificities of French society. Eschewing notions of natural law, Paradol insisted that equality in France had been "a conquest over
nature." In this conception, equality became a specifically national trait that,
and consequently, was politically appropriate for some societies and not others. "The sentiment of equality, is so strong and vivacious among us that it
would seem a second nature in France," he argued.[62]

Like other liberals, he recognized—and to some extent feared—the potential
power that political equality could bestow on any given regime. But, unlike other
liberals, since he perceived it as an inherent quality of French society, it needed
to be the foundation for democratic government. "It is wrong," he insisted, "to
consider equality to be a concession to power like a fruit of its tolerance or its
interest well-conceived."[63] To the contrary, equality "can only be maintained
within a society through incessant individual energy that prevents all attempts
at usurpation."[64] Democratic equality became a positive form of political action, and law became a means of creating equality instead of a mere protection.
Equality, he suggested, "consists in this: that all must be equally exposed to the
action of the laws and submitted to their empire."[65] In this sense, Paradol turned
the early nineteenth-century liberal conception of equality on its head: instead
of protecting naturally given individual rights or recognizing the inevitability
of equality in modern society, law became the power to act on all equally.

Reconsidering the relationship between liberty and equality in this way
challenged Napoleon III's claim that democracy reigned under restricted

liberty. At the same time, it undermined the conviction of so many early nineteenth-century liberals that democratic equality potentially supported tyranny. "According to a widely held prejudice, there exists, according to the very laws of nature and of politics, a sort of perpetual antagonism between equality and liberty; so much so that they are destined to increase and flourish in inverse relation and the simultaneous enjoyment of these two great goods of human life are forbidden to civilized societies." For Paradol this prejudice needed to be combated. First, he looked to existing examples, insisting that one had only to look so far as Switzerland, Belgium, or the United States to see that equality and liberty could coexist. Moreover, he insisted: "we can go even further and affirm that these two great possessions have an intimate relationship, that often liberty appears first and gives birth to equality, that they grow together and support one another."[66]

However, by defining equality solely as a national project—that is, by subordinating a discourse of rights to the equal power of the demos—Paradol also opened a dangerous path. While the political construction of equality was at the center of Paradol's conception of democracy, such a political understanding of equality also created a deep tension in Paradol's thinking on colonization and empire. His political construction of equality not only permitted a strong stance in favor of colonization, but in fact, since democratic equality had been made entirely distinct from a concern with the abstractions of natural rights or human equality, it opened the door to accepting colonial domination of those who were equal amongst themselves.

Prévost-Paradol's work held extraordinary influence over the founders of the Third Republic. So for all of his commitment to democracy, Prévost-Paradol's support of colonization must be considered. The colonial ambitions of the Third Republican democracy remain one of its most enduring legacies. The cohabitation of colonial antidemocracy within republican democracy requires an understanding of the grounds on which dedicated democrats were able to defend colonization. Paradol paid particular attention to the future of French colonization in Algeria. His analysis grew from his argument that European colonization had come to a crossroads. Echoing arguments of settler colonization, he argued, that there were two types of colonization. On the one hand were the "best" colonies—settler colonies—"which are founded on vacant territories or occupied by savage races that are rapidly destroyed by war or disappear on their own in the face of a superior race." Here again Britain had led the way, taking over "the colonies of North America, Australia, New Zealand, vast territories taken in one swoop by the Anglo-Saxon race, admirable establishments." There were then the colonies of a second type that should be understood as trading outposts: "those founded on occupied territories by docile races, unfit for war, easily governed and attached to the glebe or divided amongst themselves by blood and religion, in such a way as to never rise up against their conqueror: such is the case with India, or our Cochin-chine." These colonies he insisted were of no help to the "superior race that had conquered them and exploited them; the conquering race can only establish itself in small numbers, it is rather represented by the individuals who follow one another than the families that take root there." These trading colonies, however, could provide wealth far beyond the sacrifices and efforts that were necessary to establish them. The problem with Algeria, in Paradol's mind, though, was that it fell into neither of these categories. The situation had become entirely unstable under the Second Empire and could not continue.

There were indeed two further obstacles to the creation of a successful French colony in Algeria. First, there was "the existence of the Arab race that it appears equally difficult to assimilate or destroy." In other words, the racial characteristics of the inhabitants of North Africa made them formidable military opponents. The soil was occupied "and we cannot decide without scruples to hunt down and destroy those who occupy like the savages of the New World or Australia. They are not docile and soft like the Chinese, nor divided like inhabitants of India between Buddhists and Muslims; they love war and pursue it in the name of their Prophet, with a faith that survives all defeat."[67] As a result, the approach that the United States had taken on the American continent or the British in Australia, for example, was not a possibility. On the other hand, however, there was a political problem of determining the proper colonial regime: "our prolonged incertitude about the regime that must be adopted to govern and administer the colony. . . . It is time to put the great interest before all others, to establish laws in Africa that are solely conceived for extending French colonization, and that leaves the Arabs to pull out, as they may, with equal arms, in a battle for life." As a result, Algeria needed to develop into a settler colony along the same lines as Australia or North America, which meant a far greater military engagement. "It is French territory that must be populated as quickly as possible, possessed and cultivated by the French."[68]

Through this reasoning, Paradol was able to argue for a far more aggressive colonial enterprise. Speaking of those who sought to establish themselves in Algeria, Paradol insisted:

> If one goes to the South, I arm him one hundred times more and I support him with all my strength, with the hope that his example will be followed and that the limits of the fatherland will be extended so far. And I do not content myself with giving him a rifle and ammunition, I do something more important and more effective yet, I say he is right. And not the slightest hair on his

head shall be touched without being paid for with interest, for in twenty years, it will be of singular importance if there were ten or twenty thousand more French. There you have it . . . the policy that I would like to see followed with perseverance in Algeria and I am certain that if the national instinct listened on such matters we would follow it. We would escape the dead end that the Algerian question has run into, and the age of action would finally succeed the age of words.[69]

It was precisely through such a policy, Paradol argued, that France would be able to counter English imperial dominance across the world. Indeed, the British had achieved a situation that Paradol envied for his native France. Paradol was fascinated by the British ability to maintain liberty at home and conquer abroad. "The universal overflowing of the Anglo-Saxon race, this great flow that continues to run from the open bosom of Great Britain." What Paradol was most enthusiastic about in British colonization was the universal capacities of the "Anglo-Saxon race," which could expand without diminishing the potency of its source. In other words, he was captivated by the British ability to encounter and conquer other areas on the globe, to rule over them, without ever diminishing what he understood to be essential liberties. Thus the emphasis on the distinction between the subordinated colonial subjects and equal metropolitan citizens was essential. Through it, Paradol was able to conceive of the French as having a common interest that was opposed to native Algerians, at the same time that he looked to encourage the French control over the colonial territory.

Paradol therefore conceptualized the European contribution to mankind not as a discovery of human rights, but through the spreading of the national "interests" of the British and French across the world. In this way, universalism was not a given of humankind; it was the positive product of those few societies that had conquered it for themselves and sought to preserve it with proper institutions: "Such is the real issue at stake which will decide the future of humanity, and which remains open to our language and our blood outside our frontiers."[70] By conceiving of equality along social and racial lines, Paradol sought to maintain the political conditions necessary to maintain a democracy at home, while asserting that those populations that France ruled outside the Hexagon did not merit the same guarantees.

As a result, Paradol was able to draw the conclusion that France could spread out across the world as a universal power only if it first created a stable democratic government rooted in equality in the Hexagon. It was precisely here that the British had been so successful, he argued: "Do you want to see a spectacle that is entirely different, look for example at the colony of Queensland, in northern Australia. . . . Would this be possible if England still hesitated on the principles of free government, if she still doubted her legitimacy, its benefits, its very necessity for ensuring order and peace among men?"[71] Indeed, the problem with the current democratic despotism of the empire, he argued, was not its tendency to dominate the imperial possessions, but instead its incapacity to do so. This was a challenge for "the French race" itself. France needed to overcome "the two scourges on our race of despotism and anarchy that have rendered sterile the most fortunate gifts that any nation has ever received from heaven." In other words, despotism and anarchy were to blame for the inability to properly dominate France's colonial possessions. A democratic government, on the other hand, would govern the empire successfully in its own interest. Hesitations in adapting the proper democratic regime, he argued, were "nothing short of moral anarchy, more damaging and more fatal for the grandeur of nations than the material anarchy that troubles the streets and puts weapons in the arms of citizens."[72]

Paradol was thus able to maintain the claim that it was only by establishing a strong democratic state in France that the country would have the power to effectively colonize: "Because to firmly establish one's position in the world, to create nations in one's image, it is necessary to have a clear sense and knowledge of what one wants. One can only give what one has, and if the colonies emerge by some miracle out of a metropole filled with such disasters, how is it possible to avoid having something that resembles those devilish children with spoiled blood that betrays the cradle and are born as sad witnesses of their father's infirmity?"[73] And here again, the English revealed the proper path. It was their commitment to liberty and above all the stability of their regime that allowed them to so confidently expand their empire. "Supposing that England had such moral anarchy . . . what would the colony of Queensland look like? . . . Would we see anything other than a camp, a café, a theater and a prison?"[74] Constructing a government of equals in France, within the strict limits of the metropole, would create the very conditions for domination beyond—democratic equality could not spread across the world as an abstraction, but only as a particular social form.

The Democratic Origins of the Third Republic

Prévost-Paradol thus left a complex legacy for the founders of the Third Republic. While it has been widely recognized that he provided inspiration for the institutional and constitutional questions which they confronted after 1871, jurists considered that Paradol was also essential for his emphasis on the question of democracy. In particular, how this democratic emphasis released him from a commitment to any specific type of regime. Esmein, for example, noted this fundamental contribution: "Convinced that the foundation was more important than the form," he explored a series of institutions that "could be adapted almost indifferently to diverse forms of state that waited in the shadows."[75] Barthélemy also insisted that Paradol was exceptional in his enthusiastic embrace of democracy: "The most desirable constitution will be found at the junction of the previous systems and democracy; democracy is inevitable," he argued. Barthélemy therefore insisted that Paradol's work had contributed through its "quasi-indifference to the form of government."[76]

So alongside Paradol's influence on the organizational structure of the Republic was the fact that his argument for the foundations of democracy opened the door to the idea that being governed democratically had little, or even nothing, to do with the "external form" of the regime, as he called it. Paradol opened his chapter on executive power by stating that his book refused to decide on one form or the other: "Not only has this question not been treated, but by establishing the basis of a free and democratic government, and by slowly approaching the fact of this political construction, we are particularly attached to showing only those elements that could be applied to a monarchical democracy or a republican democracy."[77] Throughout *La France nouvelle*, Paradol insisted that either a republic or a monarchy could sit atop a democratic state. "The external form of government . . . I insist is a secondary question next to the capital question of the political and administrative reform of France."[78] He also made similar comments in his articles in the press. In a book review of works by Laboulaye and others he suggested that their works provided an important contribution because they were "applicable to all regimes, independent of any debate over the external form of government."[79]

In the context of constituting a new regime, this flexibility left open the essential question of how to assert legitimate authority in a regime that had declared itself a republic but was without a working constitution and locked in a generalized state of emergency during its first years of inception. In short, where could democratic authority come from in such tentative and dire circumstances? From this perspective, it is worth considering the impact of Paradol's fundamental distinction between "the external form of government" and the other question that interested him, the society-government relationship. By invoking this distinction and building the foundations of his political thought around it, Paradol was suggesting that what was peculiar to democracy was that it could be "internal" to any number of "external" regime structures—even one without a constitution at all. In other words, the actual regime was less important than matching a society to its government.[80]

No doubt, such a separation between democracy as a social-governance project and the multiplicity of regimes that could accomplish it was essential to Prévost-Paradol's rallying to the support of the liberal empire in the final year of the Napoleon III's reign.[81] But beyond Paradol's personally tragic relationship to the liberal empire, the applications of this theoretical distinction merit consideration. First, the distinction contributed to the very possibility of legitimating a democratic government without any consensus on the actual kind of regime that would govern the nation and its colonial empire. Thiers, as president of the republic, developed this idea while he attempted to rule as the executive of a country without a constitution: "Gentlemen, pacify, reorganize, raise the credit, revitalize your labors, such is the only possible and even appropriate policy at this moment. To such a policy, any reasonable, honest, enlightened man, no matter what he thinks of the Monarchy or the Republic must adhere."[82] Similarly, Albert de Broglie in May 1874 noted the influence of this distinction in the separation of powers legislated early in the Third Republic: "Principles that can be applied to all forms of government survive all revolutions; they are inherent in all legal regimes, whether they be permanent or temporary, whether they be called republic or monarchy."[83] Finally, such flexibility proved invaluable in the early years of the Third Republic as the Assembly welcomed an increasing number of deputies who were hostile to the very idea of a republican regime.

Unfortunately, however, this democratic model was also compatible with unwavering violence on the colonial periphery. As we shall see, liberals like Laboulaye and Thiers, who slowly converted to a form of democratic statehood, confronted this problem even as the republic was in toddling infancy, and, as we shall also see, each of them managed it in their own way. Paradol staked out an influential opinion rooted in a peculiarly equalitarian French society and the need for democratized government within the republic. As the republic became the guarantor of democracy on the periphery, however, Paradol's distinction between regime type and governance could work in the opposite direction as well. As he made clear, the regime type had little impact on how people were actually governed. Thus by evacuating any notion of natural right and basing equality on a solely positive internal conception of democratic society, Paradolian democracy also helped evacuate a humanitarian ideal. In this sense, Paradol embraced a positive theory of democratic government while opening the door to a radical distinction between those who were governed democratically by the republic and those who were not, depending on their social state. The demos had been assembled, but on the imperial periphery it had also potentially given birth to civil war.

3

EMERGENCY:
Edouard Laboulaye's Constitutionalism

The closer we become, the more we will understand the solidarity between the two continents and what I refer to as America's role in Europe.[1]

Napoleon withers, Washington swells.[2]

Unsatisfied with the main currents of postrevolutionary French politics, Prévost-Paradol was not alone in his attempt to reinterpret the democratic in order to break out of the political *cul-de-sac* of Bonapartist plebiscitary democracy. To be sure, there were those who looked across the Channel, but many others of this generation also looked across the Atlantic to reconceive the state through a democratized liberalism. As a constitutional historian of the United States, professor and then head administrator of the Collège de France as well as, among his other actions, organizer of the gift of the Statue of Liberty to the United States,[3] Laboulaye was one of the central figures of this push beyond the intellectual boundaries of French political theory. Laboulaye's academic studies, public lectures, and, ultimately, practice, as he played an active role in crafting the constitution of the Third Republic, uncover the glaring reality that liberal democratic theories of the French state on the eve of the Third Republic were not hermetically sealed within the nation's borders.

Any investigation into the transatlantic web of intellectual influences that nourished new thought on the state during this period necessarily falls upon Laboulaye, and upon his interpretation of the American state. First and foremost, he was in many ways *the* inheritor of the Tocquevillian problem. There were of course many others, as this book shows, who looked beyond France toward the United States to develop their theories of the state, but Laboulaye became in many ways the bearer of Tocqueville's torch after the latter's death. Therefore, his reading of Tocqueville and his attempts to elaborate on his colleague's theory of liberalism and democracy by confronting the problem of the state merit special attention for understanding the transition into the Third Republic.

Laboulaye developed an ambition to redefine the new possibilities *and* limits of a state in democracy. This new theory of the state, which was captured by Laboulaye's analysis of American institutions, may be understood as a new *liberal democratic state*. Beyond the common usage of this term, I am employing this appellation in a more specific historically transformational sense. I suggest that Laboulaye embraced the democratic foundations of government, while also insisting that the illiberal democracy of the Second Empire was highly problematic: "Many fear this democracy, which is rising incessantly. . . . I embrace it [*Je l'aime*]."[4] For Laboulaye, then, the Second Empire had not necessarily faulted in its plebiscitary democracy. In fact, Laboulaye was a great supporter of the tool of the plebiscite during the constitutional debates of the Third Republic. So in his view, the Second Empire had erred in its illiberalism. It was a regime dominated by the centralization of administrative power in the hands of a few at the expense of liberty. Laboulaye therefore thought and helped design a state with a proper distribution of power and respect for the rule of law and the individual. He sought the introduction of a liberal separation of powers, which necessarily restricted the executive's reach into all areas of government of society. However, what was radically new, and perhaps contradictory at first glance, was that the liberal distribution of power did not just limit but also strengthened the executive's power in those areas that remained under its control, and especially in maintaining public order in a democracy.[5] He arrived at this original formulation by wrestling with the problem of emergency government.

So by looking across the Atlantic, Laboulaye was able to conceive of a strong executive while critiquing both the Bonapartist and the revolutionary republican tradition in France.[6] In contrast to the Convention or the First and Second Empires, he argued, the American president had saved the nation in exceptional circumstances without claiming to be the unmediated manifestation of popular sovereignty. Lincoln further showed, according to Laboulaye, that in times of crisis a republic was best served by an executive who overstepped the legal limits of his power as long as he did not change the constitution and his exceptional powers were of a limited duration.[7] Thus, in Laboulaye's constitutional thought, the nineteenth-century American state provided one of the strongest models for thinking the state of emergency in a liberal democratic context. Laboulaye's constitutional thought—specifically his theory of a limited but potentially substantial executive power—, his distinction between constituent and executive power, and his analysis of Lincoln's use of exceptional powers became the foundation of his conception of emergency. It was, in turn, through the idea of emergency that Laboulaye was able to democratize his liberalism and develop a more robust notion of the modern state.

Tocqueville and the Origins of Laboulaye's
Theory of the Liberal Democratic State

Born in 1811, Edouard Laboulaye was one of the key members of the second generation of postrevolutionary French liberalism. A supporter of the July Monarchy, Laboulaye was trained in law and was elected to the *Académie des inscriptions et belles lettres* in 1845.[8] While his early works had earned him a prominent place within Parisian intellectual circles, Laboulaye would not become a career politician or a well-known academic voice until the 1850s.[9] A political moderate, Laboulaye maintained an institutional elasticity across the 1848 divide that would become characteristic of his political career (as well as of many liberals of his generation)—he rejected neither the July Monarchy nor the Second Republic, favoring above all the regime that could ensure stable liberal democratic institutions, protect private property and prevent revolution.

In the 1840s, Laboulaye developed the focus on the United States and its constitutional history that would become the hallmark of his oeuvre. Of course, at the center of this study was the work of his colleague Alexis de Tocqueville and especially the latter's *Democracy in America*, which had provided a privileged model for interpreting the American case and its potential for informing French politics. Tocqueville's appreciation of American democracy provided a model for liberals of his generation, like Laboulaye, and beyond. Laboulaye's description of Tocqueville's thought therefore merits reflection. For, beyond Tocqueville's actual writings, the question of his reception, especially in the 1850s and 1860s was central to the elaboration of the democratic question.

Upon Tocqueville's death, Laboulaye wrote an extensive article of almost seventy pages, which outlined both his support and occasional critiques of Tocqueville's oeuvre. Laboulaye insisted on the importance of Tocqueville's thought for French liberal democracy: "Between the institutions of the two countries there were not only profound differences, there was a radical opposition that nothing could reconcile. In France, Mr. de Tocqueville could only see the state; in America, it was always the individual that he found before him."[10] Specifically, Tocqueville's writings on executive power suggested that the American case could beneficially inform French politics by offering a model of a thriving democratic society in the minimal shadow of a comparatively weak executive. "I could have emphasized the governmental power of the King of France, stretched out and penetrating into administration and individual interests in a thousand different ways," Tocqueville wrote, opposing it to the American executive, "which is only exercised within a restricted sphere of sovereignty."[11]

In the field of constitutional law, Tocqueville, like his liberal interlocutors, also insisted on the importance of the separation of powers and the distinction between the United States and France. Here, he pointed specifically to the wisdom of the Americans, who, unlike the French, guaranteed the dependence of the American president on the legislative body. "The [French] king shares the right to propose a bill with the Chambers [the legislative]," he noted. "The President does not have the right to such an initiative." He then pointed out that "the King of France thus walks as an equal alongside the legislature that cannot act without him just as he cannot act without it," while "the President is placed alongside the legislature as an inferior and dependent power."[12] In Tocqueville's view, the legislative initiative held by the French king threatened the very stability of the political system by upsetting the separation of powers and the checks between them. To the contrary, the American constitution reduced the power and independence of the executive.

With this in mind, Laboulaye continued praise for Tocqueville's analysis. Most importantly, he highlighted that an essential feature of Tocqueville's liberalism was to argue that the growth of the state should not come at the expense of the individual: "The principal object, the essential object of politics, is not the state, but the individual. . . . Reduce the individual to grow the state is to sacrifice everything for sterile uniformity."[13] Then, lending words to Tocqueville that he would later employ himself in his own work, he suggested that "Mr. Tocqueville did not dream of a government that broke with the national tradition; he left in the hands of the state the army, the marine, diplomacy, legislation, justice, taxation, finance, the direction of general interests and the ultimate police powers; he only asked that we release the administrative knot that suffocated the individual without benefiting society."[14] What is striking is the extent to which Laboulaye witnessed Tocqueville's recognition of the potential governmental power and the regulatory state in democracy, as long as it served society. In spite of the reception of Tocqueville's work, especially in the second half of the twentieth century, his contemporary Laboulaye—like Mill—recognized that these themes were central.

However, he did find fault in the second volume of Democracy in America. It was in this volume, Laboulaye argued, that Tocqueville attempted to stretch the dangers of democracy beyond reasonable limits. "The error of Mr. Tocqueville was that he did not recognize that the word democracy applies to the most diverse societies and that each of these societies is subject to a thousand influences that mix and combine with political life."[15] Laboulaye did recognize the importance of Tocqueville's contribution, but the problem was that within this analysis, what exactly was democratic and what was not had been lost. "Too often," Laboulaye insisted, "[Tocqueville] renders democracy

responsible for the vices and weaknesses for which it is not necessarily responsible. If a taste for well-being is an essential trait of our age, is it really the fault of
equality? Wouldn't it be useful to search for the cause in the development of industry, the advantages of a long period of peace, or the progress of wealth in general?"[16] For Laboulaye, unjust as it may sound today, Tocqueville was an author
who came back to this one singular idea incessantly: "*Democracy in America*
is a book written with one single idea to which he constantly returns in all its
forms; the style is at times so austere as to be monotonous."[17] As important as
Tocqueville had been for putting the democratic question at the center of politics, Laboulaye considered that what remained to be done was a more elaborate
theorization of its exact contours.

Following his discussion of *Democracy in America*, Laboulaye focused on
Tocqueville's contributions to the constitution for the new republic in 1848.
Erupting on the heels of an obstreperous liberal monarchy, the arrival of the
Second Republic brought liberals and republicans back together to build institutions in a revolutionary context. Tocqueville agreed to participate in drafting the constitution of the Second Republic and attempted to hold to his previous positions within the Commission.[18] Inevitably, one of the key areas of
discussion was the executive power. Given his deep conviction that a strong
president might reinforce French centralization and consequently smother a
potentially nascent democratic society, Tocqueville insisted on a weak executive. Here again, Tocqueville's eyes were on the United States as his analysis
changed little from that set forth in his *Democracy*. He regularly observed
that the American president was weak and in one explicit reference he plainly
stated that "in America, the President has little power."[19] He accepted that
there should doubtless be a president in the new republic, but the constitution should check his ambitions by limiting him to one term in office. During
the debates on the 1848 constitution, he explained: "I would rather see the
Constitution exposed to an accidental and transitory danger than see society
habitually subject to the corrupting influence of a president who employs the
strength he possesses to prolong his power."[20] In other words, Tocqueville
resisted an executive who could respond to occasional threats or "transitory
dangers" because, in his view, it would necessitate strengthening the executive. Such reinforcement of the executive, even for momentary or exceptional
crises, could only undermine democracy because it was necessarily opposed
to the cultivation of a more democratic society that also respected individual
liberty. Later, in his *Recollections*, Tocqueville explicitly opposed France's history of strong executives: "I did not think then, any more than I think now,
that a Republican form of government was the one best suited to the needs
of France, meaning by 'Republican government' an elected executive branch.

Where the habits, traditions and mores of a people have assured such a vast sphere of power for the executive, its instability will always, whenever troubled days come, lead to revolution, and even in peaceful times such instability will be uncomfortable."[21] Tocqueville paired the republic and an elected executive, and he adjoined both to the French political tradition that had been unable to establish a stable democracy which would also cherish liberty.

In his *Considérations sur la Constitution*, published in 1848, Laboulaye presented his liberal ideas on the fresh republic. However, offering his opinion about the proper regime, he clearly disagreed with Tocqueville, emphasizing the role of executive power to ensure its solidity. His departure from Tocqueville's views was gentle but clear.[22] Laboulaye expressed the core of his departure from Tocqueville's earlier ideas in his comment that "politically" Tocqueville "was born in 1789."[23] Indeed, as the young Laboulaye demonstrated in his 1848 pamphlet, he too was critical of administrative centralization, but he also entertained the possibility of various levels of government and executive control (cautiously, of course, depending on where and when) alongside his adherence to some basic liberal ideals of the late eighteenth and early nineteenth centuries.

Here too, Laboulaye thought that Tocqueville's actions were left wanting. Commenting on Tocqueville's conduct in 1851 during the attempts to revise the constitution, Laboulaye could not hide his disappointment, revealing that he "would have dreamed of a more difficult and greater role for Tocqueville," whose hands were no doubt tied by "a character that was too chevaleresque to hold his party accountable in a moment of danger." Significantly, he compared Tocqueville's incapacity to imagine a revision of the constitution not to the capacities of Napoleon, but to one of the founding fathers of the American constitution, celebrating "Hamilton and a handful of devoted citizens who called upon American patriotism to pull out of a society in ruins a federal constitution."[24] Characteristically, Laboulaye insisted that the Americans did provide a model for saving the republic in moments of crisis, something Tocqueville regretfully seemed too reticent to accept.

Thus when he focused specifically on the question of the executive, Laboulaye was more inclined to turn—like Blanc, as we will see—to Mill. Citing Mill directly, he drew the idea that "as the relationships between men develop and become more complex, the task of government will necessarily increase; the entire question is to keep this increase within the sphere of the state. The life of a people is not a fixed quantity that cannot be increased on the one side without decreasing on the other, it is a force that grows indefinitely; we concede without hesitation that in an advanced civilization, the people will be free while the government is very busy."[25] Laboulaye then did not so much look to critique Tocqueville as to attempt to build a more elaborate theory of government, and particularly the executive, out of his work.

Laboulaye is indicative of a group of liberal thinkers that emerged in the latter 1850s and 1860s who were avid readers of Tocqueville and found many resources in his fecund thought, but displayed greater confidence than Tocqueville in some of the capacities of central state institutions, the executive in particular, to promote a healthy democratic polity, especially in times of crisis. From this perspective, it is of no small consequence that Laboulaye reedited his article on Tocqueville in a book entitled *The State and Its Limits*. From the outset, the title already opened up the necessity of the state as well as the necessity of more carefully defining the limits of its power. Such a title did not so much make a radical break from Tocqueville as place the cursor on a different set of problems. Of course, Tocqueville had been interested in the fundamental question of the democracy as a social condition. And of course, as we have seen, he had considered the problem of democratic administration and the state through the police powers. Laboulaye even put an emphasis on this problem in his discussion of Tocqueville. But as Henry Michel noted at the turn of the twentieth century in the heart of the Third Republic, Tocqueville "was not afraid of the idea that the state could intervene often in favor of equality and to establish justice in social relations. But what he was missing was to trace, with sufficient precision, the limit of these interventions."[26] It was precisely here that Laboulaye sought to intervene. For Laboulaye, liberty and the state could grow simultaneously as long as the limits of the state were clearly defined. Thus, while he too favored decentralization and individual liberty, he did not condemn the delegation of power to the executive as a threat to a healthy democratic society. Rather, in specific circumstances, he accepted the central government, and specifically the executive, as a solution to France's political volatility in the name of national unity. A strengthened executive, he argued, if appropriately designed, could more effectively navigate between "transitory danger" and liberal democracy.[27] What was necessary, as Michel pointed out, was a more specific analysis of the state along with when and how to establish its limits— and this was precisely the ambition of Laboulaye's book *The State and Its Limits*.

Within this vision, the United States was also of signal importance. Laboulaye's pamphlet *Considerations sur la constitution* appeared in 1848 at just the moment when Tocqueville and the constitutional commission debated the institutional shape of an executive. But from the opening pages, Laboulaye showed his differences with Tocqueville by pointing out the importance of honoring a more powerful executive. Writing in the wake of the June Days and Cavaignac's declaration of a "state of siege," Laboulaye expressed a preference for an executive strong enough to save the country from dissolution. It is no small detail that from his liberal perch (and in favor of the republic) he dedicated his work to "General Cavaignac, head of the executive power"— celebrating the Cavaignac who had crushed the last gasp of a "social" revolution in the name of the republic.[28] Laboulaye's approach was original in that he celebrated the general without looking to compromise the republican regime, even if this meant governing momentarily through the state of siege. In Cavaignac, Laboulaye argued, France had found neither a new Louis-Philippe nor a Napoleon; it had not recreated the republican Terror either; rather it had unknowingly happened upon a French version of the American tradition:

> By placing the destiny of the fatherland in your [Cavaignac's] hands, these events have carved out a position for you that is comparable to that of Washington. In a war that was far crueler than a foreign war, you have shown a strength and humanity worthy of this great man. Now in order to complete this historical parallel that you have begun so nobly, you must found, with our legislators, a truly free and truly republican Constitution. May the wisdom and the exquisite instinct of this hero of the United States serve as an example to you.[29]

For Laboulaye, events had pushed Cavaignac to extraordinary measures and he had risen to the occasion, but it was now necessary to build solid institutional foundations for the Second Republic. The executive was, then, the essential force that responded to political crises, but his legitimacy to act strongly depended on the capacity to demobilize and return to the democratic foundations of the regime in the wake of these emergency circumstances. From this perspective, the United States offered the most coherent vision of executive power in a republic: "The questions dividing us are the very questions that divided the Founders of the American Republic: the declaration of rights, the independence of the executive power, the maintenance of legislative power within the limits that prevent it from degenerating into an insufferable tyranny. Washington's solutions were accepted by his contemporaries and made the greatness of America."[30]

The role of the state in Laboulaye's vision of American democracy is striking. First, Laboulaye did not argue that the division of powers weakened the American executive but that it increased its capacities. According to Laboulaye, the real danger to France in mid-1848 was the concentration of power into the hands of any one body of government. Therefore, he was as concerned about an all-powerful, unicameral legislature as about a dictatorial executive. A unicameral legislature would, he feared, impinge on the purview of the executive: "What will your president do when the Assembly imposes its unjust will and forces him by a two-day vote to revoke a treaty that has already been accepted or declare a war that he does not condone—he who is given the responsibility of the country's destiny and is responsible before France, Europe and all of posterity?"[31] The only way to avoid such confusion, Laboulaye insisted, was to distribute power across two chambers and the executive along the lines of the United States. This division of legislative powers would in turn ensure the independence of the president. Thus to the liberal mind of Laboulaye, each power was to be strictly separated from the other, but this division of power was not designed to limit the state's power to act.

He summarized this point in an article on *La République constitutionelle*, citing Bossuet: "That which you weaken so that it will not oppress you becomes impotent to protect you."[32] The powers of the president, he argued, needed to be strictly defined, but within that sphere, they needed to be robust enough to accomplish essential tasks effectively: namely, acting as commander and chief of the army, signing treaties, and above all defending "public security." "Past experience," he argued, "and an interest and desire for all of France—all of these aspects suggest that the perfect independence of the executive power should be conserved and even expanded. . . . The head of the government must be able to decide quickly, for everything depends on him."[33] In short, by limiting the sphere within which the president could act, he would acquire greater independence and therefore would be even more effective in those areas that concerned him.

Distributing power to reinforce the state was central to Laboulaye's interpretation of the United States. Drawing from his creative reading of the American example in his essay on the US constitution from 1849, Laboulaye insisted that it was the United States that had resolved the fundamental problem of the relationship between the executive and the legislative: "Thus, for example, we all feel that the executive power requires independence and that the country must have the right to surveillance at every moment. Since 1789, we have only succeeded in invigorating authority or pinning it under the complete influence of the assemblies. Our administration has gone back and forth from impotent to despotic. The Americans have resolved this question by making the president independent from the Assembly."[34] In his statist view, the US constitution provided a third way out of the French impasse between legislative hegemony and an authoritarian executive by, paradoxically, increasing state efficacy through the horizontal distribution of power across the different branches. Later, during the debates on the constitution of the Third Republic, Laboulaye reaffirmed the American solution:

> *Revolutionary or French School*: The executive power must be a subordinate power, the simple minister of the will of the Assembly.

> *American School*: The executive power must be independent from the Assemblies; for two reasons: 1. Because it is essential to have a responsible and energetic government; 2. Because the independence of executive power maintains the sovereignty of the people in preventing the temptation of usurpation that can mislead Assemblies.[35]

In his view, then, the American state both avoided despotism and ensured popular sovereignty by reinforcing the executive's authority in specific cases. Laboulaye's broader vision of the efficacy of the American liberal democratic state suggested that it had little to envy European state powers. Summarizing his view of American institutions, Laboulaye argued:

> Open the Constitution and search for what separates the United States from European Governments. Nothing more than greater local independence; as far as political sovereignty is concerned, it belongs entirely to the President and Congress. The supreme power of the executive legislative, judiciary, the right to make war and peace, are in the hands of the central authority. . . . The diplomacy, the army, the marines, customs, the post office, money, all of these privileges of sovereignty were removed from the States and given to the federal government. The President commands the individual militias and controls naturalization; he also represents the nation to foreign powers.[36]

This was the capacious vision of the nineteenth-century American liberal democratic state, which, he insisted, only minimally departed from the European state model in its responsibilities. Alongside the reinforced local authorities, all of the essential state powers were present: the monopoly on coercive power, fiscal duties, diplomacy, the postal service, and citizenship and greater local governance—none of these powers threatened democracy; they were all essential for its effective functioning. Therefore, Laboulaye's vision of American democracy marked a subtle but important departure from Tocqueville by placing an accent on exactly when and how the state, and specifically the executive, could act to save the republic. And yet, he did so *at the same time* that he emphasized local autonomy and individual freedom. "In my system, nothing is more easily done than organizing the executive power without putting liberty in danger,"[37] Laboulaye summarized succinctly.

The Colonial State of Liberal Democracy

If Laboulaye was focused on elaborating the role of the state that he had inherited from Tocqueville's liberalism, his approach to the colonies differed more thoroughly. Indeed, his liberal democratic redefinition of state power opened a path out of the impasse of Tocqueville's authoritarian liberal imperialism. As many historians and political scientists have noted, Tocqueville's liberalism confronted its limits on the troubled terrain of imperial expansion in Algeria throughout the July Monarchy.[38] In his writings on Algeria, Tocqueville compared the French imperial project to the United States' westward expansion. In so doing, he consistently regretted (but nonetheless insisted upon) the necessity of using a powerful administrative apparatus and martial law in Algeria to promote the political stability and the glory of the metropole. Thus, it was also in the colonial context that Tocqueville theorized a reinforced administrative state power. For example, Tocqueville elaborated a central tenet of his imperial thought—and elaborated a central theme in his discussion of the regulatory police powers—when he wrote: "Civil administration should be concentrated in the hands of an official who, as the head of all the departments, would give them a common and continuous direction. This is urgent and must not be put off. Another task is not less pressing. It is the creation of a government council composed differently from the existing council and with more extended powers."[39] Such extended powers were essential for ensuring the order against native Algerians. Margaret Kohn has noted that Tocqueville ultimately settled on a dual approach to governing Algeria: a permanent state of exception for native Algerians and the rule of civilian law for the native French.[40] This analysis misses that Tocqueville had an elaborate notion of administrative intervention in the police powers which provided ample resources for keeping order in particular cases on the imperial frontier.

Laboulaye's work on Algeria was far more sporadic than Tocqueville's, although his remarks indicate that he thought heavily about the subject and had clear ideas about its proper evolution.[41] Like Tocqueville's, his vision of Algeria was directly tied to his analysis of North America. In the case of Laboulaye, however, it was not the contemporary experience of New England democracy but rather the imagined and idyllic beginnings of North American colonization. Favorable as well to the settler colonies that Paradol celebrated in the British model, his longest discussions of Algeria are therefore to be found in his first volume on the history of the United States focusing on the period from the seventeenth century to the Revolution. In this work, first published in 1855, and in stark contrast to Tocqueville's writings, he sought something more akin to a Lockean Carolina, a site from which to sketch the ideals of a system built on individualism, private property, and the rule of law.[42]

This radical shift in presenting the colonial project should be placed in the context of the 1850s when French colonization in Algeria was achieving a new stability and the question of the form of a more stable imperial state came to the fore.[43] In the 1850s, the Second Empire was confronted with new challenges in its colonial empire, especially in the realm of state building. Recognizing the necessity of a new administrative structure in the colonies, Napoleon III created a Ministry of Algeria and the Colonies from 1858 to 1860. On a more theoretical level, this transition from military expansion to state governance helps explain the shocking change in tone from Tocqueville's icy pragmatism of the 1830 and 1840s to Laboulaye's legalist approach in little more than two decades. As Tzvetan Todorov notes, "When he wrote his report on Algeria for the Chamber of Deputies, Tocqueville asked only one question: 'Is the domination that we are currently imposing on the former Regency of Alger useful for France?' "[44] Laboulaye, however, argued for asserting the power of a liberal democratic state differently.

Writing with what appears an almost total amnesia of the conquest against Abd el-Kader, Bugeaud's infamous *razzias,* and territorial expansion, Laboulaye developed a rights-based conception of French imperialism. "The age of conquest and adventure is over," he contended.[45] Instead of insisting on the role of the army and martial law in removing indigenous populations, he openly recognized that those who had lived on the territory for centuries might have land rights and that these rights should not be undermined militarily, but instead protected by law. At the same time, however, he made a distinction between these property rights and sovereignty. Spinning his argument out of a seventeenth-century reference, he explained:

> [William] Penn held his charter to colonize the province to which he left his name from James II and he certainly did not believe that an Indian deed could change the charter of his master. It was simply the possession of the land that he purchased from the Indians. In other words, he acted as we have acted in Algeria. Our sovereignty over the lands occupied by tribes who are nominally independent will allow the French and foreign immigrants to buy an Arab deed, the property of the soil where the tribe leaves its beasts to roam; but we would never accept that the Arabs, by selling the fields which they occupy, could sell a portion of Algerian sovereignty to England.[46]

In Laboulaye's view, native populations could be removed from occupied land only by consent and contract, just as William Penn had done in early North American colonization. However, Laboulaye insisted, their ability to dispose of the land did not mean that the native populations had any sovereign claims over the territory. Laboulaye, in effect, asserted a "legal" imperialism by decoupling indigenous property rights and the sovereignty of nations.

This new *constitutional imperialism* developed out of an international network of state theorists that united Laboulaye with Johann Caspar Bluntschli and Francis Lieber. Together, in the 1860s, they theorized state sovereignty through constitutional and international law as well as war codes.[47] Their common project came to fruition when Laboulaye prefaced the French edition and translation of Bluntschli's *Code of International Law* to which he appended Lieber's *Instructions for the Government of Armies of the United States in the Field*.[48] In words that Laboulaye echoed almost verbatim in his historical analysis, Bluntschli included a chapter on territorial sovereignty in which he noted: "The forms admitted in private law, such as the purchase, sale, exchange, transcription, usufruct, and mortgages, even if they were frequently used in the middle ages, cannot be applied to the acquisition of modern sovereignty. . . . The sale, according to which one party cedes its sovereignty and the other pays in compensation a sum of money is unworthy of our age."[49] For Bluntschli, property could be sold, but national sovereignty could not; as the cornerstone of international law, national state sovereignty was inviolable. Therefore, unlike Tocqueville, Laboulaye could not justify French expansion into sovereign Algerian territory either through a language of glory or political necessity, because such justification would have undermined the basic tenets of his international legal theory. Laboulaye could, however, legally justify French colonization by granting property rights to native populations while conveniently arguing that they had been ignorant and bereft of territorial sovereignty. State sovereignty could only be established through the imperial expansion of a sovereign nation state like France, he argued.

It should be noted that this decoupling of property rights and territorial sovereignty became an essential feature of Napoleon III's Algerian policy in the 1860s, especially after 1863 when the Second Empire passed a new law guaranteeing indigenous populations the usufruct of their land. Just two years later, on July 14, 1865, another law made the fundamental, and hitherto almost unthinkable, distinction between French nationality and citizenship for indigenous populations. These laws have been attributed largely to Napoleon III's "indigenophilia" and the influence of Saint-Simonians such as Frédéric Lacroix or Ismaÿl Urbain.[50] However, the fact that Laboulaye and his circle of constitutional theorists had been making similar arguments through their analyses of the United States suggests that the origins of this new distinction between property rights and sovereignty as well as citizenship and nationality were responding to a much larger international movement. In the case of Laboulaye, these distinctions generated the stunning paradox that liberty should be the foundation for colonial rule: "We stubbornly insist on administering Algeria from afar, and have not yet understood, after so many failures, that the first foundation of any colonization is liberty."[51]

Laboulaye's approach to the colonies differed then from that of Paradol, even if the effect of metropolitan dominance remained the same. Shifting from a discourse of equality to one of liberty and sovereignty, his constitutional imperialism was not divided into metropolitan, which had conquered equality, and colonized spaces, which had not (as was the case for Prévost-Paradol); nor did he rely on the repressive capacities of the police powers (as had been the case for Tocqueville).[52] His conception of imperialism was in fact guided by a conception of international law. One question however remained: Who was legitimately endowed with the right to be protected under such law? Obviously, the metropolitan French, who had become sovereign, had accomplished the fundamental step necessary to participate in an international law governed by sovereign nation states. The indigenous populations of Algeria, however, had not formed into a sovereign nation state and therefore needed to be ruled by the French to acquire the same benefits of sovereignty in such a context. So this approach to the colonies opened up a new problem: sovereignty was granted by a democratic authority that ruled in the name of the whole, even if it was an external imposition for a portion of the population. In other words, the popular sovereignty that ensured a democratized liberalism also provided the universal foundation for imperial expansion. To come to terms with such an original vision of the imperial state Laboulaye returned to his analysis of the American state and, increasingly in the 1860s, to its Civil War president.

Laboulaye's Lincoln

The American Civil War and the ostensible disintegration of the American republic was especially important for those liberals who had been attentive to the American case, such as Laboulaye. In this context, the bloody conflict between former compatriots and the ultimate success of the Union became a reservoir of political theory on the executive. In particular, the political juxtaposition of the Second Empire and the American Civil War (especially Lincoln's presidency) reinforced Laboulaye's conviction that the Americans were equipped with a liberal democratic state that could maintain the unity of a democratic nation without sacrificing necessary liberties, even in the most difficult circumstances.

Laboulaye often referred to the political limitations of the Second Empire's overburdened central administration and personal rule, which he accused of destroying French democratic life: "As a republic or a monarchy, France is forever an army which must live out the thoughts of its leaders," he wrote.[53] He further argued, in veiled (and sometimes less-veiled) words, that the regime of Napoleon III had failed to establish the desired reign of liberty: "Today, just as it was during the years of the First Empire and the First Restoration, they explain to us that France has been misguided by vain phantoms and that we are not fit for liberty. It is in the name of this tradition, or the French genius, that the necessary changes, which would lead to pacific and fecund progress, are pushed aside."[54] In Laboulaye's view, Napoleon III was guilty of the same errors as his uncle: an overbearing and deeply illiberal state that prevented the reign of liberty: "We have never been more than half-free. The administration has always dominated the majority of our rights," he insisted.[55]

As a result, Laboulaye built his interest in the United States during these years on overcoming the perceived need to ensure national unity through ever-greater political and administrative centralization. For Laboulaye, it was Lincoln's use of executive powers that opened a path toward the hitherto contradictory position that greater liberty and decentralization could ensure national unity. Lincoln, Laboulaye argued, demonstrated the importance for a democratically elected and liberally bound president to be able to rise above strict institutional boundaries in response to the crises of a nation, without undermining the constitution, the rule of law, and therefore the cause of liberty. Lincoln, in his view, had deployed the full weight of the modern state, grounded in popular sovereignty, in the service of his nation. "What is the war in America, which has been fought with such tenacity and courage, if not the supreme effort on the part of the people to sacrifice everything in the name of unity?"[56] Laboulaye asked in his preface to *Les États-Unis et la France*. This question cut to the heart of Laboulaye's interest in the American Civil War: in contrast to the overbearing centralized administration of the empire that justified itself in the name of national unity, Laboulaye discovered a polity that was "free," but willing, for a brief moment, to sacrifice "everything" to maintain its unity. He juxtaposed this "sacrifice" in the name of liberty to Napoleon III's state control: "As for national unity, we are more committed to it than anyone else; we have little time for federations. But national unity has nothing to do with absolute power, nor with centralized uniformity, nor arbitrary administration."[57]

Moreover, Napoleon III's empire, he insisted, had enrolled liberty and order in a zero-sum game, when a true liberal democracy required precisely the reverse: "Public order is a big word; but if it is separated from liberty, it is just another name for force." "We all desire public order," he continued, insisting that "the primary condition of civil life is security."[58] Order was a precondition for liberty and according to Laboulaye, it could be achieved in two ways. In some states, he argued, pointing toward the Second Empire, "it is the administration, that is, a certain number of civil servants" that are responsible for maintaining public order. He suggested that the United States, however, had revealed a different path: "There are two ways of asserting public order; the rule of law or the rule of men. In constitutional countries, it is the law, protector of all rights, that maintains the public peace through the magistrates."[59] Order was to be established and maintained then by protecting the law and the people, not by increasing the number of civil servants or expanding the administrative and centralizing capacities of the state. He concluded with a question that cut to the heart of his rejection of the empire and his sustained interest in the United States: "Is it not time to put an end to these old-fashioned politics?"[60]

Laboulaye remained convinced that Lincoln's success in maintaining the Union had been the result of the potent combination of respect for the constitution and the executive's robust executive powers. While the liberal executive could never threaten the constitution, Laboulaye argued that he should be able to employ almost any means necessary for a short duration to save it. Through this theory, Laboulaye proposed an executive with the ability to exert absolute power in exceptional circumstances in order to protect the liberties of the people. Such an approach differed radically from the regime of the Second Empire because the use of these absolute powers was restricted to a brief moment, whereas the administrative centralization of the empire instituted a permanent state of servitude. In the immediate aftermath of the Civil War, Laboulaye, together with colleagues Augustin Cochin, Henri Martin, and Agénor De Gasparin, argued that the denouement of the Civil War provided a model for executive action in extraordinary circumstances. In their celebration of the end of the "Lincoln dictatorship," they wrote:

> Following in Mr. Lincoln's footsteps, he [Andrew Johnson] has understood the necessity of putting an end as speedily as possible to the period of exceptional powers; he has set the example of the head of a government hastening to abdicate all dictatorship and to restore the national liberties in full. We are in a good position to applaud—we who have consistently predicted that you would crown your struggle by thus pardoning the vanquished, disbanding your armies, re-establishing the regular working of your institutions, and showing the world for the first time a constitution emerging intact from civil war.[61]

In spite of the exceptional powers that Lincoln had exerted in the early moments of the Civil War, Laboulaye and his colleagues insisted that he had
clearly not opened a dangerous path to extended "dictatorship" or "despotism."
Laboulaye was of course aware that the president had acted under exceptional
circumstances and had even suspended *habeas corpus*, but in this context, he
was acting to save the constitution: "Was Mr. Lincoln a despot who violated
his oath and threw national liberties to the ground? No."[62] Even if the American executive had bordered on despotism, he had indeed *served* the constitution, and the end of the period of exceptional powers was proof of this in
itself.

Toward a Liberal Democratic State

The collapse of the Second Empire, the declaration of the Third Republic, and
the revolutionary upheaval of the Commune brought the full complexity of
building an institutional architecture in a contentious republican empire to the
fore. During this period, Laboulaye mobilized his previous work on constitutional history to become an active participant in designing the new republican
constitutional laws and the formation of a liberal and democratic state. That
is, he sought the construction of a state that was divided (i.e., liberal) and took
deep roots in French society through mass participation (i.e., democratic), but
used these techniques of limited powers and greater accountability to make the
state more effective rather than less. During this period he also filled the role of
weathered liberal statesman that Tocqueville had occupied in the constitutional
committee of the Second Republic.[63] He quickly overcame the tarnish that his
support for the Liberal Empire of 1870 had placed on his political reputation,
and rallied to the republic while presenting his candidacy in the legislative elections held in July 1871. In this election, he won a seat to the National Assembly
representing the Department of the Seine. Once seated in the Assembly, he
maintained his social conservatism and took on an important role in the *centre
gauche*. His election by the *centre gauche* to the Senate in 1875 was a sign of the
esteem in which his party and the conservative Assembly at large held him.[64]
Throughout this period, he hoped to establish the republic permanently and
avoid any further revolution, preferring his own appellation, the "République
constitutionelle," to that of Thiers', "République conservatrice."

During the constitutional debates, Laboulaye reedited many of his earlier
texts with new annotations and new chapters. In particular, his *Questions constitutionelles*, published in 1872, reproduced his *Considérations sur la Constitution* from 1848 with a new preface and notes and included a number of new
articles on the essential questions of constituent powers and sovereignty.[65]

These reedited volumes reveal Laboulaye's continued conviction that the theory of a liberal democratic state he had been forging was relevant for the constitutional debates of the 1870s. In particular, he insisted upon separating the representative institutions of the state and the constituent power; sovereignty should necessarily remain in the hands of the people and therefore the constitution could be approved and changed only by the people themselves. As he wrote in his article entitled "Sovereignty," "before and after the election, there is only one sovereign in France: the Nation."[66] Laboulaye was therefore convinced that constitutional ratification through plebiscite was a fundamental necessity.[67] For Laboulaye, any constitution not approved by a plebiscite would reproduce all the errors of French politics since 1789: "Our fathers saw founding or reforming a constitution as a magical process that could be confided to a unique assembly convoked extraordinarily and given full power to redefine the very relationship between state and society. Not only was all power concentrated in the hands of one body, which is the very definition of despotism itself, but this authority was also given to the constituents such that they could impose their government onto the nation without consultation or asking for any opinion. The nation was then forbidden to touch it."[68] According to Laboulaye, the social contract, or the relationship between state and society, could not be established by an extraordinary assembly, but only by the nation itself. If the government could create and approve of a constitution on its own, Laboulaye feared, it could also amend it or draft a new one. This, he argued, was why France had suffered such political instability during the previous century. By separating the government that drafted the constitution from the constituent power itself, he attempted to give the constituent power back to the people and thereby limit the government's ability, under any circumstances whatsoever, to change the constitution toward its own ends.

To prevent further the state from confiscating sovereign power, he reiterated his argument that each branch of government only partially represented the people. The government should consist of a mixed regime grounded in bicameralism and a robust, but independent, executive. Only a bicameral structure could ensure that the legislative branch should not become "despotic": according to Laboulaye, the Assembly did not constitute the nation, but served it. "The people are sovereign over everything that touches upon the general interest. This sovereignty cannot be delegated. To give the Assembly the power to reign in the place of the nation would be an abdication, a nullification of itself."[69] Laboulaye shunned the traditional republican ideal in which the nation became a "corps" through the legislative body: to his liberal mind, the nation existed independently of its representation in the legislative body.

It was precisely in the space between the indelegable sovereignty of the nation and the incomplete representation of any branch of government that Laboulaye redefined the resources of the executive power in a democracy. The executive, he argued, was "created in order to act"; it needed "full liberty in its actions."[70] However, in a sentence that epitomized the originality of Laboulaye's theory of liberal democratic stateness, he insisted further: "It is possible to reduce its attributes, but it must not be limited within the sphere that it is granted."[71] Confining legislative and executive power and removing all constituent power from government therefore *reinforced* the executive's ability to react to potential threats to national unity. As David Bates has noted, "efforts throughout the Third Republic to legitimate the 'legal state' were deeply affected by the persistence of intense conflict and violence and by the imagined possibility of civil war."[72] Laboulaye shared these concerns in his attempts to define state power. However, he was convinced that his liberal democratic theory of divided powers, reduced attributes, and greater accountability actually improved the state's capacity to maintain order in moments of social or political conflict. Laboulaye's theory of the liberal democratic state therefore garnered a new legitimacy for the executive in moments of emergency. "To weaken [the executive]," he argued, "is to discourage justice and compromise public security."[73]

Pasquino and Ferejohn have noted that the separation between constituent and emergency powers has been at the heart of theorizing a state of exception based on the rule of law: "There is still a distinction between emergency and constitutive powers. . . . In exercising legislative emergency powers, the executive is supposed, normatively, to be acting only to resolve the emergency and restore the normal legal order."[74] By removing any constituent power from the legislative assembly or the executive power, Laboulaye was making precisely such a move, ensuring that any exceptional measures could be invoked only to restore the normal constitutional order. Herein also resided his critique of the Convention, which according to his analysis had created "a permanent dictatorship." In a direct reference to 1793, he first criticized the Convention for its inability to conceive of a separation of powers: "A legislative power tempered by nothing is despotism."[75] He further argued that this permanent dictatorship came from the Convention's inability to make a clear distinction between its constituent and legislative powers.[76] Writing in the early 1870s, Laboulaye insisted that only the executive—stripped of all constituent powers—could effectively save the constitution and preserve liberty. Once the sovereign people had spoken as free individuals, their sovereignty was guaranteed because no single branch of government had the power to overturn it (not even the government as a whole because it was not

greater than the sum of its parts). The protection of the constitution, even if it
meant the temporary suspension of rights by the state in moments of crisis,
respected the constituent power and the inalienable sovereignty of the people:
"When a new government establishes itself after a revolution, all we ask of it
is order and peace in the streets, that it provide security. We do not negotiate
its power, nor even, alas! its arbitrariness. All is permitted and everything is
done easily. There is no resistance, no opposition. Dissidents are damned on
grounds of sedition. But this absolute obedience of a people is only momentary. Once order is restored, and interests are reassured, the country requires
liberty once again."[77] In a regime in which popular sovereignty could never be
fully captured but only partially represented, in which government was necessarily divided, constitutional law was inviolable, and national sovereignty
was guaranteed by international law there was still room for a momentary
declaration of authoritarian rule. However, this state of exception became a
tool for preserving national sovereignty and the constitution instead of undermining it.

Thus, while Laboulaye's work on the 1848 constitution emphasized the importance of the executive power for guaranteeing popular sovereignty, and his
work on imperialism and slavery had sanctified national sovereignty in the
context of international law, the young Third Republic forced him to mobilize
his constitutional thought toward the founding of a liberal democratic executive. In January 1875, as the National Assembly set out to solidify the constitutional foundations of the new republic, Laboulaye introduced an amendment
to the floor of the Assembly which stated: "Art. 1. The government of the Republic is composed of two Chambers and a President." This short article carries
the essence of Laboulaye's ideas on liberal democratic institutions and reveals his
influence in shaping the institutional matrix of the Third Republic. His broader
aim in presenting the amendment was to definitively institute a republic as
a mixed regime by establishing the powers of the legislative and executive
and removing MacMahon's identification with the latter. While Laboulaye's
amendment did not pass, a version of it, proposed by Henri Wallon in the
weeks that followed, was adopted (353 to 352 votes), a decision that, as Adhémar Esmein observed succinctly, "became the cornerstone of the new form of
the state: the Republic was founded."[78] Laboulaye's vision of the separation of
powers and the executive was, indeed, at the heart of the new republican state.[79]

The focus on the executive in building a sound set of liberal democratic
institutions in the uncertain political climate of the early 1870s also revealed
the importance of confronting the problem of the state of emergency. As the
dust settled from 1870 to 1871, the question of the longevity of the Third Republic turned around the fundamental issue of the executive power in general and

MacMahon's power in particular. From 1870 to 1877, the republican regime was governed through a generalized state of emergency: for much of that time it had no constitution, only ill-defined institutional outlines of the regime, and, after 1873, a military and monarchist executive who remained convinced by a version of the liberal authoritarianism that had guided France for much of the century. It was precisely in response to MacMahon's attempted "coup d'état" in May 1877 that this state of emergency came to an end and the ideas of liberals like Laboulaye, who had consistently fought against the politics embodied in his coup, were established. But the fact that the republic was being founded under the auspices of a generalized state of emergency did raise fundamental questions of its legitimacy.

As Léon Duguit, a celebrated jurist of the Third Republic, revealed in his writings on constitutional law, the last time the state of siege had been declared in a republic by the Constituent Assembly of 1848, it had no doubt been lawful "because [the Assembly] was the constituent power."[80] However, as Laboulaye insisted in his writings from the Third Republic, the constitution could be legitimately ratified only by plebiscite and not by a Constituent Assembly. Could then a democratic constitution be protected by the state of siege when it had not been voted by the people? Moreover, who, in such a context, should be able to declare the state of emergency or the state of siege in the republic? These questions plagued the founders of the new constitution and became increasingly problematic as the Third Republic wore on.

On April 3, 1878, a new law was passed changing article 2 of the constitution of 1852 that had given the head of state, followed by approval by the senate, the right to declare the fictional state of siege. Article 1 of the law of 1878 removed this presidential initiative, stating, "The state of siege can only be declared by the legislative bodies for a limited time."[81] However, article 2 of the law qualified article 1, establishing that in cases when the legislative body was not in session, "the President of the Republic could declare the state of siege on the advice of his council of ministers, but the Chambers (legislative branch) must be convened within two days."[82] Esmein, who recognized the potential danger of such an article for the parliamentary regime, posed the question of this article's constitutionality, but he concluded that even with this power, the president would not be able to overstep the constitutional bounds because the legislative power was to be called back with full powers so soon after.[83] Beyond its constitutionality, what was of primary importance in this article was the recognition within the republican constitution itself that the fictional state of siege could be declared by either the legislative or the executive and, furthermore, in either case only for a limited time. As a result, this law was an essential indicator of the potential powers of the executive in the Third Republic. It was also an indication that legal conceptions of executive emergency powers, which would in the first half of the twentieth century become so central to public law jurists such as Joseph Barthélemy, Mauric Hauriou, and Louis Le Fur, were already present in the gestation of the Third Republic's constitution.[84] The law was designed to ensure that any exceptional measure to maintain order should be controlled by the rule of law, thereby serving popular sovereignty and the constitution instead of transforming it. It therefore confirmed the broader liberal democratic vision of the state that Laboulaye crafted, and it solidified his contribution to the development of a legal foundation for emergency powers that would come of age in the Third Republic.[85]

But Laboulaye's legacy was also limited in some essential respects to the extent that he remained part of a group of liberal theorists who attempted to gather the demos into a collective order through a somewhat partial conception of the state. While, like many liberals of his generation, he brought the question of democracy and the importance of the state forward as a means of reinforcing individual liberty, his treatment of the liberal democratic state focused overwhelmingly on its emergency powers. As if he were unable to come to grips with the full social capacity of the modern state, he focused relatively little on the quotidian role that the state might play, insisting on its limits on the one hand and its absolute power in times of emergency on the other. Such an approach to the state would not be uncommon among liberals in this new age of state conceptualization, but it did leave a troubled legacy for how to manage many of the most important challenges that democratic states would confront in the decades to come. In particular, amidst the social struggles that would gather steam in the Third Republic, the ability to conceive of a robust interventionist state in a liberal democracy largely as a force to maintain order comforted an increasingly untenable position toward repression instead of social reform. Moreover, it also contributed to a paternalistic conception of colonial rule that was now integrated into the very texture of an international law grounded in sovereign states. These were all questions that the following generation of state thinkers would have to confront.

Nonetheless, Laboulaye did contribute to the constitutional thought of the early Third Republic in his analysis of exceptional powers rooted in Lincoln's presidency, and in particular the relationship between executive power and exceptional circumstances in a liberal democratic regime. Through this analysis, he stepped far beyond the liberal republicanism and the various forms of liberal authoritarianism that had marked French liberalism in the first half of the nineteenth century. Moreover, Laboulaye's theories of the executive, international law, and constitutionalism show that exceptional circumstances *and* the rule of law were among the essential concepts that shaped this new theory of the liberal democratic state. Laboulaye was particularly well positioned to appreciate the full weight of Lincoln's presidency because he had been studying American constitutional history for more than a decade and was already one of the great specialists on the American constitution when the Civil War broke out. In fact, as we have seen, he had already found a model for the executive in the United States before Lincoln, having compared Cavaignac's conduct during the June Days to that of Washington in the early years of the American republic. But with Lincoln, he had an even stronger illustration of how the American state's delegation of power to the executive could save the unity of the nation and serve the constitution, even if it meant temporarily assuming absolute powers.

Considering the importance of Laboulaye in the founding of the Third Republic, this analysis suggests that European historians of the state entrenched in a reading of a weak American liberal polity may have overlooked one of the most potent intellectual resources in nineteenth-century European state building, the American state. In particular, the American state provided a model for how to pose the problem of emergency circumstances and executive power. Laboulaye, of course, was not the only one to explore this heritage. Others, including one of the pillars of nineteenth-century French and European politics, posed a similar problem, in strikingly quotidian and pragmatic terms.

4

NECESSITY:
Adolphe Thiers's Liberal Democratic Executive

One cannot govern without being a philosopher.

ADOLPHE THIERS[1]

Adolphe Thiers stood as a towering and troubling figure of nineteenth-century French and European politics. From his *History of the French Revolution*, written in the 1820s during the Restoration, to his inaugural presidency in the Third Republic, he cleared a liberal path across every regime before helping to set the republic on track to a lasting institutional structure. Over the course of his histories, political theory, parliamentary mandates, and executive power a central question emerged that transformed his liberalism: How to secure a stable French polity by crafting a modern state in a democratic age?[2]

This chapter investigates Thiers's ideas on the state through a reading of his voluminous historical works, political writings, parliamentary speeches, and letters. With Thiers, we are confronted with a peculiarly tight-knit relationship between the conceptual and the immediate political demands of government. As he stated in a letter to Comte de Saint-Vallier in 1872, "I am a philosopher in power [*je suis un philosophe au pouvoir*]."[3] Out of Thiers's back-and-forth between the conceptual and politics emerged a consistent response to the problem of building a stable polity in a democracy, necessity. Indeed, it is possible to read the problematic of necessity [*nécéssité/notstand*] diagonally across his vast oeuvre of political discourses, historical frescoes, and political mandates and decisions.

When examined from this perspective, what emerged in Thiers's expansive career and oeuvre was a complex and robust conception of the state in which government power built on the resources of civil society and the creative capacity of the law. Unlike many early nineteenth-century liberals, Thiers began to see civil society and law as a means of extending and empowering government's reach into the everyday lives of French citizens. The vehicle for this transformation was the concept of necessity.

The notion of necessity, as Giorgio Agamben notes, does not make reference to a specific formal legal apparatus. As a result, Agamben and many others have suggested that necessity implies the suspension of law.[4] With Thiers, however, we are confronted with a very different, antiformalist conception of necessity. Thiers did not theorize necessity as an extralegal decisionist force but rather as a part of the legal and political capacities inherent in liberal and democratic states. Necessity originated and legitimated legal action and its capacity to respond to the constant, everyday problems that confronted government. Law, in his view, was never suspended; indeed, in his antiformalist vision of legal power, it need never be. Rather, law became a means of exercising the necessary powers of government in the constantly improvised contexts of rule.

To this extent, Thiers's theory of necessity was more capacious than the exceptional circumstances explored by Laboulaye. While they shared an interest in statecraft in Algeria and in the model of Abraham Lincoln, Laboulaye remained deeply concerned with conceiving the state's limits and could only envision a more capacious interventionist state in contexts of emergency. Thiers, on the other hand, began operating under the more pragmatic idea that government was largely a question of ruling through the management of everyday problems. Thiers's doctrine of necessity therefore attests to a strong tradition in France of "a close interconnection and interpenetration of sovereignty, necessity, police, and the rule of law."[5] Such a realist conception of legal power was essential to building a more capacious interventionist state across the nineteenth century, for it challenged the early liberal ideas on the law that suggested the sufficiency of a night-watchman state neutrally governing through legislation, laissez-faire, and political economy. It therefore broke down some key liberal assumptions inherited from the eighteenth century, which argued that the state could do little more than protect individuals from injurious force and distantly steer a self-regulating economy. Thiers's conception became far more robust because necessity propelled the state into a much broader realm of social activity from managing floods to putting out fires and from protecting the national economy to civil war. Through this approach, an increasingly powerful and interventionist state took form year by year and came to fruition in the crisis moments of the Third Republic's first years. The difficulty of course in assembling democratic power in this way, however, was that such a doctrine left very little sense of exactly where government should stop and when—Thiers's reputation as the butcher of Transnonain and the Commune has justly made sure that this challenge was not forgotten.

Following a braided narrative, this chapter traces how necessity democratized Thiers's liberalism in powerful and sometimes dangerous ways culminating in his presidency. It weaves this narrative with his interpretations of the liberal democratic model of the American republic. This narrative reveals that in Thiers's conception of necessity, a robust civil society, individual liberty, and the law became the means of broadening the reach of the state instead of limiting it. Moreover, his timid but growing attachment to liberal democracy, especially in opposition to Napoleon III, convinced him that the state needed to retain the necessary powers to act in order to combat the potentially deleterious effects of democratization without systematizing an overt suspicion of democracy pace Guizot on the one hand or an illiberal democratic dictatorship like the Second Empire on the other.

Thiers, Tocqueville, and the French and American States

Thiers enjoyed an extraordinary popularity in the nineteenth century, when he published two widely read multivolume histories, *The History of the French Revolution* (which scandalized Tocqueville) and *The History of the Consulate and Empire*, selling by some estimates over 1 million copies of the latter. Immediately following the revolution of 1830, to which he contributed, he participated in the successive ministries of the July Monarchy. At age thirty-three he held his first position as undersecretary within the Ministry of Finance, by thirty-five he was appointed minister of the interior, followed by minister of agriculture, and head of the government in 1836 and 1840. After 1840, he continued to serve in the legislature of subsequent regimes, saving his most important political appointment for the end of his career when after the collapse of France's last engagement with a Bonapartist empire, he became the first president of the French Third Republic and the first republican president in French history to leave office without a coup d'état or revolution.

Thiers was a constant of French politics, and his voluminous writings, correspondence, and parliamentary speeches have left a complex picture of a deeply committed French liberal who was incessantly entwined with the key political questions and governance of his day. It has generally been argued that Thiers was fascinated by English constitutionalism. His famous statement on constitutional monarchy, "the King rules, but does not govern," has been interpreted as a commitment to the British parliamentary system.[6] And yet, while Thiers did demonstrate a consistent affinity for the British system of rule, he also demonstrated a strong interest in American government. In a key speech given to the National Assembly in 1851 as Louis-Napoleon was planning his coup d'état, Thiers outlined his acceptance of the republic born in 1848, admitting that he had been misled in his previous search for models of liberal government. He explained that while he had been convinced of the supremacy of the English model of constitutional monarchy before the consolidation of the Second Republic, he was ready to rally to the republic's cause because of the American example. "What I have to say is so difficult, delicate and important that I beg you not to interrupt me," he began.

> I never dreamed of anything more than the form of liberty that can be found in England and its Monarchy. For me, this was the most liberal form of government, that which brought together to the greatest extent the two necessary conditions for my support, order and liberty. But, I misinterpreted the great and beautiful model that America has provided . . . 1848 arrived. Oh! Did I experience profound regret? You know what I told myself? Not that I had been wrong to believe that the form of the English Monarchy was the most liberal in the world; but that, in spite of the excellence of this form, the destiny of modern nations was leading them toward the American form rather than the English form of government. . . . Yes, I told myself that perhaps I had been mistaken and that while I had been correct in preferring the English form, perhaps our European societies were driven by the force of circumstances to the American form.[7]

In the waning moments of the Second Republic then, Thiers was convinced that the American form of government, or some form of it, could be established in Europe. The question was then, just what were these "circumstances" that had transformed the United States into a model? How did he understand American government and its potential contributions to the creation of a liberal democratic state in France? What emerges in response to this question is a somewhat surprising vision of the American state and its role in building a modern polity.

One of the pillars of Tocqueville's analysis of American democracy was his argument that associations were a vital vehicle for American democracy and the stability of democratic life more generally. "Americans of all ages, all stations in life, and all types of disposition are forever forming associations," he argued, comparing this to the French case where "at the head of any new undertaking . . . you would find the government." This argument appeared in the second volume of *Democracy in America*, which appeared in 1840, one year after he entered the French legislature. Indeed, Tocqueville's theory of civil and political associations was written within a specific context of vast debates on the role of associations in French democracy. In particular, it was Adolphe Thiers who had led the Orleanist charge in this debate, arguing for the importance of civil and political associations, but also insisting on the role that the state should play in structuring them.

These debates had been launched in the early July Monarchy when Tocqueville left for the United States. They then came to a head after his return while he was drafting his masterpiece in 1834. While they served as the political backdrop for the writing of his chef d'oeuvre, he did not participate directly because he was not yet a member of the legislative body. The debates turned on the government's desire to limit political association in the context of the powerful wave of democratization that continued to gain momentum after the revolution of 1830. Extensive civil and political unrest had continued to threaten the solidity of the regime since its inception. As a result, the July Monarchy looked to limit the number of individuals that could join any given political association to twenty. To defend this claim, Thiers presented his vision of the relationship between the state and associational organizations in a liberal democratic context. In so doing, he provided a very different perspective from Tocqueville.

As the cornerstone of American democracy, associations served primarily two purposes for Tocqueville. On the one hand, they were to serve as intermediary bodies that could limit the reach of the central state. Outside the central state's control, they also protected the citizens from any excessive reach of the state. On the other hand, they also provided a "school" for learning how to participate in democratic society. In both cases, they protected and cultivated democratic customs within individuals by grouping them together with their fellow citizens. Tocqueville argued in the second volume: "If the men who live in democratic countries do not have the right nor a taste to unite toward political aims, their independence runs a great risk, but they can conserve their wealth and their intelligence; as long as they do not have the right to associate in ordinary life, civilization itself is in peril."[8]

Thiers shared a sense of the importance of associations: "We have spoken extensively about the spirit of association; we have stated that it is a great principle of civilization, a principle respected by all governments and that we are going to do it serious harm. No, gentlemen, we recognize that the principle of association is founded on the nature of man; that individual men are weak and that men associated with others are powerful. It is by putting men next to men, generations next to generations, that we will produce the marvels of civilization."[9] The deep similarities in language suggest that both men were in agreement on the importance of associations and their role in strengthening society and cultivating "civilization."

Where they differed, however, was in their understanding of the proper relationship between these associations and the state. Thiers recognized the social power of associations and the importance of their development, but in his view, social power was not opposed to the state or completely outside of state regulation. In his discussion of mutual aid societies, for example, he staked out a classical liberal position insisting that the state had few resources and that much of the mutual aid needed to be provided by private individuals: "Whatever the state may do is of minimal importance next to what men can do for themselves. What the state can do is infinitely limited."[10] However, this did not imply that the state was to take a straightforward laissez-faire position, leaving the poor to be managed solely by private initiative. It meant to the contrary that the state had an important role to play, but could only play that role through cooperation and contracting certain services to private associations.

> The liberty of these associations must be scrupulously respected. They must be free to form, to administer themselves, to dissolve themselves. But, by looking over their statutes, keeping their funds and serving their interests, the state may provide them with services that are within its reach, and which do not extend beyond the limits of intervention indicated by their true principles. By giving the mutual aid societies the status of legal entities, who may operate according to justice and receive gifts and inheritance, an attribute that the state has the right to give or refuse through its cherished laws, the state must maintain the right to revise their statutes and hold their hand to ensure that their statutes are equitable, well-conceived and protected from all fraud.[11]

Thus while the state could not take on the direct cost of providing social security or retirement for the workers, it could provide the legal framework and key statutes, such that they could equitably redistribute resources amongst themselves. The state therefore needed to facilitate the services provided by the mutual aid societies by offering them a legal structure while not directly intervening itself.

Elaborating a key principle of liberal stateness in the French context, Thiers argued that law and an associative civil society did not limit the state. Instead, both fostered the conditions for a more robust state, which in turn became more capacious *through* law and associations.[12] This, however, did not mean that the state would never provide direct and visible intervention. Revealing a key thread in his interpretation of liberal governance, Thiers argued that the state should play an important role in times of emergency or crisis.

> When a city is consumed in flames, or an entire county is inundated, private help takes the lead, goes to work, and individually takes care of a great deal of misery. Beyond this, the state, the most powerful of all, enters in and giving by millions, repairs a portion of the problem, repairing it within the measure

of what is necessary and possible. Thus a few years ago, when taking care of those who were flooded by the Loire, the state was able to repair much of the damage, without it taking an important financial toll. . . . There is no danger in such charity because the state can come to the rescue without impeding or violating any of its principles, because the state may deliver charity without it coming at the expense of the individual.[13]

Here, and elsewhere in his historical and political works, Thiers insisted upon the role of the state in intervening and acting decisively in exceptional moments of disaster, war, or civil unrest. Under such circumstances, state intervention was not opposed to individual initiative. As a rule, then, the state acted through law and associations while reserving the capacity to act directly and forcefully under necessary circumstances.

Comparisons with the conclusions of recent work on the liberal state and civil society in the United States suggest that Thiers's approach to social security and mutual aid was startlingly similar to some of the actual practices of the US state. Elisabeth Clemens has suggested that there were primarily three ways that the civil society and state relationship operated in the United States, what she refers to as "congruence, conflict, and collaboration arguments." She further suggests that scholars have largely emphasized the congruence and conflict and the expense of collaboration. "A third line of argument emphasizes the potential for cooperation between state and associations. Lacking the concern for the formal congruence between liberal democracy and the internal politics of associations, these analyses explore the division of labor between governments and private or not-for-profit organizations. Here, the critical aspects of association-state relationships center on delegation of authority, public subsidies or contracts, and formalized arrangements for consultation or policy formation." She concludes that "through the cumulation of legislative statutes and judicial decisions, associational life in the United States has become increasingly structured by political outcomes rather than sheltered in some separate civic realm."[14] Much the same may be said of Thiers's ideas, which insisted upon effective political outcomes instead of a constant state intervention or retreat.

Moreover, Thiers's arguments reveal an attempt to formulate these modes of the state-society relationship into a coherent principle of governance. For Thiers such a state neither controlled nor completely ignored the social power unleashed through a vibrant civil society. Rather, as he argued, the state accomplished its essential goals through society:

Examine what government actually is? Of what does it consist? You see the numbers that compose it and you see where its force is, one hundred thousand civil servants, some one hundred thousand soldiers. What are these three or four hundred thousand individuals in the midst of 32 million people? It's nothing in terms of numeric force, material force. What makes the force of the government then? Its organization, the cooperation [*concert*] with which it acts, it is the faculty to give orders and to be obeyed, it is the power to unite in Lyon, in an instant, ten thousand soldiers, a prefect, and generals; to do the same thing in Strasbourg, in Marseille, in Bordeaux, at the very same moment that the government acts in Paris with the same collective harmony (*ensemble*), with the same vigor. Its force is in its organization, its cooperation, the vigor of collective harmony resulting from association; and this faculty, contains the entirety of the social power [*puissance sociale*].[15]

This paragraph was a key example of Thiers's ability to introduce the conceptual into contemporary political debates. It also marked one of his most comprehensive statements on the ideal state-society relationship. The argument on the nature of state power relationship bears three essential claims. First, he recognized the presence of a great number of civil servants in the French administration. However, he insisted that this great number of employees and military officials was not in fact what made France a potentially strong state in the context of effectively governing 30 million French persons. Such an assessment pursues a very different line of argument to the traditional approaches to state development growing out of state theories that have counted the number of civil servants and military agents as a key indicator of the growth of the modern state. For Thiers, and this was the second point, if the actual size of the state was of little importance, it was because the state's strength should actually be measured by what he called *concert* or "cooperation." It was not so much the ability to hire and enlist greater and greater numbers of individuals in the state's employ or even to centralize those capacities, but to organize those soldiers and that administration and, most importantly, as he said, "to be obeyed." In short, it was the capacity to achieve the ends through *concert* rather than the specific ability to accumulate individuals within a centralized state. The third essential claim then was that the vigor of this capacity was determined by the state's penetration into society through "association." He understood the state's capacity as, in his own words, a "social power [*une puissance sociale*]." Although he persisted in his distrust of democracy, Thiers's arguments on state power did show a deep awareness of its role as a source of social integration. This power did rely to some extent on coercion, but it depended equally on association and *concert*.

William Novak has argued that there was a similar relationship between the state and civil society in the nineteenth-century United States: "Beneath the language of consent and contract, elements of coercion, restriction, and inequality remain irreducible parts of American associationalism."[16] In this sense, the new interpretations of the relationship between the state and American civil society may be used effectively to understand convergences in liberal democratic state practices between France and the United States. Moreover, these new readings suggest that a certain reversal may be in order in thinking about the construction of a liberal state in France. Building on the growing literature of a vibrant civil society in nineteenth-century France, it would appear that the United States was not the only country to conceptualize state power through civil society. In France, too, such liberal techniques were used to augment state power. This state was neither the Jacobin centralized menace abhorred by a key circle of French liberals known as the Coppet Group, including Germaine de Staël, Benjamin Constant, and Alexis de Tocqueville, nor was it a laissez-faire weak state that allowed civil society to develop freely without interference as in the dreams of an idealized nineteenth-century America.[17] Rather, this liberal state required a constant interaction with and through social organization, albeit oftentimes on the terms of the state. In other words, Thiers's conception of the state was predicated on the creation of a robust civil society, but the line between this civil society and state power could be drawn only in shades and squiggles.

Thus, it should not be any more surprising that Thiers, like Tocqueville, also defended his vision of the liberal state by looking across the ocean to the American model. "Do you know what we do through associations?" he announced in the debates of 1834,

> I would like to borrow the language of Washington. In a republic where there is no doubt that all of the rights of man are respected, Washington stated that an opinion formed within an association was artificial and factious; that it was not a natural or true opinion. He said, "Any opposition to the execution of laws, any association whose aim is to bother or hinder the action of government is directly contrary to the fundamental principles that we have established. These associations are designed to organize factions and to give them an extraordinary and artificial strength as well as to substitute for the will of a party a weak minority, which is ambitious and without principles, etc." As you can see, the head of the republic recognized that in a well-organized country, the opposition and resistance must be produced by public opinion, through the vote and not by associations where an artificial and false opinion is formed. One that can only be transformed through conspiracy . . . I insist then. Yes, you have the right to association, but you cannot exercise this right without the intervention of public authorities.[18]

As Thiers's conclusion made clear, he was not employing Washington to argue entirely against civil society, but rather to insist that associative life could not function politically without state intervention. What is of great importance for understanding the transformation of the liberal state in France is Thiers's defense of the argument for the intervention of public power into associational life through an analysis of one of the founding fathers of American democracy. Thiers was reading from a script that would have direct influence on French policy. The American state that he was using as an ideal type in these debates was one that refused "to idealize civic association and to exaggerate its separateness from state power and other forms of social, economic, and political organization."[19]

The Liberal Democratic State of Necessity

Alongside Thiers's interpretation of the modern liberal state as a social power, he consistently confronted the fact of democratization. Thiers's conviction that 1789 (and later 1830) provided the only legitimate foundation for a modern French regime, as well as his gradual embrace of public opinion, universal suffrage, and majority rule, betrayed a seemingly ineluctable resignation toward democracy. By the time he became president of the Third Republic, his commitment to the broad outlines of a democratic regime was unshakable thanks to the elaboration of the concept of necessity.

But by the same token, establishing democracy in France ran up against serious obstacles for Thiers. First, he remained haunted by his conviction that the horrors of the Terror were the product of a democratic regime run amok; second, he remained committed to a colonial regime in North Africa that had a troubled relationship to democratic rule; and, third, he was convinced that the silly excesses of Napoleon III's regime were the product of the latter's creative mix of democratic legitimacy and illiberal governance. Each of these arguments contributed to a typically liberal suspicion of democracy and ensured that in spite of a gradual embrace of democratic foundations, Thiers's conversion was slow and careful. This slow adaptation was achieved through a series of small incremental steps which passed through the essential obstacles of the modern state: historical analyses of the French Revolution (especially the Terror) and the First Empire, as well as interpretations of the revolution of 1830, colonization in Algeria, Louis Napoleon's coup, and the Mexican debacle. One finds in each of these cases, a theory and critique of the uses and abuses of the state of necessity. Ultimately, through his histories, speeches, and political analyses, Thiers carved out a space for ensuring order within the liberal democratic state. In so doing, he both set aside the

Bonapartist tradition, which he considered either impossible to reproduce (as in the First Empire) or politically bankrupt (as in the Second), and provided the groundwork for his presidency, which would set the Third Republic on the road to institutional stability.

NECESSARY CIRCUMSTANCES IN
THE FRENCH REVOLUTION

Recounting his first reading of Thiers's *History of the French Revolution*, which appeared between 1823 and 1827, a horrified Tocqueville wrote: "I was ablaze with the loyal simplicities natural to youth; besides, the traditions of my family still kept their primal power over my imagination. So the *Histoire de la Révolution* was peculiarly horrifying and caused a violent hatred of the author. I regarded M. Thiers as the most perverse and dangerous of men."[20] Tocqueville's own admittedly innocent reaction nonetheless captured what would become a common theme in his distaste for Thiers, who he long suspected of a facile interest in things basely political and instrumental. Essential to Tocqueville's history of the Revolution was precisely his critical distance from the actual events and circumstances of the Revolution. Tocqueville cultivated a sociological and conceptual detachment in his attempt to understand the unfolding of the Revolution, and the Terror in particular. For Tocqueville, the tragic circumstances of 1793–94 could in no way explain the Terror, which had been yet another important, and unfortunate, moment in a long history of centralized administration. As Tocqueville's reaction implies, however, Thiers wrote his *History of the French Revolution* from a profoundly different perspective. Embracing his potent mix of the conceptual with a taste for realpolitik, he wrote his history as a member of the liberal opposition against the Bourbons. Thiers ignored the deep structural origins and emphasized the immediate and exceptional circumstances of the war and internal revolt in his explanation of the authoritarian turn toward Terror in 1793.[21] Moreover, and this was particularly distasteful to the young Tocqueville, Thiers like Blanc ascribed to the theory of circumstances to justify the early phase of the 1793.

Historians have long noted the importance of Thiers's *History* as a key, early liberal reading of the French Revolution, which—much to Tocqueville's dismay—would greatly influence liberals such as Guizot and Augustin Thierry. Thiers and his close friend François Auguste Mignet have been considered the founders of the "fatalist" school in French revolutionary historiography.[22] However, while historians have amply read this work and its interpretation of the Terror and placed it within the context of French Revolutionary

historiography and French liberalism, such a focus has come at the expense
of the other important intellectual currents with which it intersected. In
particular, they have missed the privileged place this interpretation of the
Terror has as the first, and in some ways paradigmatic, account of Thiers's theory of governing through necessity and the broader context of theories on
exceptional circumstances in Western political thought.

His *History*, and specifically its interpretation of the Terror, provided an
initial outline of key elements of Thiers's theory of governing through necessity. First among these elements was Thiers's refusal to condemn exceptional
measures on either a moral or legal basis. He accepted that the regime of 1793
had been at times morally reprehensible, but it could not be dismissed on
these grounds because these actions had been a necessary response to exceptional circumstances.[23] Thus, while they had broken with the high-minded
constitutionalism of the bourgeois elite during the first years of the Revolution, the fierce democrats of 1793 merited recognition for their stunning
and successful response to the very real threats to the French nation. "The
first murders, committed in 93," he wrote, "were the result of a real threat.
They were motivated by danger."[24] Indeed, Thiers's history betrayed a certain respect for the Convention's sang-froid in 1793: "The convention, in the
middle of the extraordinary circumstances in which it found itself, was not
troubled in the least."[25] Rising to the occasion of extraordinary circumstances
he further insisted that "the means employed to arm, house, and nourish the
soldiers were in keeping with the circumstances." The government of 1793
had acted "energetically" and appropriately, he argued. There was then, according to Thiers, room for extraordinary measures within a constitutionally
just regime.

By extension, Thiers refused to condemn 1789 because of the events of
1793. This was the second key element of the theory of necessity present in
Thiers's *History*: government violence could not condemn the entire regime
or revolution. According to his account, the year 1789 had given birth to a
strong, legitimate regime led by bourgeois elites and bound to the constitutional law. It did not then, in itself, bear the seeds of 1793: 1789 could have
persisted without 1793, which had in essence been brought on by factors outside the Revolution itself. The fact that the government had been in a situation to take such drastic and necessary measures in 1793 was therefore more
a sign of 1789's strength than of its weakness or some inherent fault in revolutionary logic. In Thiers's analysis, it had not been the necessary measures
taken by the government, but the unnecessary excesses of 1794 that ultimately
brought down the regime. For him, once 1793 had engaged the path of Terror,
the republic was incapable of stopping the violence. In short, 1793 had been

necessary, but because it had taken place within a democratic republic there were neither the men nor the mechanisms to bring the exception to an end.

In Thiers's view, this had been the true failure of the democratic republic established in 1792 and this is the point where Thiers's reading of exceptional circumstances during the Revolution departed radically from that of Louis Blanc. Of course both employed the theory of circumstances, and both needed to make room for the Terror within their theory of the liberal democratic state instead of understanding it as an event that condemned a liberal democratic regime. But where they differed was over the transition from 1793 to 1794. Blanc's wholehearted embrace of the creative powers of democratic rule meant that even in the final throes of the Terror and a suspended constitution Robespierre's execution ensured democratic principles had been maintained. For Thiers, however, while 1793 was necessary, 1794 could have been avoided. In Thiers's view, 1794 had been the product of a regime bound too tightly to a democratic rule that was wholly incapable of wielding the full capacity of a modern state responsibly. So while both Thiers and Blanc integrated the power revealed by the Terror into their theories of the state, they disagreed on how it provided the foundations of democratic rule.

Thus, in spite of his objective approval of 1793, Thiers did insist upon the dangers and excessive violence of the Terror as it spread into 1794. This marked a third element in his theory of circumstances: the need to bring any and all necessary measures to an end when the circumstances that made them legitimate were over: "On this day [1794], when the perils had ceased and the republic was victorious, people were massacred no longer out of indignation but purely by deathly habits that had been acquired through murder. This tremendous machine that needed to be built to resist enemies of all types was no longer necessary; but once it was put into place, it was impossible to stop it."[26] The problem then, according to Thiers's *History* and the broader theory of exceptional powers it opened into, was not the use of necessary powers in exceptional circumstances—for the ability to navigate crisis was essential to the success of any modern liberal democratic state. Rather, the essential issue was that exceptional measures needed to come to an end as soon as the circumstances that required them were over: "All governments must have their excesses, and will only perish when they have fulfilled those excesses. The revolutionary government did not finish the very day that the enemies of the republic were sufficiently terrified; it had to go further, it had to continue until it revolted every heart through its very atrocities."[27] All governments would be forced into excess and such abuses would not naturally end on their own. Thus, it was necessary to place temporal limits on any government's use of exceptional powers.

Thiers' reading of 1793–94 coincides with a long line of theories of crisis
government developed in the eighteenth century in France, England, and the
United States. For example, emphasis on temporal limitation was in keeping with the leading theories of legitimate crisis government that had been
outlined by eighteenth-century liberals like Montesquieu and Blackstone. As
Bernard Manin has shown, establishing temporal limitations had been fundamental to the legitimacy of exceptional powers in the works of these theorists: "By casting the issue in temporal terms and by stating that parting with
liberty for a while was justified as long as it served to preserve liberty for the
future, the two writers were in effect making an argument that conformed to
a key liberal principle, namely the principle that liberty may be restricted only
for the sake of liberty, not for the sake of just any kind of common good, such
as, for instance, the public welfare."[28] Moreover, the English jurist and French
Anglophile were not the only political theorists of the eighteenth century to
explore this territory. Legal scholars have suggested that there are also similar
grounds in the American constitutional tradition. For example, As Levinson
and Balkin point out, "In *The Federalist* No. 41, Madison added the brac-
ing assertion that mere 'constitutional barriers' cannot deter 'the impulse of
self-preservation.' Trying to erect such barriers would simply 'plant [] . . . in
the Constitution itself necessary usurpations of power.'"[29] According to this
reading, even in the context of American constitutional law, necessary powers were not necessarily seen to be inconsistent with the law. Thiers, then, was
in good liberal company. But his reading of necessity went somewhat further
than Blackstone. His conception of necessity was profoundly historical and
creative. That is, it was not bound to a formal rule of law upon which necessary action was impinging. Indeed, it would seem that for Thiers, legitimate
political action was driven almost solely by necessity just as law was a creative
source of power. He revealed a further dimension of this idea a few short
years later, in the wake of the next French revolution of 1830.

1830: A REVOLUTION OF NECESSITY

In his history and theory of the state of exception, François Saint Bonnet
argues that Guizot provided an original reading of the revolution of 1830
through the lens of the state of exception. In his view, Saint Bonnet argues,
1830 was a revolution of necessity; as such, it was "the revolution without
revolution, or," he writes, "a kind of reversed state of exception."[30] This reading of the revolution of 1830 by Guizot was the product of the contested political legacy of the three glorious days (July 27, 28, and 29, 1830). Thiers, like his
colleague Guizot, hoped to establish the legal and constitutional legitimacy

of the new Orleanist regime, under which he would soon be appointed minister, without recognizing that the regime had been born of a *revolution*. To
do so, Thiers explained the July days as a popular movement of necessity—
necessitated by the constitutional abuses of Charles X. From this perspective,
the revolutionary actions of the Parisian people were a "revolution without
revolution" because they had taken place within an exceptional set of circumstances that provided the opportunity to reestablish the true constitutional
order instead of transform it. Thiers summarized this point in the preface to
his treatise on 1830: "We defend with perseverance and courage a government
which is neither the result of a popular caprice nor court conspiracy, but of
sole necessity." By choosing the new Orleanist regime, the French people, he
insisted, "had neither given in to a revolutionary tradition nor a fascination
for a man or a dynasty, they had saved themselves."[31] As he wrote in the pages
that followed, 1830 "was a profound, universally felt necessity."[32]

   With this analysis, Thiers added another key component to the history
and theory of crisis government in France. As Margeret Kohn has pointed
out, research on theories of the state of exception has placed an overwhelming focus on the paradigmatic case of Weimar Germany, and especially Carl
Schmitt's decisionist theory of dictatorship, without paying proper attention
to earlier generations' attempts to explore the conceptual challenges brought
on by the necessary suspension of law in liberal regimes, in particular in the
context of democratic revolution and colonization.[33] Thiers's reading of 1830
provided just such a contribution to the theory of the state of exception in
two ways. First, it demonstrated a strong commitment, typical of the French
tradition of constitutional dictatorship, to the legal dimensions of exceptional
powers. Throughout his political career and even during his presidency,
Thiers insisted that governance through necessity could not be the sole prerogative of the executive—to his liberal constitutional mind, this smacked
entirely too much of the Restoration and Bonapartism—but rather needed
to be considered a means of exercising legal power. As we shall see, even
the expansion into Algeria and the crushing of the Commune would bear
this obsession with acting through the empire of the law. Second, and as a
result, it made an original move away from a decisionist reading of the state
of exception. Instead of focusing on the power of the state or the executive to
declare an emergency in a moment of crisis, Thiers's reading of 1830 pursued
the idea of "a reversed state of exception" in which the people had the right
to overthrow the regime if it consistently abused its power. The focus on legal
and popular legitimacy of the exceptional circumstance of 1830 became two
essential elements of Thiers's theory and practice of necessity.

   Critical to Thiers's reversal of the state of exception away from executive decisionism was his claim that the Bourbon Restoration had broken with the just constitutional order established by the Charter of 1814. At the heart of this critique was Thiers's argument against the abuses of Article 14 of the Charter, which granted the Bourbon monarch executive prerogative and exceptional powers to preserve the state and ensure the execution of the law. This article, which states that the king *"fait les règlements et ordonnances nécessaires pour l'éxecution des lois et la sûreté de l'État,"*[34] holds an important place in the history of French legislation on constitutional dictatorship for the extensive and ill-defined powers it granted to the king in the postrevolutionary regime.[35] While Louis XVIII demonstrated a certain retinue even during the hundred days, Charles X took advantage of the article's imprecision. The second king of the Restoration did so to such an extent that, in the eyes of a liberal critic of the Restoration like Thiers, the king's abuse of this power had hollowed out the very essence of the constitution: "After 1815, the Old Regime reacted first in the spirit of vengeance; then, when things were more calm, with a spirit of avidity until 1830 when it acted as a stubborn criminal."[36] In such a context, the revolution was necessary because "a government that violated the law could not be tolerated,"[37] repeated Thiers. From this perspective, the July Monarchy had not been founded to replace the Restoration of 1814, but had been an extraordinary movement to restore the just constitutional order betrayed by its kings. The revolution of 1830, he argued, "only reestablished the natural movement of our institutions, which had been undermined and paralyzed by a corrupt dynasty; all that was left to do was continue the spirit of perfection that had already been introduced by it."[38] The revolution had taken place in a state of exception because it was a circumscribed exceptional moment, necessitated by the crisis perpetuated by an authoritarian monarchy. "Without a revolution," Thiers claimed, "abolition would only have been possible over time, through a thousand and one detours. This way, we erased article 14 immediately."[39] The revolution had simply accelerated a process that would have naturally emerged, but had been hindered by the abuses of the king.

According to this argument, the Parisian revolution had been exceptional, but it had also been "legal" because it had never broken with the constitutional order that was threatened by Charles X: "Our revolution [1830], in spite of a few wild and impotent outbursts," he insisted, "remained calm, clement, and legal."[40] He continued, insisting that "above all, it remained legal" since its aim was to "allow everyone to benefit from the laws."[41] Essential to Thiers's popular reversal of the state of exception was his claim that no one person or group had been behind the exceptional events that had overthrown the regime. It had been an act of the people as a whole, who could not call upon an earthly judge, but who could act legitimately to the extent that their revolution was spontaneous and unanimous.

Thiers, of course, recognized that there appeared to be an inherent contradiction between his analysis of the state of exception in the revolution of 1830 and the one of 1793. And yet, in his commentary on the revolution of 1830, he refused to forsake what he had written on 1793, and even insisted he had been consistent in his interpretation of exceptional measures:

> Please hear me when I say: by supporting this, I am perfectly consistent with what I have said, written and thought about the French Revolution. . . . I invoked the impartiality of my century in favor of men who, after so much effort and pain for themselves, regenerated France. I have shown the results that may emerge from the political passions that may drive otherwise calm and clement minds. I have shown the weakness of men in the immense tempest of revolutions; and amidst so much misfortune, I have insisted upon covering them with the merit of a regenerated France, saved from a foreign threat.[42]

Thus, in 1793, the state had acted out of necessity against its own people to save the regime. In his defense of 1830, on the other hand, it had been the people who had acted in the name of the constitution to save themselves: under what circumstances, then, was it legitimate for the state to invoke exceptional circumstances and when could the people rightly do so precisely to prevent such abuses? This was a question that would haunt Thiers even into his presidency. But with his analysis of 1830, he already suggested a response. Thiers responded by insisting on the essential difference between the Revolution of 1789 and that of 1830: "One of the things that needed to be repeated was that we did not want a transformation or a revolution; we did not want to reproduce the violence of 93 or even the theories of 89." The revolution of 1830, he insisted, had not been an attempt to redefine the relationship between the social and the political as 1789 had been. He insisted that 1830 had merely been a political revolution. "Not every revolution entirely renews society."[43] "This revolution," of 1830, "I repeat, was purely political."[44] In Thiers's view, the Revolution of 1789 had the immense ambition of regenerating France and even Europe. Such a project, he reminded his readers, had been in part responsible for the horrors of civil war and a devastating conflict across the continent. Subsequent revolutions, even if they were necessary, needed to avoid such upheaval.

Drawing political lessons from this history, he insisted that exceptional measures, even if necessary, could also be dangerous:

> In administration, extraordinary measures can be effective, but only by ensuring ultimate ruin. The requisitions exhaust and waste ten times more than the

resources they produce; new money [*the assignats*] may serve for a few days, but at the expense of bankruptcy in a few months. Nonetheless, I concede that in a moment of imminent peril, with the Vendeens in Saumur, the Austrians at Lille, we may need, for a month or two, during a campaign, to force the journals to silence, contain the agitators, find food reserves, print paper to allow for a few more days of existence.[45]

Thus, Thiers maintained his claim that employing necessary measures was not to be condemned in its entirety especially in 1792–93. But even in these moments, employing necessary means was not an easy or straightforward solution, because "we contained, we survived, but by irritating; afterwards, it is necessary to calm, which is slow and difficult."[46] Therefore, since the use of exceptional measures was already weighty and dangerous under circumstances of necessity, to employ them unnecessarily—for example in the context of the mere political revolution of 1830 when the people were acting justly—would have been unjustified: "If, for example, we are not in a pressing crisis; if we don't have an important reason to restore the calm or resources during the time of a campaign; if it is only because of impatience, out of a desire to bring a quick end that we employ exceptional measures; then, please allow me to say, that this system which is already highly contestable in a time of crisis, becomes even more so when we are not in crisis. It becomes absurd and guilt-ridden."[47] The revolution of 1830 had been the political crowning of the bourgeois revolution of 1789. The social fabric had already been changed, the bourgeois elites were ready to govern, and, as such, no further social transformation was necessary. As a result, it would have been useless and even dangerous to suspend the law or employ the exceptional measures required in 1793. "The men who believed that the idea of the revolution was essentially tied to ideas of violence and exceptional measures, also believed it was tied to war and conquest. Here again they were wrong: fortunately the government was not mistaken with them. Peace was conserved outside and law was respected within."[48]

The distinction between the state of exception in his analysis of 1793 and that of 1830 demonstrates important elements in the development of Thiers's conception of necessary governance: in particular, attention to what constitutes necessary circumstances. While he recognized the necessity of 1793, he insisted that such circumstances did not exist for the state in 1830. The first French revolution had redefined the very relationship between the social and political. The profound impact of this situation inevitably required, and more importantly, justified, exceptional measures on the part of the state. But Thiers insisted that this could happen only once, that this kind of sovereign decisionism in which the state had the capacity to enforce social transformation through emergency powers was limited to the extraordinary and unique experience of the Revolution. As non-impartial as his analysis of 1793 had been, it was not a call for the consistent employment of exceptional measures. Moreover, the success of 1830 had been the proof of precisely this. "Violence like 92 and 93 would have brought civil and foreign war upon the revolution of 1830; the calm and legality of 1830 ensured internal serenity and foreign peace."[49] He therefore opposed to a decisionist state of exception a popular exceptionalism, in which the people had the right to overthrow an executive who broke with the legal constitutional order. This highly innovative invocation of exceptional circumstances, or *reversed state of exception*, provided an important contribution to the broader theory of necessary circumstances for a politician that both accepted and feared democratic revolutions. Through this analysis, Thiers could insist on the legality of the democratic revolution—it was legitimate because it restored the constitutional order rent asunder by the Restoration.

LEGAL NECESSITY IN ALGERIA

"Ah! No, gentlemen, we have no intention of returning to the imperial system."[50]

As already discussed in the context of Prévost-Paradol, Laboulaye, and Tocqueville, one of the most important legacies of the July Monarchy for the modern French state was the colonization of Algeria under a parliamentary regime. Squaring a constitutional, representative government with the expansion of the empire was a challenge that would emerge in every French regime that took the law and legislative procedure seriously. Within this project, French liberals played a central role. From the earliest moments of the expansion into Algeria, they were among the strongest supporters of this colonial enterprise. As France pushed further into Algeria during the July Monarchy, liberals such as Alexis de Tocqueville and Adolphe Thiers theorized and made policy on the process of colonization. Numerous historians and political scientists have recognized the importance of Tocqueville's writings on Algeria for conceptualizing the liberal foundations of Empire and the state of exception. But while Tocqueville's support of Algerian colonization is no doubt one of the more eye-catching of the period, it was far from unique and in many cases it was not the most emblematic or even influential. A liberal of the state, like Adolphe Thiers, however, who was a leading minister under the July Monarchy, was confronted with the full complexity of the challenge of defending both the colonial enterprise and the constitutional monarchy he had worked so hard to put in place. Most of all, he was confronted with very

practical challenges posed by empire such as accounting for the military excesses of soldiers on the ground and justifying the massive budget that the
colonial enterprise required. Here too necessity provided the means for theorizing the relationship between colonization, law, and wartime.

Thiers's first extended speech on Algeria came with the debates on the budget for pursuing military deployment in Algeria in 1836 following the bloody
and disastrous campaign of Maréchal Clauzel. In the early years of the July
Monarchy, the question hovered as to whether France should remain on the
coast of Algeria controlling just a few key cities or push inland, expanding its
control into the hinterland. While many members of the government, including the influential Duvergier de Hauranne, petitioned for the more limited position, Thiers argued that France needed to control a vast inland territory and
therefore insisted that greater financial and military resources needed to be
deployed to ensure a successful colonization. This position in favor of a surge,
however, had been weakened in the chamber by the massacres that the French
army was accused of in Médéah, Tlemcen, and Mascara in the previous military campaigns. Thus, Thiers set out—not for the last time—to reassure the
legislative body that these massacres had not tarnished the constitutional
regime. He did so by insisting upon the importance of maintaining the force
of law and justice throughout the colonial endeavor, even amidst the necessary brutalities of war and colonial expansion.

Thiers set out to convince the chamber that expansion into the Algerian territory through military means was a necessity for maintaining French prestige
internationally. His chief concern was to preserve French "glory" within the
context of a parliamentary regime. France did not require an imperial regime to
pursue this new colonial expansion, he argued; it could remain a constitutional
monarchy: "The triumphs of the Empire cannot be promised to the country; a
different system is necessary, other sentiments must be celebrated in the discussion of our affairs so that powerful men will dare to aspire to great and useful
things."[51] Conversely, without colonization, he argued, the democratic tendencies of the July Monarchy could be perceived as a sign of weakness by other
more authoritarian countries. It was precisely against the apparent weakness
of the liberal regime that he argued insistently: "We must never say that liberty
destroyed our sense of grandeur and patriotism. This would be deplorable, a
grave accusation against representative government; and I, who cherish this
form of government and who would like to see it achieve the highest degree
of splendor possible, I would be deeply disappointed if we could say that since
France has benefited from a representative regime, any ambition to grandeur is
forbidden because every time that we attempt something great and useful it is

hindered."[52] The challenge, according to Thiers, was to demonstrate that France was equally, if not more, powerful under a liberal, constitutional and representative regime than it had been under an authoritarian or absolutist government. There should be no danger, he claimed, that a representative government would be incapable of bold action. Rather, it was precisely the regime that was best equipped to conquer and establish a vast empire. Of course, an empire conquered by a representative regime would necessarily be of a different sort than those of authoritarian empires. Most importantly, the same parliamentary procedures used to establish all laws in the metropole should be used to decide all political or military engagement.

This emphasis on the law and the legitimacy of parliamentary procedure within the context of brutal military expansion became a hallmark of Thiers's vision of governance. Thiers sought to avoid at all costs—from the July Monarchy to the Commune—the creation of a generalized state of war that formally posited the rule of law on one side and the need for exceptional powers that broke the rule of law on the other. "Does this mean that we will establish forever and always a system of permanent war with the Arabs?" he asked. "No, certainly not,"[53] he responded immediately. To the contrary, he argued that the norms of parliamentary governance should be at the foundation of any military endeavor, and as such would actually strengthen the imperial expansion into Algeria. Otherwise, if it expanded through a system of lawless conquest, the constitutional monarchy necessarily undermined its own political foundations, when Thiers's aim was precisely the opposite. Thiers's was a new type of empire, which operated through representative government and law.

Imperial war and the necessities it engendered, then, did have their place within Thiers's adherence to law and proper parliamentary procedure. War, in his view, was a legitimate means of pursuing national interest in a constitutional regime: "This is what we search for with peace when war is unnecessary, or with war and peace when one or the other is necessary."[54] War and peace were part of strong foreign policy; both existed side by side. However, neither meant the negation of legal rule. In fact, Thiers insisted, military expansion and colonial occupation should play an essential role in bolstering the international reputation of representative government and its commitment to proper parliamentary procedure. Essential to these claims, again, was the separation between the Napoleonic Empire's drive to conquest at the expense of any constitutionalism and the liberal regime that Thiers defended. In an argument that bears a striking similarity to his reading of 1830, Thiers even suggested that the wars in Algeria were no more than the natural outcome of French presence in the Mediterranean: "The government did not engage in war deliberately; it was brought to war necessarily by the same situation as any people who, arriving in a new country with different moeurs is sooner or later forced into war."[55] Thiers's argument that the war had been brought on by "the situation" returned to a common feature within his vision of governance: state-sponsored violence was a necessity brought on by external circumstances.

In Thiers's view, then, the actions that took place in a situation of necessity did not mean the suspension of law or the constitutional order. Rather, the war and the battles it entailed were brought on by circumstances that required creative legal action. Necessity therefore operated within the legal order, instead of sitting somewhere outside of it: "If it is this system of war that we are referring to as anxious and agitated, it is not the work of the cabinet, it is the product of previous and obligatory circumstances,"[56] he explained, in an argument reminiscent of his reading of 1793. Thus, he insisted that within the system of war and peace, there would necessarily be unexpected, and at times exceptional, events that required a freedom of action from men on the field. No matter how procedural or representative, circumstances of necessity could arise within the military expansion: "I am not saying that our efforts will always have a happy ending, that they will be masterfully directed; I am not saying that there will never be misfortune, offenses or excesses. Ah! What government could be so presumptuous going into a distant land and employing the means of war to assume that everything would be wisely and humanely accomplished?"[57]

Even if war could be pursued legally, the possibility or even necessity of radical violence could never be precluded. But, once again, even amidst such allowances for excessive behavior, Thiers insisted that the neither the law nor the legal justice that France represented and defended was suspended in these moments of excess: "I declare, if there were excesses, the government will punish them. I do not think that it is true that our soldiers cut the throats of women and children; I do not think that they would sully their names with such excesses. But the government will put great effort, you can count on that, to ensuring that justice prevails alongside force in Africa. If there were acts that merit punishment, it will be applied and we will do our best to prevent its return."[58] If any excessive force had been employed, the government would ensure that the individuals who were responsible would be properly punished. It must be underlined then that an essential principle in his support of imperial war was that it did not mean that the acts brought on by external circumstances and committed out of necessity took place outside the rule of law. Rather, he insisted, law would in turn be used to pursue retroactive punishment for unnecessary excesses. This was a cornerstone of his colonial policy:

"What I can promise, is that the government, jealous of French honor, jealous of the honor of its armies, jealous above all of its flag, will march with force but also with justice."[59] Excesses of violence and brutality were an unfortunate part of war. Thiers was more than willing to accept this nasty fact, but he was unwilling to accept that this, in any way, undermined the legal foundations of the French parliamentary regime. "I will repeat, because it is the truth. I do not think that any party will find that the army violated the law, because the law is in everyone's spirit."[60] Law was not a self-constituting, formal set of strictures that applied in all times and all places; it was a spirit, revealed by circumstances external to it.

Since French colonization was animated by the principle of law, the wars in its favor were also driven by a desire to ensure security and justice in Algeria. "A government that is charged with governing another can give two things, security and justice—ensuring that no one invade the land that you have cultivated, that violence is not brought upon peaceful laborers, and, second, if two laborers have a contention, an equitable and enlightened judge will make a decision."[61] By embarking on the colonial project, Thiers argued, the French state was operating through law. In his mind, the exceptional circumstances necessary for colonization were an expression and commitment to this legal order.

In keeping then with his reading of 1793 and 1830, he recognized that abuses and excesses were inherent in any regime and were, in some cases, necessary. However, they could not be used to condemn a parliamentary regime precisely because they were responses to external and exceptional circumstances; and because they were limited in duration and subject to retrospective judgment and punishment. For Thiers, the conquest of Algeria was an important step in demonstrating that a parliamentary regime could use law toward decisive and glorious action and the creation of an empire. He therefore dislodged the national benefits of military expansion from its previous attachment to authoritarian empire. Such a legal regime would be essential to the Republican commitment to an overseas empire.

NAPOLEON: GENIUS AND CIRCUMSTANCES

"Two conditions are necessary: genius and the situation."[62]

Sudhir Hazareesingh has recently demonstrated the importance of Thiers's *Histoire du Consulat et de l'Empire* in the making of Napoleon's liberal legend during the Second Empire.[63] Not only did he explain and celebrate Napoleon's "remarkable accomplishments," Thiers also provided an interpretation of *how* he had achieved them. Thiers echoed many of his generation in insisting that the bedrock of Napoleon's rule resided in his "genius." Nonetheless, as Thiers explained, "however great the genius of one man, he must never be completely entrusted with the destinies of a nation." In other words, while Thiers's interpretation of Napoleon's legend provided a reconciliation between Bonapartism and the Republic, it also presented a problem: a stable liberal democratic regime could not be founded on genius. Fortunately, this unique gift was not the sole quality that had allowed for Napoleon's legendary political deeds; for, his greatness was also due to his capacity to act according to specific circumstances and take necessary action: "The circumstances favored the man of genius who was to emerge, just as the genius himself requires circumstances."[64] For this reason, he argued more generally: "To judge accurately the acts of the heads of government, one must always take into consideration the empire of circumstances under which they were acting."

According to Thiers, Napoleon's genius was in part the result of his extraordinary judgment in all circumstances. In the first volume, he described how Napoleon's rise to power was the result of favorable circumstances that he had known how to take advantage of: "The general had in his favor his genius and the favor of circumstances."[65] He then compared this capacity to act in accordance to circumstances to the philosophical rigidity of Sieyès: "In each period, he reconsidered his work; and finally he decided and once he decided, he refused to change his plan. He refused to sacrifice anything to circumstances, even to the principle of circumstances, to the General Bonaparte, whose place he needed to prepare, aligning it with the genius and the character of the one who was to occupy it."[66] Sieyès, Thiers insisted, remained locked in the formalism of the eighteenth century, incapable of adaptation and realistic assessment.

Thiers therefore also needed to explain within such a theory how Napoleon had ultimately failed to ensure a lasting peace and government. It was here that Thiers's liberalism and his lasting commitment to ministerial responsibility came forth. In his view, Napoleon's genius ensured that he would make the best decision for each circumstance. Thus he could only fail if he were unaware or refused to recognize the true situation. This was particularly dangerous for the more distant campaigns such as Portugal where he was not present or during those moments when he refused to listen to his generals and advisors. Recounting General Foy's defense of Masséna, Thiers argued: "It was general Foy who still brought most of the news to Napoleon. He was warmly greeted because he knew how to please, but he was not listened to when he tried to present the defense of his head General. Napoleon, who had only himself to blame as the supreme leader of the events, remorselessly criticized his illustrious lieutenant, who he should have consoled instead of crushing, acting like a blind audience that was only capable of judging the result and refused to take the circumstances into consideration."[67] In his ascent and at the height of his power, his attentiveness to circumstances had been precisely Napoleon's strength. When Napoleon either witnessed the conditions himself or listened to his advisers, his genius ensured that he would systematically make the right decision in any given situation. However, even Napoleon's genius could not win out "when he did not look with his own eyes, and let himself be informed by courtesan ministers who only said what he wanted to hear."[68]

Using this interpretation of Napoleon's failures, it was in the volumes written in the 1850s (volume 12 was published in 1855) that Thiers began to demonstrate how he intended to recuperate Napoleon while criticizing Napoleon III. In spite of his vastly divergent appreciation of their "genius," he argued that Napoleon III had failed for the same reasons as his uncle: he refused to listen to his ministers. Thiers critique of the Mexican debacle for example was based on his conviction that Napoleon III had not properly consulted his cabinet: "It is here that the truly serious fault begins," he wrote of the emperor; "if what I call control had existed to the extent to which I desire it, it is not possible that a responsible cabinet, deliberating under the eyes of the sovereign, composed of men of a certain capacity, because the Sovereign gives them the honor of calling them to his side, it is not possible that deliberating issues in the way one must deliberate within a truly constitutional monarchy, that serious objections would not have been raised."[69] The emperor would never have even launched the Mexican campaign had he listened properly to competent ministers, Thiers argued.

What could be saved from the First Empire, then, was the need to pay exhaustive attention to detail, to listen to one's cabinet, and to trust one's generals and ministers. Thiers would stand by this idea during his crushing of the Commune and during his presidency: "I grant you permission to speak on my behalf to all administrative and judicial authorities, to stimulate their zeal and indicate to me those who do not fulfill the duties dictated by the circumstances," he wrote in a telegraph to Le Comte de Saint-Vallier in 1872.[70] But Napoleon I's genius could not be imitated; no theory could replicate the genius of his decisions. This too was one of Napoleon III's great weaknesses. For, in Thiers's view, he had attempted to turn Napoleonic rule, which was based on genius and circumstances, into a political system. Such ambition was the pure mark of hubris. "Every period when a superior man executes great things, not according to theory, but circumstances, imitating minds

follow, creating systems instead of the great things that genius makes naturally."[71] Napoleon, Thiers insisted, had never attempted to create a lasting or
durable system. Significantly, Thiers suggested that this attention to circumstances could even be used to justify a limited dictatorship, as long as it was
not transformed into a lasting dictatorial regime: "In his [Napoleon's] most
intimate interviews, he repeated that dictatorship could be a concession given
for a couple of years to a man of his genius, but a concession of a couple of
years only; and when he decided to return liberty, he gave it entirely [during
the constitutional projects of the hundred days]."[72] Thus, what Thiers had
consistently criticized in Napoleon III was not the arbitrary or exceptional
measures in themselves, but rather their transformation into the foundation
of a regime. "When we consider the history of the last 75 years, we are struck
by the following observation: France can, at times, set aside its liberties to the
point that it appears to have forgotten them. And then, when spirits become
calmer, the liberties return with a singular perseverance and an almost ir-
resistible force."[73] Thiers's *History of the Consulate* did indeed contribute to
"a powerful constellation of intellectual forces," as Hazareesingh argues, that
would sit at the heart of the Third Republic. But, it was not only a celebration
of Napoleon's administrative legacy. At the same time that he developed a
more robust notion of a liberal democratic state, Thiers also conceptualized
the capacity to act in a state of necessity. These acts could not be systematized
in advance, but the intellectual space within which they were to take place
had been created.

Toward a Republic of Legal Necessity

"The Republic is a necessity [*La République, c'est la nécessité*]."[74]

Adolphe Thiers's conception of necessity proved essential in the construction of the new French state. Through the problematic of necessity, Thiers
bolstered his liberalism at the same time that he overcame his deep distrust
of democracy. "In my opinion," wrote Thiers, confessing this conviction toward the end of his long career, "it is impossible to put an end to the principle
of universal suffrage today."[75] Through his historical, theoretical, and political
positions, Thiers adhered to a liberal and democratic state grounded in law
and universal suffrage. The dominant features of Thiers's leadership, first as
an *homme fort* of the government of national defense from the fall of the empire to the negotiation of the Versailles treaty, then as head of the executive
from February 1871 through September 1871, and finally as president of the
Republic from 1871 through 1873 built on the broad outlines of his previous

conceptions. He showed a willingness to use necessary force to impose what he considered a legitimate government against popular insurgency through the positive role of law.

The situation in France as Thiers assumed the office of the executive was dire, to say the least. The rapid defeat of the French imperial forces in the Franco-Prussian war confirmed much of the essence of Thiers's arguments against the Second Empire. Having established a democratic dictatorship, Thiers had consistently argued that Napoleon III had actually sapped the French military and the state of much of the power that would have allowed it effectively to succeed or even avoid war. Thiers had consistently argued that war in western Europe was to be avoided as he fiercely criticized Napoleon's policy in Italy, for example. But the war did come, and it came at a tremendous cost for France, including a sustained siege of Paris that reduced the city to a shell of its imperial self and the loss of two departments, Alsace and portions of Lorraine, to its imperial neighbor. This was not a glorious beginning for a republic. The defeat marked the Third Republic for much of the next thirty years, creating what some historians have referred to as "a culture of defeat" that contributed to the support of colonial expansion and mobilization for World War I. But the irony worth exploring is that the only French republic born of defeat was the only republic to survive.

Moreover, following the treaty, the legislature that came out of the elections of February 8, 1871, was one of the most unpredictable of the entire regime. Filled with men from throughout the political spectrum, it also contained a majority who were hostile to the very regime itself. Beyond the republic's institutions, mobilization in Paris and provincial cities since the war was without precedent and distrust of the government ran high. Finally, Thiers, elected to the position of the first president of the republic, was no George Washington or Lafayette; he was a Thomas Jefferson at best. Indeed, his voluminous writings and philosophizing filled the bookshelves of many a Parisian and provincial bourgeois home. His history of the French Revolution was among the most widely read of the nineteenth century and his presence in the French Academy since the 1830s had made him a man of letters of great renown. A historian of generals he was, a general he was not. Thiers seemed only capable of expressing himself in multiple volumes and lengthy speeches, which wore out even his auditors. And yet, he was the first of a long chain of presidents that have continued with only a brief and devastating four-year hiatus during Vichy up to the present day.

This relatively grim picture of the advent of the Third Republic returns us to the paradox we have followed throughout this book. Why was this regime— which suffered a humiliating defeat, fundamentally lacked legitimacy for having ceded a prized portion of its territory, was deficient of a brilliant general (the general who did appear was neither brilliant nor the initial executive power) to guarantee stability in the wake of war, had elected one of the most varied and uncontrollable legislatures in French history— able to succeed where the other two republics failed? The answer lies in part in Thiers's informal and positive capacity to deploy law according to necessary circumstances within the constitutional vacuum of the early republic.

Serving as the country's president, Thiers was able to deploy precisely the kind of violence that Cavaignac had used in June 1848. Like Cavaignac, he acted without a constitution. However, unlike Cavaignac, he lacked the legitimacy of military glory. As a result, from the outset of his presidency, Thiers met the fundamental challenges of the regime in a deeply liberal mode. Order could only be maintained through law and parliamentary procedure. In so doing, he called upon a mainstay of his arguments since the Restoration: the force of law could be sacrificed at no cost. "I declare," he explained, "Paris, we are full of pain and affection for you; we know how much Paris has contributed to the glory of France that has been in such need of support in recent times; but I repeat, we cannot sacrifice our duties, our conscience and France; we cannot sacrifice law to Paris."[76] As with his arguments for Napoleon, he recognized how Paris granted France the gift of glory, but glory at the expense of law was inconceivable.

In his analysis of the Commune, Thiers revisited the opposition between dictatorship and liberal democracy that had been at the heart of his work—as well as that of Blanc, as we shall see. "On the one side there is a handful of dictators, who have taken over the strayed multitude, who tyrannize them and push them, in spite of themselves, toward the fire. On the other side, there is the representation of the entire country, assembled in this room."[77] This revolutionary regime functioned only through tyranny and dictatorship, he argued, as with the emperors that had preceded it. As dictators, he insisted, they could not rightly call upon the demands of necessity: "In Tours and Bordeaux, there are governments composed of three members that have never received the endorsement of the country's will and who enlisted necessity as the reason for their existence. I recognize that necessity can be a noble title; but, this time it is usurped. As for the actual will of the country, that is something entirely different."[78] Thiers's argument over the legitimate claim to necessary action recalled his previous analyses where he had asserted that extreme measures had been needed, at least for a moment, in the early moments of the civil and foreign war of 1793, but had been inappropriately invoked in 1794. The attempt to reclaim the legacy of 1793 was echoed in the *Journal Officiel* in the heart of the Commune: "It would be entirely too honorific to compare the Parisian insurrection to the regime of 1793. In 1793 a love of France and the cult of the fatherland remained in the hearts of the most ferocious. The acts were terrible, but they were accomplished by men devoted to national unity who acted against men suspected of negotiating with the enemy and dreaming of federalism in the presence of enemy armies."[79] This battle over the heritage of 1793 in the early moments of the troubled regime revealed to what extent the debate on necessity opened a space for reconciling the Terror and the new republic. "In 1793, Terror was but a means, victory was the goal. In 1871, Terror is the only goal," the article concluded.[80]

At the heart of this argument was once again the claim that any extraordinary measures taken would not become systematized into dictatorship. It was law supported by force that would do the work of justice, not the executive: "law will maintain its force [*force restera à la loi*]" Thiers insisted. The law therefore found itself at the very heart of Thiers's deployment of military violence against his fellow Frenchmen. In fact, they were profoundly intertwined from the very outset. While he knew that the republic would be maintained by military force, he had gone to extraordinary lengths to insist that these military actions were the only legal means possible. The birth of the liberal democratic state combated "dictatorship" with a fierce deployment of necessary force.

At the heart of this vision of governance, then, was his argument that the extraordinary military measures would be temporary. "The army is a generous and noble means of repression, but it is not a means of government."[81] It was essential that the republic bring an end to all military threats immediately following the repression. "Laws alone will intervene, but they will be executed with all necessary rigor," he insisted. "Gentlemen, expiation will be completed, but it will be, I repeat, the expiation that honest men must inflict when justice demands it; expiation in the name of the law and through the law."[82] The Communards would be severely treated, but all justice would be achieved through the pursuit of law, Thiers insisted. "We are pursuing victory at this very moment. But after the victory, it will be necessary to punish: yes, legal punishment is an implacable necessity. Yes the public conscience must be implacable, but it must do so by following the law, with the law and through the law."[83]

Thiers remained remarkably consistent in his position against the Communards. First, much as with his arguments for Algerian colonization, he remained convinced that state-sponsored violence was a necessity in order to maintain order and preserve national glory. In this sense, neither law nor the foundations of the nascent liberal regime were being called into question in the deployment of military force against the Communards. Violence was possible within the context of the legal regime in moments of necessity. Similarly, justice would continue to be enforced after the violence had stopped. So, essential to Thiers's use of the law was its positive function. Law was not to be used in his liberalism to merely protect individuals from one another and from the state. It was a positive force that could be used to initiate, forge, and maintain national unity in the most extreme instances. In short, law became the powerful arm of a just liberal regime.

Thiers's novel conception of the liberal and democratic state was dependent on using law as an expression of state power, instead of as a means of limiting it. Hardly designed to limit the state, it was at the heart of the liberal democratic state's capacity to unify and strengthen the republic. Thiers insisted that it was precisely this use of law that distinguished his presidency from the regime of Napoleon III: "We have recourse to all legal means, that is all there is. You can modify those that you bring to bear, but it is the only option, all else is dictatorship. The dictatorship of great mean led you astray; that of lesser men will do so as well, minus the glory."[84]

Indeed, it is reasonable to suggest that Thiers's use of law in the Commune was part of a series of dramatic changes underway in the nature of nineteenth-century governance on both sides of the Atlantic. In the United States, Lincoln's use of executive authority was emblematic of a newly emerging form of state power that was consonant with a new breed of liberal and democratic states. Thiers was hardly blind to this larger transformation. Napoleon III's defeat, his abdication, and the declaration of a republic in the face of a loss to Prussian troops in 1870 ultimately gave even greater influence to Lincoln's memory among French liberals. Lincoln's moral authority and capacity to mobilize the Union toward his cause provided a model for Thiers as he rose to the seat of the executive to become the first president of the Third Republic. The anatomy of the American state was of enough interest to Thiers that he corresponded with a friend in Washington, Adolphe de Chambrun, and encouraged his French colleague to pursue one of the first histories of American executive power, which the latter completed in 1873.[85]

In many ways, Thiers's renewed interest in American executive power should not be surprising, especially in the context of the Commune. Lincoln's war powers, and in particular the Emancipation Proclamation, were reflective of a larger transformation in American public law that was quickly overturning reigning antebellum ideas about governance and the state. Though the transformations were epitomized by Lincoln's ascendency during the Civil War, these legal developments were not the exclusive province of American history. During this period, for example, the official newspaper of the French government made regular reports on the international situation that could be of interest to the nation.[86] On April 12, 1871, the newspaper chose to high-light a recent legal decision in the United States: "Washington.—The House of Representatives has just passed a law rendering the crimes of the Ku-Klux in the south accountable before federal courts and authorizing the president to suspend *Habeas Corpus* anywhere that this illegal and dangerous organi-zation exists."[87] Printing this decision was no accident; interest in American legal decisions was at an all-time high. Thiers was aware of the importance that suspension of habeas corpus had already played in the United States dur-ing the Civil War. Building on the moral authority of the American republic, he insisted during the height of the Commune that those who had chosen to make enemies of the republic could not necessarily be guaranteed all of their rights. The affinity between these situations in the United States and France only gave strength to the government's position.

As Thiers prepared for the military invasion of Paris and the final assault on the revolutionaries, Lincoln's presidency and the context of the Civil War were called upon with greater regularity. Thiers repeatedly argued that the Parisian insurrection was not a legitimate revolution, but a civil war, in which he was responsible for ensuring the unity of France. "What! You think that it is without fear and suffering that I preside during this civil war thanks to the title you have bestowed upon me!"[88] He then repeated once again: "The criminal insurrection has brought a civil war on the heels of a foreign war, which is no less harmful."[89] By invoking the idea of civil war following foreign war, Thiers was attempting to draw a direct parallel between his role as ex-ecutive, Lincoln's war powers, and the distant memory of 1793. The American state and the revolutionaries of 1793 had demonstrated their extraordinary capacity to act, even assuming quasi-dictatorial powers, in order to preserve a liberal democratic republic. Citing the American example directly, Thiers stated: "All attempts at secession, on the part of any portion or the territory will be forcefully put down, just as they were in America—A. Thiers."[90]

But the weight of the American model went beyond the immediate con-text of the war. France also looked to the US state as a model for fiscal author-ity in the aftermath of the Civil War. With the end of the Franco-Prussian War and the Commune, the fiscal situation of the French state was desperate. The budget of 1870 was in deficit 645,448,625 francs out of a total budget of 2,730,156,000 francs and at the end of 1871, the deficit climbed to 1,005,727, 735 francs. The indemnity that France owed Prussia as a result of the Treaty of Versailles was 5 billion, one-quarter of France's gross domestic product, to be paid in gold or foreign currency, and equal to two years of state revenue.[91] Considering the drop in state revenues during the war and the Commune, the total for the double deficit of the two years in June of 1871 was 1,651,176,735 francs. Moreover, Thiers estimated that the cost of the war totaled 7.8 billion including the reparations, which would be covered in large part by loans and the 325 million for the purchase of railroads in the departments lost to Germany. The total cost of these loans per annum was to be approximately 566 million—this included 200 million toward an amortization of the loan taken out from the Banque de France. In June 1871, the government proposed an increase in revenue of 446 million in new taxes but this sum proved insufficient to cover the new expenses in the state's budget and the payouts on the loans. Ultimately, the sum was closer to 600 million out of a budget that was estimated at approximately 2 billion francs (2,023,215,951) or approximately an overwhelming 25 percent.

In this context, the fiscal system developed by the United States in the wake of the Civil War was regularly invoked as the model for the French state. In the discussions on indemnities to the cities and departments that had suffered during the war and the rebellion, one legislative member argued: "Let me cite you an example. After this incredible struggle that we call the war of secession in the United States, the question of asking the state for an indemnity was posed. They did not hesitate to respond that no indemnities would be permitted after the war."[92] During the debate on raising taxes, the United States was once again seen as a model. "We must adopt all of these new taxes," argued another National Assemblyman, "in order to create a system which is analogous to that of the United States after the war of secession, which cost them 20 billion."[93] He continued by insisting that the US government had increased old taxes and created new ones and in so doing paid off a portion of their war debt each year. He cited, for example, a tax on alcohol suggesting that in spite of the drastic raise in taxes, the country was still in need of liquor. He then came to what might appear to be a surprising conclusion with regard to taxation, suggesting that it was fundamental to examine "the United States, whose example is always cited when we need to find more money."[94] This deputy was not alone in this assessment. Another member of the legislature announced to the chamber: "We never miss an opportunity to invoke the example of America."[95]

But what exactly was the nature of this model of American fiscal power? Thiers's minister of finance also argued for the American model at the beginning of the year 1872 as France continued to look for new resources to pay the war reparations: "Gentlemen, let us take the example that is the most reasonable and the most similar to our own" he argued, "that of the American nation." What the minister was particularly interested in was the United States' capacity to raise armies and funds with great rapidity without creating over the long term a crushing fiscal or military structure: "The American nation does not have enormous military armaments, nor does it have a large army, but they know how to create, in an instant and with an extraordinary effort . . . the necessary force to respond to any eventuality. This is what they did during the war of secession."[96] The American state of the nineteenth century was not a model for its low tax rates, but for its ability to raise taxes and armies quickly. This would seem to have been at the heart of the liberal state model that appeared so attractive to the new French government.

So as the French attempted to found a lasting republic key liberals like Thiers and Laboulaye argued that the United States provided one of the most successful models of fiscal and war powers ever seen in a republic. The fact that the United States had found a militarily and fiscally successful response to rebellion and civil war—the greatest possible threat to a polity rooted in the people—only solidified the conviction that the Americans provided an important model for a viable state in a democratic regime. From the invocation of extraordinary powers, the suspension of *habeas corpus* and the bloody crushing of revolt to the dismantling of the military mobilization, the fiscal apparatus to pay for the ravages of war, and the ultimate amnesty of the rebels, the construction of a modern liberal democratic state was hardly contained within the limited purview of France.

As Thiers began preparing a military response to the Commune in March 1871, he presented his conception of the new republican regime: "We have found a Republic already established, like a fact without an author. I will not destroy this form of government that I am now using to maintain order."[97] There were two key elements to this declaration before the Assembly. First, the republic was not the work of any one individual. It had imposed itself like a fact without being the product of the will of any specific individual. As we shall see, this argument would reemerge when Blanc challenged Laboulaye's amendment a few years later. Since it had emerged without being the product of any one individual's will, there was nothing that could be done but serve it. Second, he insisted that this impersonal republic, and not the very personal power of the emperor, was the most effective means for maintaining order. A point he would bloodily prove some two short months later.

Thiers outlined a theory of the liberal democratic state that would find itself at the heart of the construction of the French state in the nineteenth century and beyond. He conceived of a state that was limited in its ability to act directly only by necessity and was able to achieve its ends by mobilizing social power through law and civil society. Such a perspective emerged out of his conviction that the state operated according to circumstances with necessary force. This necessary power could be deployed in everyday governance just as it could be deployed in a context of natural disaster, economic need, internal revolt, or foreign war, but in any of these instances, the state did not confront a rule of law which bound it; through necessity, law became the mechanism through which it intervened. That the man who developed such a vision of the liberal democratic state became the founder of the Third Republic requires us to reconsider arguments which suggest that France lacked a vibrant liberal tradition because it fostered a strong state under the Third Republic. To the contrary, Thiers's liberal and democratic commitment to law was precisely one of the key features of his conception of the state. Moreover, the fact that at key moments in his reflection, the United States provided an ideal type for thinking through these problems should also indicate that many of our assumptions on the place of American democracy and state power in the world and its relationship to law have a more complex history than we may have recognized.

5

EXCLUSION:
Jenny d'Héricourt on the Edges of the Political

A nous deux donc, monsieur Proudhon!
JENNY D´HÉRICOURT[1]

For all the capacities of the new democratic state described in the previous chapters, there remained the equally fundamental problem of exclusion. As a new vision of democracy came onto the horizon, formulated against the problems of inequality, equality, emergency, necessity, and the Terror, there was still the question of how a robust relationship between the individual, the social, and the state could be assured, when both rested on the fundamental bias of being a "male individual" and therefore a "male state." To be sure, some men took this problem very seriously, as we shall see, but this foundation of exclusion also generated one of the most original theories of the political in a democratic state of the second half of the nineteenth century in the work of Jenny d'Héricourt.

As an outspoken activist for women's political and civil rights, d'Héricourt had been doubly deceived by the Second Republic's refusal to grant women the vote and its collapse into the hands of a paternalist Bonaparte. However, this disappointment only stimulated her intellectual development. After 1852, d'Héricourt set out on a new intellectual path, influenced by a stronger international women's movement.[2] Innovating on many of the ideas that had guided her during the July Monarchy, Jenny d'Héricourt became a social theorist and philosopher of the first order, developing a sophisticated theory of the democratic state and society.[3] To present, the tradition to which she belongs has been largely accredited to . . . men: Charles Renouvier and his Third Republican followers like Alfred Fouillée, Henry Michel, Emile Durkheim, Léon Bourgeois, and Celestin Bouglé.[4] And yet, d'Héricourt's political theory of the democratic state had close intellectual affinities with these figures just as it has been noted how key aspects of her sociological theory are strikingly similar to those of Durkheim and may have influenced him as well.[5] The fact that d'Héricourt has been overlooked within this tradition is particularly problematic for at least two reasons: she was a first-rate philosopher and her gender critique provided a deeply insightful perspective on how to theorize the democratic state in response to the crippling fact of exclusion.

D'Héricourt confronted the problem of gender exclusion by embracing differences and theorizing an adversarial conception of the political. By challenging even the most "natural" assumptions of her day on the distinction between man and woman and the "nature" of gender, she broke down the last elements of certainty and "metaphysical abstractions" inherited from the eighteenth century. D'Héricourt posed gender and all social questions in a profoundly political way: nothing could remain uncontested. Her aim therefore was not to create a homogeneous collective identity that could unite against the paternalist state. Rather, her ambition was to create the conditions for each individual to live his or her ideas, ambitions, and gender according to their own design in society. At the root of this vision was an adversarial notion of the political, which focused less on the question of representation than on the question of difference. This adversarial political model was built on a thick definition of the social individual in which the individual's expression of his or her capacities in his or her own way could only be guaranteed by the state, not in opposition to it. In this way, exclusion was not a means for building the polity by deciding who was in and who was out, but a threat to the political itself because it prevented each individual from participating in the agonistic foundation of the democratic state.

While this vision led d'Héricourt to a certain suspicion of representation and the vote, it also pushed her to consider the potential contributions of other democratic regimes. In particular, d'Héricourt spent ten years in the United States working within the women's movement and developing original observations of American institutions. Upon her return in 1873, then, as the fledgling Third Republic was still searching for a sound institutional foothold, d'Héricourt posited the potential contribution of the organization of American institutions to accommodate her theory of agonistic democracy.

Beyond the Absolute Republic? D'Héricourt's Early Feminism

During the decades between the revolution of 1830 and the revolution of 1848, the question of social and political justice united radical and event centrist republicans. As Pierre Rosanvallon has shown, republican and socialist reformers of the period understood suffrage and social equality to be inextricably linked in what he has called the "Republic of Universal Suffrage."[6] After 1830, he argues, "reference to the republic neatly concentrated a whole ensemble of social and cultural aspirations into a single word. The republic of universal suffrage implied, above all, the search for a society without divisions."[7] Rosan-vallon's compelling analysis of this process demonstrates that throughout the July Monarchy, popular sovereignty suffered from a kind of reversed absolut-ism, lacking any substantial difference with the old regime by substituting the people for the king as a total and unified sovereign. According to this logic, all social injustices and divisions were derivative of limited suffrage. Because the sovereign was indivisible, giving voice to the entire people through universal suffrage would eliminate all social difference and inequality; the unified body of the king would find its fullest expression in the unified body of the people.[8]

While this assessment proved true for many in mid-nineteenth-century France, recent work has suggested that some key figures of the left developed a different form of republicanism that was not so at odds with forms of liberal pluralism as well as socialism. Insisting on both individual rights and social cohesion, Pierre Leroux was among the first, with Louis Blanc, to open the promising path of a new republicanism that navigated between liberalism and socialism. As we shall see, this tradition attempted to frame the individual as a social being. Like Louis Blanc, Leroux sought a middle road between the radical individualism of a Bentham and the collectivism of the Phalanstère, insisting that the social bond was necessarily reinforced by the recognition that liberty was ensured through social organization.

Within this debate on the intellectual history of republicanism, however, the question of women's politics has been almost entirely ignored. And yet, it may not be a coincidence that Pierre Leroux, who was at the origins of this hybrid political and social theory, was so often cited (even into the early Third Republic in 1874) as one of the leading male supporters of women's rights. Indeed, the nexus of French republicanism, utopian socialism, and feminism generated a particularly rich resource for innovating on republican ideas be-fore 1848 and after. The women's movement was in fact central to crafting an original republican "third way" between liberalism and socialism through the notion of the "social individual." While the dominant tradition of French republicanism may have insisted on the univocal nature of republican sov-ereignty, key women suffragists fought for women's civil and political rights based on complementarities between genders, opening the possibility for a more complex and even pluralist theory of egalitarian society.

In the work of these feminist theorists, gender was one social distinc-tion that would not be overcome through universal suffrage. The women's movement of the July Monarchy found strong support among utopian social-ists.[9] Key Saint-Simonians, for example, understood the exclusion of women from public life as the simple rejection of one half of humanity and therefore a profound disruption to social equilibrium. As Prosper Enfantin wrote in 1831, "The man and the woman, this is the social individual."[10] Similarly, Charles Fourier argued that "freedom must be simultaneously extended to men, women, and children."[11] The tremendous development of the women's rights movement in the 1830s and 1840s was thus spurred on by a drive for social harmony based on the social complementarities of gender difference. As feminist historians have shown, this period stood as a high point of one brand of French feminism founded on radical claims of difference.[12] Hence, women like Jeanne Deroin, Pauline Roland, and Jenny d'Héricourt, among others, who wrote about and fought for women's rights within this tradition, focused their attention on what women offered the social sphere as women.

According to these theories, universal suffrage and social equality would reveal an equality in difference that would be essential for the march toward social progress. "Thus women are not similar to men and yet they are equals," it was argued.[13] While the social difference between a worker and a bourgeois would supposedly cede to the ballot box in a system of absolute republican sovereignty, it could never, in the minds of women's activists, undermine the difference between man and woman—a difference that remained essential in the construction of a harmonious society. So, in the specific case of gender difference, universal suffrage would actually guarantee the proper relationship between equal differences. "We cannot conceive of the idea of privilege being associated with the idea of democracy," Eugénie Niboyet argued in the first issue of the La Voix des femmes, in March 1848, confirming the essential outlines of the Republic of Universal Suffrage. "Yet," she continued, "while the least intelligent citoyen has the right to vote, the most intelligent citoyenne is still deprived of this right." The women's republic of universal suffrage was to be both socially just and built on difference; alongside its commitment to socialist ideals and universal suffrage in a republic, it was not entirely antithetical to key aspects of pluralism designed to preserve individual difference.

To this extent, Mona Ozouf's claim that Enfantin's "'social individual' [was] a figure that blurs the distinction between individual and society [and] was not the individual in the sense given that term by the Enlightenment and the Revolution"[14] is less a limitation than precisely the germ of an attempt to combine liberalism and socialism through the perspective of gender. As Pierre Leroux argued, "I don't know anything that is as much an individual right as marriage."[15] For Leroux, the opportunity to join into a man-woman partnership was rooted in individual choice. In this view, social progress would only become possible as each individual fulfilled his and her social and political roles by freely joining in a common bond. When considering feminists' contributions to a new republicanism, it is also worth noting John Stuart Mill's support of Pierre Leroux's proposition for women's suffrage in 1851. Mill wrote a letter to Leroux following his speech in the National Assembly, "Please allow an English democrat, joined in spirit to the French socialist struggle for the regeneration of human institutions, to pay homage and give recognition for the noble initiative that you have undertaken on one of the great questions of the future through your proposal to the National Assembly to recognize the political rights of women."[16] As Serge Audier has noted, Mill's move away from classical liberalism to an increasingly new position that made room for the social individual was closely tied to his work with Harriet Taylor on the woman question. Early French feminism therefore played an important role in laying the groundwork for a new conception of individual liberty which broke down the individual/social divide.

Coming of age intellectually in the July Monarchy, d'Héricourt (then Poinsard) bathed in the radical political ideas of the period, in particular the Saint-Simonians, and alongside them the rise of a feminist movement in France. Working with Etienne Cabet as a writer for his newspaper, *Le Populaire*, she also published a novel under the pen name Félix Lamb, developing the foundations of her radical feminism.[17] Jenny d'Héricourt continued to endorse some of the key ideas of utopian socialism, even if she disagreed with some of their "metaphysical" and utopian claims. Moreover, she continued to demonstrate a particular affinity for the ideas of Pierre Leroux.[18]

Fighting for both civil and political equality in the eruption of the Second Republic, she was a key contributor to the women's movement in early 1848. At the outset of the revolution, she participated as secretary in *La Société pour l'émancipation de la femme*, a leading feminist organization for social and political equality in the context of a new republic.[19] Working with figures like Jeanne Deroin, Eugénie Niboyet, and Désirée Gay, she attended political campaigns and rallies, arguing for women's suffrage. As the *Manifesto of the Organization of Women Workers* by the Society for the Emancipation of Women argued: "The keystone of the edifice of their emancipation [is] political rights. How is it possible to pay taxes that one has not voted by oneself or through a representative of one's choice? How can one accept laws on which one has not been consulted? Such are our goals."[20]

So the refusal to grant women the vote in 1848, especially in the context of the declaration of universal manhood suffrage, marked a double failure. First, it did not help overcome all social difference as the Second Republic was quickly drawn into social conflict. The closing of the National Workshops, the conflagration of June, and the election of Louis-Napoleon Bonaparte at the end of the year ensured that social division would remain central to this Second Republican experiment. And second, the republic did not grant the

138   CHAPTER FIVE

vote to women. Lamenting the short-sightedness of the 1848 male revolutionaries years later, d'Héricourt argued:

> Nothing is equivalent to the generosity and the devotion of advanced women, who serve the projects and ideas of democracy. The representatives of Paris owed their nomination in part to their efforts. Then the representatives in their stupid pride and unintelligence, detached them from the movement by rejecting the bill on divorce, by closing their meetings and pushing their brutality and scorn to such an extent that they refused women entry into their meetings; they could not even learn! . . . Once women were removed, the Revolution was bound to perish and perish it did.[21]

From this perspective, the problem of the Second Republic was hardly its absolutist republicanism, but rather the short-sighted pragmatism of its provisional government in the form of a refusal to realize one of the leading drives behind the radical republicanism of the preceding decade.

For d'Héricourt, a republic that denied the participation of women undermined its access to the full weight of social resources available to it. Therefore, excluding women and depriving itself of half of its support system, the republic was bound to fail. The absolute republic thus disappointed on both counts: it was neither utopian nor universal enough to allow for real difference. The republic fell far short of realizing one of the most important claims for instituting a unified social body—not because it tried and failed, as in the case of universal suffrage or the national workshops, but because it proved entirely unwilling to provide for women's civil and political equality. For all of the impact of French feminism on liberal socialism, the end result was the republic's double failure, both to deliver as guarantor of social unity and to prevent the foundations of a potential positive division with the social.

Looking back on the experience of 1848 during the Second Empire, d'Héricourt highlighted the major transition that took place in the wake of what she perceived as the revolution's failure:

> I don't deny that women caused great harm to the February Revolution, for they are only as intelligent as men and have great influence upon them. But what did this Revolution do for them, I ask? Those who ruled over public opinion still needed them: the most active put themselves in their service, without any agenda and total devotion. And once you were well established, through a decision in the Chamber, you closed the doors on the meetings where they opened their hearts to understand the greater national interest and universal fraternity. . . . Women, like the people, will have none of our revolutions that destroy them for the benefit of a few chatter boxes.[22]

Considering the revolution of 1848 from the depths of the Second Empire, d'Héricourt was not suggesting that the inclusion of women would have been a panacea to the revolution's problems, an argument she repeated time and again in her work following 1848. Indeed, in a view that broke with the utopian ideal of universal suffrage, she insisted that women and men, as individuals, were no doubt equally intelligent as well as foolhardy, so there was no reason to assume that the same proportion of intelligent and foolhardy people would have changed the outcome of the revolution in itself. However, by refusing women's formal participation, d'Héricourt became convinced that the republic did not give itself the tools for social improvement and was therefore bound to fail.

D'Héricourt's International Turn

So while the women's movement of the 1840s had been central to the development of the key concept of the social individual, the collapse of the Springtime of Peoples, the refusal to grant women the right to vote in a republic of universal suffrage, and the conservative turn of the Second Republic in 1849, marked a transition in the history of the feminist movement that would have a profound effect on the work of Jenny d'Héricourt. Many of the feminist 48ers shifted away from a direct political engagement. And some, like the activist Eugénie Niboyet, even seemed to denounce their role in 1848 in the new patriarchal and imperial context of the Second Empire.[23] D'Héricourt's work in the Second Empire, however, built on the ideas that had germinated during the July Monarchy, building on the truncated legacy of 1848: "What did Jean Deroin, Pauline Roland and many others, do here in 1848? What am I doing today, in the name of a legion of women for whom I am the interpreter? All women do not make reclamations, no; but do you not know that every demand of right is made at first singly."[24] The collapse of the ideals of 1848 and the Second Republic became an invitation and even an obligation for d'Héricourt to elaborate a political and social theory of the state in democracy.

In the years that followed, d'Héricourt insisted on both individual liberty and social cohesion, entering into a profound dialogue with some of the most important philosophers and social theorists of her day such as Charles Renouvier. Through this collaboration, she created a deeply original theory of the social individual and the political from the perspective of gender at the same time that she turned away from the fundamental idea of women's natural difference, insisting instead on a more radical vision of the social and cultural construction of gender.

The foundations of her new theory were formed by participating in international intellectual circles and a rapidly internationalizing women's movement. She insisted on the importance of the international intellectual network, writing: "It is equally appropriate that I offer my recognition to the Italian, English, Dutch, American, and German journals that translated many of my articles; to the men and women of these diverse countries. . . . It is to you my French and foreign friends that I dedicate this work."[25] This internationalism was buttressed by her integration into women's activist movements across Europe and the Atlantic. As Karen Offen has noted, the 1850s marked an internationalization of the women's movement in general. "Although there were never official international organizations, which would have allowed it to survive, the movement gave radical feminists in Europe and the United States contacts and liaisons as well as ideas and strategies. The revolutionary year of 1848 was a volcanic eruption of activities, in particular for national women's movements; but during the 1850s, it was an international network that helped support feminists after their revolutions had failed or turned conservative."[26] In this informal system of international feminism, d'Héricourt both learned from and shared her ideas with feminists from around the North Atlantic world. Looking to the United States, for example, she argued: "What are a host of American women doing at the present time?"[27]

It was in this context that Jenny d'Héricourt—pushed into the international arena by her radicalism in the conservative context of the early Second Empire—slowly became an essential figure in an international nexus. "Some women particularly embodied these international connections," Bonnie Andersen writes. "Anne Knight in England and France, Lucretia Mott in Philadelphia, and Jenny d'Héricourt in Paris and then Chicago—all functioned as important nodes in the radical feminist network, traveling, corresponding, and seeking out like-minded visitors from other nations."[28] D'Héricourt's initial decision to use international outlets for the publication of her articles was the result of the radicalism of her feminism in the context of the Second Empire. Her collaborators in Paris encouraged her to publish abroad, fearing the consequences that a Parisian publication might bring. As Alice Primi suggests, "since 1852, no woman had risked demanding equality of the sexes publicly in France. . . . It was only in December 1856 that d'Héricourt was able to publish texts there [in France] as radical as those that appeared in *La Ragione* [in Italy]." Writing at an increasingly feverish pace during the late 1850s, d'Héricourt published twenty-six articles in France and Italy.[29]

D'Héricourt was also drawn to the American women's movement during the Second Empire for its intellectual and social resources.[30] Among these new influences, d'Héricourt's role in the international women's movement

led her to write a biographical article on Ernestine Rose, "the foremost fe-
male orator in the United States,"[31] following Rose's visit to France. In her
article, d'Héricourt insisted on the advancement of women's rights in the
United States. "Today, in the United States, there are one hundred thousand
women enrolled under the banner of emancipation. . . . In the American
West, married women administer their own wealth. Women are embracing
careers hitherto reserved only for men: women are now accepted as medical
practitioners, and soon there will be women doctors of law. . . . Conventions
composed of men and women assemble each year in one state or another to
discuss the laws that must be changed and to petition for their repeal."[32] Her
interest in the American women's movement and its foundations continued
to grow in the coming decade. Indeed, d'Héricourt progressively became engaged in the women's movement in the United States until she ultimately left
for Chicago in the mid-1860s, where she would participate in some of the
most important debates on equal rights in the wake of the Civil War with
such figures as Susan B. Anthony, Lucy Stone, and Frederick Douglass. But,
by the time d'Héricourt left for Chicago, she had produced an oeuvre, amass-
ing articles and a book on women's *affranchisement* that would mark her
generation.

D'Héricourt's Gender Critique of the Demos

During this period of intense intellectual production, d'Héricourt contributed
to a new theory of the state rooted in her gender critique. Here, her position
on gender was not only political but also the point of departure for proposing
a radical theory of democracy that challenged many of the leading philosophers of her day. At the center of this radical theory were two essential traits.
First, her theory refused the inherited certainties of universalist abstraction,
insisting that any full notion of political organization needed to be based on
observation of facts on the ground, and specifically the observation of gender. Second, highlighting the radical diversity across gender in intelligence,
capacity, and strength her new theory of the democratic state navigated between the liberal ideals of individual liberty, by building on earlier theories of
the social individual.

To the extent that she refused to build a notion of the state on a metaphysics inherited from the eighteenth century, d'Héricourt was very much of her
time. But she also pushed far beyond her contemporaries as she scrutinized
the logical conclusions of her contemporaries' philosophies through the lens
of gender. D'Héricourt crafted a critique of the most prominent political and
social scholars of her day, arguing that their vision of women was not only

unjust but also revealed fundamental contradictions in their methods and conclusions, especially those of the fledgling positivist school. Her ambition in doing so was to root out the last semblances of metaphysics in political and social theory and in so doing reveal the profoundly contingent, and necessarily political, nature of all collective organization.

Reserving her sharpest critiques of contemporary social and political theory for the father of nineteenth-century positivism, Auguste Comte, and the socialist Pierre-Joseph Proudhon, she demonstrated that when their writings on women were examined, many philosophical abstractions remained at the core of their system, in spite of their claims to the contrary. Her focus on these two figures is in one sense quite surprising. Indeed, she was convinced of many of the basic arguments of Comte's positivism and his critique of eighteenth-century metaphysics, just as she adhered to many of Proudhon's radical socialist ideas. Her attacks then were not "ideological" to the extent that she agreed with many of their philosophical presuppositions. Rather, her critique was based on her claim that when one examined their philosophy and theories of political organization through their writings on women, they had actually been unsuccessful in realizing the full ambitions of their own systems—that is, in undermining the basic metaphysics that underpinned much of their own critiques of eighteenth-century social and political theory.[33] Using a rhetorical method that she developed to great effect throughout her work, she quoted Proudhon back to himself, revealing through his own work his contradictions on women: "'Most aberrations and philosophical chimeras come from the fact that we attribute a series of logics to a reality that does not exist; and we attempt to explain the nature of man through abstractions.'"[34] She continued, insisting that Proudhon's observations on women were the result of his abstractions and his metaphysics: "Your contradictions, Sir, are real and good contradictions. For you, as for us, there is only one kind of woman: the one who lives in a society of men, who, like him, has flaws and vices and influences as much as she is influenced; the other woman has only ever existed in the minds of mystics and hallucinations."[35] There were no "natural" facts; political and social theory needed to recognize the constructed and therefore contested nature of every element of social life.

The fact that Proudhon could recognize social inequality, but could not recognize gender inequality meant that, for d'Héricourt, it was in fact Proudhon who had *only paradoxes to offer*.[36] "Very well. Your theory, if theory there is, is nothing but a fabric woven of paradoxes; your ostensible principles are *challenged by the facts*."[37] She continues further on, "If I were a lover of paradoxes like you, I would say: man is an incomplete woman, since it is the woman who produces the seed, men's role in the reproduction process is highly dubious and science may one day learn to do without them entirely. That is the paradox of Auguste Comte; it is worth as much as yours."[38] For d'Héricourt, the paradoxes emerged out of the perspective of male republicans and socialists who could not fully embrace the conclusions generated by their methods.

So at the center of d'Héricourt's philosophy was her critique of gender as an a priori concept from which one could deduce difference within a political system. D'Héricourt insisted that unlike most of her contemporaries, her political philosophy was truly rooted in the facts of social life. From this position, she elaborated her fundamental observation that the variation in intellectual and physical difference across men and women was the same as those between individuals of the same sex: "Now gentlemen, what becomes of these pretensions in the presence of *facts* that show you all unequal in strength and intellect? What becomes of these pretensions in the presence of *facts* that show us a host of women stronger than many men; a host of women more intelligent than the great mass of men?"[39] Thus the blanket assumption that men and women were born equal was a useless abstraction. Instead, examination of society revealed radical inequalities across genders: individuals of all genders shared in a given society a profoundly unequal ability to develop their individual capacities according to their own desires just as they were unable to contribute to society equally according to their own abilities. The problem, however, was that such radical inequalities were masked by those who posited male equality and the divergent social and political functions of men and women based on gender: "The law of sexual differences is not manifested through the several characteristics which have been laid down. That these characteristics may be only the result of education, of the difference of prejudices, of that of occupations, etc. That as these generalities may be the fruit of the difference of training and surroundings, nothing can be legitimately deduced from them as to the functions of woman."[40] One's political, social, and cultural surround, d'Héricourt insisted, determined the "function" of a given gender. Therefore, gender was more accurately understood as a vehicle for expressing one's liberty within society according to each individual's capacities, desires, and needs. "In *fact*, I know not, and you know no better than I, what are the true characteristics arising from the distinction of the sexes, and I believe that they can be revealed only by liberty in equality, parity of instruction and of education."[41]

Shifting from her arguments on gender equality that had driven the women's movement up to 1848, d'Héricourt developed a highly differentiated notion of gender as a form of individual liberty—liberty for women, in this view, would not come as a collective, but as individuals. In a statement that echoed key elements of contemporary forms of liberal pluralism, d'Héricourt asserted: "Those who have a disposition to go to the Church, the Temple, or the Synagogue should have full liberty to receive the blessing of their respective priests! This does not concern Society." However, she did not, in consequence conclude that individual expressions of gender could be achieved by freeing the individual from the social. Instead, one could only fully realize one's individual liberty through the opportunity to fully express his or her gender as he or she saw fit *in* society. She continued her argument: "What we need is that, if afterward their vows should not seem to them binding, social authority should not make them obligatory; they have a right to be absurd, but society has no right to impose absurdity on them." Note that she refers to the state here as a "social authority." This was common in her work and attested to the fact that the state could not be seen as a power that imposed itself from the outside. Rather, individuals were to be free to choose on those issues that "did not concern Society." Therefore, "social authority" was necessary to ensure that they could do so. But it was also necessary to ensure that they could change their minds; that is, that the individual would not be prisoner to previous decisions or to the inherited choices of groups.

Through gender, then, individual choice became politically charged and as such, it became a problem of state because only the state could provide the generalized educational opportunities necessary for cutting through the social and cultural prejudices. Education could not be left to religious bodies any more than it could be left to local communities, because in each case, such instruction would only reinforce the social construction of gender that already existed. The state was the necessary guarantor of such order, d'Héricourt insisted: "Its [social authority's] duty is, on the contrary, to enlighten them, and to render them free."[42] Only the state could adjoin individuals such that they could pursue their social capacities free of superstition or unchallenged cultural practice. To be sure, she was not arguing for a central state that would impose the abstract ideal of equality. What she did insist on, however, was that the state provide the conditions for each to develop fully his or her individual capacities within society.

D'Héricourt's attempt to integrate gender and individual ideals into the social milieu contributed to the construction of a broader theory of the social individual that shared many similarities with Louis Blanc's ideas. Seeking to overcome the opposition between an overwhelming democratic-socialist emphasis on social equality and classical liberalism's unbendable embrace of individual liberty, her theory of the individual took into consideration the sanctity of the individual *within* the collective order.[43] As d'Héricourt wrote in the Italian journal, *La Ragione,* her ideal was "*the creation of individual liberty through social equality.*"[44] Such a call for equality was hardly utopian; based on observation of individual differences, she proposed a theory of individual specialization as a constituent part of modernity, building on the key idea that realizing one's capacities within the social matrix, regardless of one's gender and without determination, increased one's liberty.[45] This was the ultimate impact of refusing the abstract rights of men and women: only through empirical knowledge could an effective organization of the collective order take form and individuals develop their *functions* and *capacities* as men or women in society. "Functions belong to those who prove their aptitude for them, and not to an abstraction called sex," she argued.[46]

The state therefore ensured the proper functioning of a social division of labor.[47] "There is no need to be a great student of philosophy or economics, Monsieur, to know that a contract is a sign of personal insufficiency," she declared. "In a common project, one brings forward an idea, the other his arms, the third his money, and the fourth the clientele; if each one of them had all of these things on her own, there would be no reason to associate." She then concluded: "A happy insufficiency has brought them together and helped them establish an equivalence between each of their contributions that could not be established by some common measure [*fait établir l'équivalence entre chacun des apports qui ne pouvaient être soumis à une commune mesure*]."[48] Social progress, she claimed, was to be attained by bringing forward each individual's specific capacities, and it was the state that provided the coordinative capacities for such complementarities to be pursued. It should be noted that d'Héricourt's notion of public authority paralleled those of Blanc and many that would follow to the extent that the state was not supported by a universal abstract identity or homogeneity that cut across the polity, nor was it an external force that guaranteed order by imposing equality from the outside. Instead it was a means of articulating the social relationship between individuals, by guaranteeing contracts, education, knowledge, etcetera, which allowed each individual to contribute through their difference. Through this "infrastructural power of the state," men and women could develop and contribute to society in ways that would reveal the full wealth of all social resources.[49]

D'Héricourt's conception of the state therefore refused any emphasis on universal abstraction at the same time that it denied a classical liberal opposition between the individual, society, and state intervention, insisting, like Blanc, that individuals were necessarily social beings. In this sense, d'Héricourt provided a strong contribution to a nineteenth-century republican position on the state that was both anticollectivist and anti-atomist, and she fits squarely within the pantheon of French republican writers that have slowly been uncovered from Louis Blanc, Pierre Leroux, and François Huet to Alfred Fouillée and Celestin Bouglé. Through her gender critique, d'Héricourt provided a particularly valuable and original contribution to this intellectual current of French republicanism that focused on a radical individual autonomy within a robust theory of social equality guaranteed by the state. But by placing gender at the heart of her social theory, she was also able to contribute something more: because gender was established within the social surround, it was in the deepest sense not natural, but political. Every element of social life, even the most fundamental distinctions like those between men and women, could be contested, challenged, and discussed. To this extent, d'Héricourt attempted to open up a new space for a politically saturated society that could take no position for granted. In her challenge of one of the most fundamental "natural" distinctions within modern political organization, there remained no utopian lines cutting through the polity, no metaphysics, as d'Héricourt would put it; instead there was only uses of the political.

On the Edge of the Political

By placing the political at the core of her theory, d'Héricourt opened a path toward an agonistic conception of democracy that challenged many of her contemporaries and would have a long life, well into the twentieth century. At the core of this project was a narrative strategy of remarkable originality, which she displayed in her magnum opus, *La Femme Affranchie*. Within this extraordinarily complex work, d'Héricourt brought together radically different writing styles, narrative positions, and literary mechanisms, provocatively combining form and content in a staging of the agon. This work places her among the most thought-provoking and challenging philosophers of her day.

The book opens by presenting the leading antagonists with which she engaged, offering multiple-page quotations to assure the reader that she will be entirely faithful to her interlocutors' arguments, in their own words: "Since the reader might suspect us of malicious exaggeration, please read the following pages, which emanate directly from the inventor of the system, attentively," she explains.[50] Authors were invited to speak in the forum of her book, demonstrating her embrace of contradictory positions. She therefore presented the vast spectrum of intellectual positions from the far left to the center, lining up the "Modern Communists, Saint-Simonians, Fusonians, Phalansterians, Ernest Legouvé, Emile de Girardin, Jules Michelet, Auguste Comte, et Joseph Proudhon." Navigating among them, she dialogued with each group or philosopher, providing the key tenets of their philosophy and then fleshing out her conception as a response. The work then pursues a consistent attempt to recognize the positions of her interlocutors, both fictional and real, both those with whom she was in agreement and those with whom she disagreed. The format of the book therefore unveiled an emphasis on contradiction and even antagonism between different individuals, uncovering the idea that at the core of the polity was not a set of agreed terms, but a constant attempt to claim and redefine one's position. Contradictory debate was therefore at the heart of the polity. The result is an arresting reading experience that throws the reader into an intellectual and political struggle.[51]

The agonistic structure of d'Héricourt's thought is captured in her preface entitled "To My Readers; To My Adversaries; To My Friends." The addresses in the title are striking as they invite her readers to experience the book as a joust. The choice of words, between *friends* and *adversaries,* places the relationship with the author at the center of the reading experience. Encouraging her friends, she insists that she will respect her adversaries, but she will attack them unabated: "If I am brutal and do not go easy on my adversaries, it is because the ideas presented are of reason and justice."[52] And indeed, she does not tread lightly; her adversaries, she argues, are the well-armed and the dominant force, who insist on the weakness of their opponents when it is precisely because of them that women appear to be weak: "It is because they are strong, well armed, and attack brutally a sex that they have worked so hard to render timid and disarm; it is because I think it is entirely appropriate to defend the weak against tyranny that has the audacity to place itself on the side of right."[53]

D'Héricourt's reference to debating with adversaries opens toward key aspects of her use of the political. First, it suggests that she sought to maintain a clear and decided opposition among members of the political community without escalating to the level of potential dissociation and dissolution of the political community itself. Second, the polity was to be constructed through a process of engagement, disagreement, and discussion. The polity was not, and could not be, a given—there were no abstract concepts, basic lines of agreement, or uncritical points of view from which to build the polity. Rather, for d'Héricourt, cultivating the political required a vibrant but respectful debate that could take place among all of the community's members. The sheer fact that all members should be able to participate equally guaranteed the proper development of the polity.

However, her work also set out to demonstrate the possibility of the breakdown of this system in a polity in which women were not recognized as equals: "Gentlemen, woman is ripe for civil liberty and we declare to you that we shall henceforth consider whoever shall rise against our lawful claim to be an enemy of progress and of the Revolution."[54] D'Héricourt made very effective use of the distinction between "enemy" and "adversary" throughout the book. While

the preface emphasizes her engagement with adversaries, she pushes on occasion to what appears to be the breaking point for the political community
of opposition between enemies, revealing the slope from the friend-adversary
toward the friend-enemy distinction that potentially breaks the political bond.
When responding to Comte, d'Héricourt indicated precisely where the social
foundation of the polity could break down: "To say to these women that they
will be nothing within the state, in marriage, in science, art, industry or even in
your subjective paradise is something that is so outlandish that I cannot conceive of a more outrageous aberration. You will never find an interlocutor. You,
sir, who seeks to annihilate woman."[55] Denying an individual's basic role in the
state meant bringing annihilation and the end to any potential conversation.
Those who denied the basic recognition of women's civil liberties and equality
were evacuating the power to build an agonistic forum for social progress. As
a result, the refusal to recognize all members as participants equally capable of
staking out a legitimate position could only usher in arbitrary decisions as the
foundation for the regime. Exclusion from the political could only be the result
of a tyrannical decision.

It was precisely this breakdown of communication and hence the disintegration of the staging of the political that she explored in her chapter on
Proudhon. This chapter is by far the most vitriolic, riveted with tension as she
reproduces the debate that had gone on between them through their publica-
tions and open letters. The chapter introduces their "dialogue" with her quoting
one of her own actually published articles on Proudhon from the *Revue Philos-
ophique*: "Women have a weakness for fighters, they say. . . . I am a woman and
Mr. Proudhon is a great fighter of ideas, so I cannot help but hold him in my
esteem and sympathy, sentiments which should encourage moderation in the
attack that I am leveling against his opinions on the role of women in humanity."[56] She opens the dialogue then recognizing him as her equal, though he remains her adversary: "You will only step out of this circle vanquished either by
me or by yourself."[57] And from this moment, she opens the joust: "It's between
you and me now, Mr. Proudhon! [*A nous deux donc, monsieur Proudhon!*]"[58]

The subsequent dialogue consists of her quoting his responses from their
published public exchange of letters and articles. Organized as a narrative
in which Proudhon himself writes twice that he is awaiting the book that
d'Héricourt has promised and within which he is now published, the series
of exchanges read as a process of increasingly embattled disagreement. She
quotes Proudhon's second response to her: "Voilà, Madame, look at the conclusions I have come to in a few lines and that any reading of your book
will certainly not modify." "However," she continues, "good faith within the
debate, respect for our readers and ourselves requires that before we open

the controversy, a reciprocal communication be established between the two of us based on all the materials collected."[59] She then exposes her ideas to conclude their first exchange. Their first exchange maintains their radical disagreement on the position of women in society, but a basic respect for each other's right to make these claims. It is however, this basic recognition that is slowly pushed aside as their debate escalates.

The debate continues with a quote from Proudhon's response to her: "'You ask for it and, then, like a woman, you claim that you are tyrannized.'"[60] D'Héricourt responds, taking the notion of tyranny very seriously as the debate proceeds: "Yes, monsieur, to present, men have subordinated women, have been tyrants over them, their enemies. I agree with you on page 57 of your first essay on property where you explain that as soon as the weak and the strong are not *equal*, they are *foreigners* to one another; they cannot form an alliance, *they are enemies*. Yes, three times yes, Monsieur, as long as women and men are unequal women have the right to consider men *tyrants, enemies*."[61] She then continues, explaining her choice of the term "enemy": "To my eyes, you are a demolition expert, a destroyer, in whom instinct carries over intelligence, who hides the clear consequences of his writings: naturally struggling, you need adversaries; and without enemies, you fire cruelly upon those who combat by your side."[62] D'Héricourt did not challenge the need for disagreement ("you need adversaries"); what she challenged was that Proudhon transformed those who disagreed with him into his enemies. He could not see that those who disagreed could be part of the same struggle—they necessarily became his enemies, and therefore needed to be eradicated.

After reproducing their exchange, she explains that he refused to respond to her third publication. And it is in this context that their dialogue ultimately breaks down. Their exchange escalates with each *prise de parole*, until Proudhon refuses to respond and d'Héricourt reproduces Proudhon's "credo" in his place, quoting his own words—forcing him to participate in the conversation by making him speak for himself through a series of quotations gathered from his works. She concludes, "Do not accuse me of being brutal; with regards to women, Mr. Proudhon has revealed himself to be of a brutality and an injustice that exceeds all limits. . . . Well, Monsieur Proudhon, you wanted a war with women! A war you will have!"[63] Proudhon's intransigence and unwillingness to continue the debate and therefore accept the legitimacy of her opinion opened the door to war. It was through the very question of war that d'Héricourt introduced the limits of civil engagement and debate, the very possibility of the breakdown of the polity from within.

By refusing to continue their dialogue, she argues, Proudhon attempted d'Héricourt's "social annihilation." "Mr. Proudhon, the greatest enemy of the revolution is the one who raises it up to women as frightening event; . . . who dares, in the name of general emancipatory principles, proclaim the social anni-hilation and conjugal servitude of an entire half of humanity."[64] For d'Héricourt "social annihilation" meant the refusal of the right to participate in debate and therefore denial of access to an agonistic relationship. It therefore meant exclu-sion from participating in the construction of the political as such.

Proudhon himself, d'Héricourt noted, considered the existence of unrem-edied inequality grounds for a breach in the social contract. Perpetuating a distinction between strong and weak made enemies of members within the political community.

MR. PROUDHON. 'Social balance means establishing equality between the strong and the weak. As long as the strong and the weak are unequal, they are foreigners, they do not form an alliance; they are enemies.' (1er Mémoire sur la propriété, p. 57.)

ME. And yet, according to you, man is stronger and woman is weaker within the same species. So, the social balance must make them equal, so that they are no longer foreigners nor enemies.

MR. PROUDHON. This is logical, but I claim that they must remain unequal in society and in marriage. Man must be prepotent because he is the strongest.

ME. Contradiction, Master.[65]

Without any attempt to establish equality between individuals (either socially or across gender) then the political dissolved; individuals became foreigners, enemies to one another. To be an enemy did not mean that they were op-posed—rather, it meant something far more radical: that the very possibility for debate and disagreement was removed. A system that perpetuated inequal-ity at its root effectively evacuated the political as an agonistic realm in which all positions could be expressed and challenged. In this case, the constructive opposition between friends and adversaries that d'Héricourt placed at the cen-ter of her work, was challenged by a conflict between enemies that could only be maintained through pure force: "You base right on force, the superiority of faculties; that is, you accept inequality, despotism, deny individual liberty, and social equality, and do not believe in the correlation between rights and duties."[66] A regime that attempted to make enemies of those within the polity placed arbitrary decision above political recognition. In the ultimate denial of basic equal civil rights, the collapse of the political into arbitrary patriarchal decision became the only possible rule. The "social annihilation" of women could only be maintained as a purely tyrannical and despotic act.

Recognizing the potential breakdown of the political, d'Héricourt sought a way back from the position of the enemy/foreigner. However, she did not do so by seeking their agreement. Rather she attempted to attenuate their war by insisting that even in the face of Proudhon's refusal to recognize her as equal, she had the power to use the asymmetrical relationship to recognize him. If, she insisted, he was only her adversary (and not her enemy at war), the possibility of debate on equal footing reemerged:

> I have been so harsh with such a firm and resolute tone that I would regret leaving you without expressing a few words from the depths of my heart. You can be my adversary: I will never be your enemy, because I esteem you as an honest man, a vigorous thinker, one of the glories of France . . . Please understand something, which I am expressing without anger: that you are incapable of understanding women, and that by continuing the struggle, you are placed under the banner of counter-revolution.[67]

In recognizing Proudhon as her adversary and *not* her enemy, d'Héricourt's aim was precisely to prevent the need to invoke the voice of a single authority bolstered by rationalism or sheer force. In d'Héricourt's social democracy, discussion, not decision; contradiction, not consensus provided the foundations for the political.

This approach to the political provides insight into one of the more unexpected shifts in d'Héricourt's thought in the early Third Republic: her turn away from a strict focus on women's suffrage. D'Héricourt, one of the most outspoken and radical feminists of the Second Empire; the woman who had fought side by side with Jeanne Deroin and Eugénie Niboyet and other women 48ers; who published across Europe and traveled to the United States to participate in the feminist movement no longer sought immediate universal suffrage for women? This startling fact is even more troubling on this side of the long struggle for women's suffrage. And, it is particularly arresting considering her staunch emphasis on the question of political rights in 1848. From the perspective of the twenty-first century, d'Héricourt seems to be heading backward. Her views on suffrage have perplexed the few scholars who have considered her work and remain largely unexplained. And yet, in some ways it is consistent with the theory of the state generated by her political conception. It is worth engaging with her work to understand the contours of this other field of rights that had become so central to her on the eve of the Third Republic.

Women's antisuffragism has been studied extensively, especially in the American context.[68] But this is not a useful way for understanding d'Héricourt's shift in position during these years. Studies of antisuffragism have focused primarily on the ostensible contradiction of women who campaigned against their own right to vote, which does not apply to d'Héricourt. Without neglecting the importance of antisuffragism, robust social and political theories of democracy and democratic engagement that look specifically beyond the vote as a positive modality of building democratic life must also be considered.[69] And this was something radical women philosophers like d'Héricourt were particularly well-positioned to do. While she recognized the importance of the vote, the real contribution of her social and political philosophy lay elsewhere as she refused a thin conception of politics in which the vote could entirely absorb and saturate the political field.

From this perspective, her post-1848 work fits into a long line of political philosophers on democracy who have seen the vote as only—one essential, but only one—portion of popular democratic rule. Considering the importance of looking outside the vote in the twentieth century in the works of such prominent figures as Hannah Arendt, Jurgen Habermas, Judith Butler, Chantal Mouffe, and Pierre Rosanvallon—to name but a few—it is important to reconsider some of the earliest manifestations of theories of democracy that looked in this direction. Indeed, these authors, like d'Héricourt, have consistently sought a robust notion of social democracy that did not necessarily place an overwhelming emphasis on the vote, but rather on the full capacity to participate as an equal member in an agonistic democracy. Recognizing the essential social aspects of democratic engagement, they too have insisted that social equality was a fundamental condition of ensuring a proper democratic polity.

Indeed, the context of the Second Empire was particularly propitious for thinking about a democratic life beyond the vote. In Napoleon III's regime, as we have seen, the vote was as much a problem as a solution. Thus during the reign of "illiberal democracy" under Napoleon III, d'Héricourt like other male republicans began looking elsewhere to reinforce democratic life. In particular, she proposed the idea that acquiring key civil rights and access to education was foremost.

READER. What should be these conditions for the enjoyment of political right, in your opinion?

AUTHOR. Twenty-five years of age; and a certificate attesting that the individual knows how to read, write and reckon, that he possesses an elementary knowledge of the history and geography of his country; together with a correct theory with respect to Right and Duty, and the destiny of humanity upon earth. The knowledge of a small volume would be sufficient, as you see, to enable every man and woman, twenty-five years of age and healthy in mind, to enjoy political rights, after having been subject to an initiation by the enjoyment of civil rights.[70]

The author of *Woman Affranchised* was able, in part, to challenge the throne of suffrage because in the wake of 1848 she saw the dangers of suffrage on the one hand and developed an agonistic theory of democratic engagement on the other. Her theory of the social individual *did* require the state to ensure education and civil equality, for such a system could only work in a context where all individuals had access to the foundations that nourished social debate. Moreover, as mentioned above, it did require the state to serve as a social authority to help coordinate social individuals' relationship to the collective whole and to ensure that individuals had equal access to participation.

In this sense too, d'Héricourt was an integral member in the nineteenth-century tradition of redefining democracy through the state. She sought to reconfigure the foundations of the political by reconsidering its relationship to politics. Politics and voting existed alongside the political. But the state was less important for its repository as a site of representation and more important for its ability to ensure that each individual could effectively express him or herself. The complex place of the state in d'Héricourt's philosophy came from the fact that while she was heavily focused on the individual and individual choice as the foundation of the polity, this individual was defined socially. That is, she did not break the link between the individual's liberty to choose to pursue fulfillment and the social surround. In fact, it was society, through the state, that guaranteed and gave meaning to the development of individual capacities. As a result, it was necessary to build a state or "social authority" that could maintain a collective order and ensure the individual's ability to express him or herself *in* society. What was profoundly original in her vision was that this collective was to remain saturated by conflict and contestation. The contestation inherent in the political was to be preserved precisely in order to ensure progress. But it was following her extended stay in the United States that d'Héricourt was able to formulate a more thorough conception of the actual state institutions required to preserve her adversarial theory of the liberal democratic state.

The American State and the New French Republic

Jenny d'Héricourt returned from the United States in 1873 to find a Third Republic in the making. It has been suggested that she returned with a manuscript on the United States, which was burned upon her death. But while this manuscript has been lost, there are remnants of how she planned to elaborate the American influence on the creation of a new liberal democratic state. The ideas she gathered in the United States and intended to publish in her book may be gleaned from an article she wrote in 1873, which applied her understanding of American institutions to the construction of the French state.[71] In this article, she unabashedly insisted that American institutions were the key to France's political woes: "Does the nation want a Republic of order and peace that closes the door on exploitation and tyrants. . . . Then it would be fruitful to consult the political establishments of the United States."[72] Building on her democratic vision of adversarial debate and her softening on the issue of suffrage, her analysis on the contribution of the American republic placed an emphasis on American institutions, the freedom of expression, the importance of the state for guaranteeing education for its citizens, an insistence on the distribution of power, and a surprising argument for the right to bear arms in France.

The article began by laying out a series of oppositions between French and American democratic systems reminiscent of Laboulaye. She then came to the fundamental question: "Do you sincerely believe that two so completely different nations [*peuples*] may be ruled by the same constitution?" The answer, she insisted, was yes. While she recognized the singularity of the French institutional past, the American republic did have essential lessons to offer, in particular the institutional structure of the United States and the liberties that ensured that they would not be abused. She affirmed "that the nation is everything, and those who govern are nothing; that they act in the name of the people, the people are made for no-one but themselves; that which makes civil servants and pays them is the master and possesses alone the right to demand and command."[73] The state, in her view, remained the sole expression of popular sovereignty, and as such required proper reflection.

She also looked to the United States to ensure the proper relationship between institutions and the people upon which the republic depended. This could be achieved through greater liberty of ideas and expression. The United States, she argued, had achieved this because they "respected the rights of each individual; there is no fear of ideas; they are generated without any other control than public opinion; those who govern respect that opinion and conform to it."[74] The respect for rights and the right to debate established an appropriate relationship between the government and the governed because it was constantly subject to public opinion.

Like many of her contemporaries discussed in this book, d'Héricourt was less interested in showing the classical opposition between civil society and the state than in showing the permeability between the state and civil society. She insisted, for example, that the American approach to politics was the product of its institutions and that these institutions opened constant doors back and forth between the people and the state:

> It is easy to conceive that a people formed by such institutions; that a people
> who freely examine those who administer and govern them, who prevent

them from staying in power too long to separate from the masses and have the idea of creating laws that they will never be subject to as citizens; that a people who judges themselves, who is always armed, has numerous schools, makes laws by opinion, can say anything, write anything, believe anything that he pleases; that such a people, is reflective, serious, enterprising and free.

This was a direct response to the French experience in the Second Empire when plebiscites were a regular strategy for granting legitimacy on imperial decisions. Voting then was not listed as an essential aspect of what made the American regime successful; rather it was the institutions and the freedom to form opinions that shaped those institutions.

Because of her emphasis on ideas and public opinion, she did not place voting rights at the center of her democratic emphasis (although she recognized that they did have a place). Rather, she focused on the contributions that a secular education could contribute to founding the polity. "The first thing that the people should demand of their representatives is a law that makes education free, obligatory, and serious. All religious officials should be removed from the schools as well as all religious programs, which should remain within the family."[75] The essential responsibility of the state was three primary tasks: "executing the law for all, demanding the creation of sufficient schools, and calling for public works designed for collective utility." Furthermore, she insisted that it resided in "an autonomous Commune" that would ensure the political and administrative education of the people and help it to expand beyond its local interests. She therefore was willing to delegate a great deal of authority to the state, but only to a state that was responsible for education as well as public works and that distributed its power to local bodies.

The state then was to play an essential role in guaranteeing the law and providing the essential task of education, but it was not to do so through a centralized administration. For, alongside her insistence that state institutions had a strong role to play in ensuring equal access to a secular and free education, she also sought a wide distribution of power. "Paralyze, as much as necessary, the central power's exuberant appetite for control of ideas and interests." The commitment to the liberal distribution of power from the center of government to society took three forms in her work. First, she argued that the *départements* in France should have as many of the same powers as the American states without becoming a full-fledged confederation of republics. The general councils should have the power to declare war or peace through a vote of two-thirds among them. Here we are confronted with a theme that has been essential in the rediscovery of the American state in the nineteenth century. While federalism was long seen in the United States as a model of limiting government, using Michael Mann's notion of infrastructural power Daniel Ziblatt has shown it to have had quite the opposite effect in Italy and Germany. Indeed, the varied, multiple seats of state power in the German contexts was one of its most important features for expanding the reach of the state. D'Héricourt seems to have already learned this lesson, hoping that the state would do more in the areas of law and education without accumulating too much power in the center.

Second, d'Héricourt was pushed to engage with the critique of democracy provided by many key republicans in the 1860s. As we have seen, Napoleon III's illiberal democratic regime placed democracy, and specifically voting, at the center of its political legitimacy. The result was an emphasis among some important republicans of the early Third Republic on a republican elitism. D'Héricourt shared these critiques of democracy, but she did not necessarily share the conclusions. Building on republican critiques of democracy from the Second Empire, she looked to American institutions to search for a way out, insisting that in the United States "people govern themselves in the commune, the states and the confederation." "In France," she argued, "the law comes from above; the people are governed, formed under passive obedience, with limited confidence . . . so that suffrage, supposedly universal, simply serves individual ambitions, a method for giving one over to masters."[76] Because the French lacked a strong political education, having been subject to distant and manipulative political leaders, suffrage in France could keep the strong and wealthy in power as it had during under Napoleon III. She made specific reference to women's right to vote suggesting that it was as poorly organized in the United States as in France, but "if it gives less terrible results, it is because there are more enlightened people and more liberty."[77] It was therefore by observing the American state that she came to terms with the problem of suffrage. If France were able to create the same distribution of power and limit the central government, then, she declared, women should be able to vote on the communal level. They would therefore be at the foundation of the republican institutional structure.

Third, writing in the wake of the Commune and having followed from a distance the state's violence against its own people, she insisted that the French should have the right to bear arms—for only by carrying arms would they be able to prevent the government from firing on its own people. "As long as there is a permanent and extensive army in the hands of a governing caste and personal ambitions, all citizens' liberty is threatened and they must have the means to make themselves respected and to respond to brutal force with intelligent force." In short, d'Héricourt's conception of the agon was extreme. Concluding her analysis, she argued: "Don't kid yourselves: if only your work can save France, it will be long and very difficult because of those who have rank, fortune, and influence. . . . In short, I repeat they are wealthy, numerous, and influential . . . may the gods help you!"[78] Here we see the extent to which d'Héricourt maintained her political conception of an adversarial state. She refused to look for the place of rational consensus in her republic. Looking in precisely the opposite direction, toward the United States, she did not find an ideal of calm local government, but a model for her antagonism.

From this perspective, d'Héricourt understood the state as both a solution and a constant danger. Her democratic theory in the early 1870s was grounded precisely in her deep conviction that free, educated individuals could engage with each other in radical debate and that it was the state's responsibility to ensure that each individual had the ability—intellectual and material—to express fully his or her identity and position. Her article on American institutions attested to the fact that d'Héricourt had long abandoned her Saint-Simonianism and her 1848 calls for immediate and universal suffrage for women. Her utopian republicanism was a thing of the distant past by the time of the Third Republic. But in the meantime, she had developed one of the most sophisticated social theories of gender in the long tradition of the French women's movement, found a home and important political influences in the United States, and a robust political conception of the state. This new republic, she concluded, should ensure the individual's ability to pursue his or her own capacities *at the same time* that, because the individual was socially defined, the state provided the conditions for this fulfillment.

D'Héricourt's work therefore merits discovery and deep consideration because of its originality and its place within a rich line of democratic history and theory that would thrive in the twentieth century. Her originality emerged out of her attempt to push beyond three dominant modes of casting the polity in the first half of the nineteenth century. First, her critique of Comtean positivism spread into her disagreement with all of those theorists who attempted to evacuate the political in the name of the social. For those like Comte who understood the ideal to be observed in the social organism, the foundation for all political organization was ultimately to be uncovered within the social realm. In their view, the state could only provide a corrupting and troublesome hand, or alternatively, as was the case of the Saint-Simonians, provide a cadre of expertise for the improvement of social well-being. Politics, debate, discussion, and power put up a false front, hiding the deeper social harmonies that could be revealed only through social transformation. D'Héricourt, however, denied the idea that even the most rational social science could supplant the need for struggle and contradiction. In short, for d'Héricourt the political was a mainstay of democratic modernity.

At the same time, she rejected the idea that a politics of universal suffrage could overcome all social tensions. Even generalized political rights would not overcome basic social inequalities or fundamental differences of opinion. It was not sufficient to give the vote to every adult in order to reveal the ideal and perfect voice of the people. Instead, by emphasizing dissensus and the agonistic relationship at the heart of public debate, d'Héricourt argued that political unity was not a product of specific political techniques (no matter how important) such as the vote. Rather, even in the context of universal suffrage dissenting opinions and contradiction would remain. Moreover, it was precisely these disagreements that were to serve as the foundation for a lasting liberal democratic state. Instead of seeking to overcome difference and the unity of the sovereign, d'Héricourt's state was organized to ensure adversarial opposition.

Finally, hers was also a radical critique of the Second Empire's illiberal democracy. Napoleon III's claim to incarnate the democratic ideal as a despot supported by universal suffrage was founded on the basic idea that popular participation depended on a deeper, unified will that could only be expressed and executed through a unified sovereign, the emperor. D'Héricourt's work attempted to shatter the ideal of such patriarchal authority. She revealed that this will was not nearly as unified as it claimed: the regime of (supposedly universal) suffrage among males had in fact been built on the exclusion of women (as well as some workers, and colonial subjects). In such a context, she insisted, a unified popular will was not necessary for government. Instead, what was necessary was the cultivation of difference, expressed forcefully and with passion.

6

TERROR:
Louis Blanc's Historical Theory of Circumstances

Times of heroism are generally times of terror, but the day never shines in which this
element may not work.

RALPH WALDO EMERSON[1]

Republican conceptions of the democratic state before 1870 necessarily navigated upstream against the main currents of nineteenth-century French conservatism. In these deep waters the Terror treaded, the threat to be avoided
at all costs. Prescient as always, historian Edgar Quinet captured the conundrum when he wrote, in a letter to Saint-René Taillandier in 1865, that the key
to his opus was its "critique of the French Revolution in the name of the Revolution."[2] With this statement, he revealed that the problem of the Terror for
postrevolutionary republicans was a problem of self-nullification: while they
naturally refused the wide palette of authoritarian and conservative solutions
already explored in an eventful nineteenth century, the Terror consistently
reminded them that the great example of institutional organization within a
democratic regime had also been one of the most devastating and traumatic
expressions of state power in modern history. In this context, interpreting the
Terror became essential to thinking through the very historical possibility of a
democratic state in the nineteenth century because, in a very acute sense, the
earliest manifestation of the democratic republic in France had been unsuccessful precisely for its betrayal *and* its power.

François Furet insisted decades ago now on the importance of nineteenth-
century historians of the Revolution for resolving the institutional questions
that plagued republicans before and during the founding of the Third Republic.[3] Indeed, as historians have continued to demonstrate, readings of the Terror in the nineteenth century begged the question of when and how to bring
an end to the Revolution and find a resolution in the Republic.[4] But behind
this great conundrum of the Revolution and the writing of its history, the Terror also begged the question of defining what form a democratic state could
take in a republic and what it would do, without unleashing uncontrollable

public passions or leading necessarily to sustained and uncontrollable state violence. Using historical interpretation to stake institutional claims thus became a bedrock on which a just democratic state was conceptualized in the years leading up to the Third Republic.

As Patrice Gueniffey has shown, explanations of the Terror in the nineteenth century fell into largely three categories. The counter-revolutionaries presented the Terror as inevitable and integrated within the logic of the Revolution itself—any 1789 would necessarily produce its 1793. Those who defended the Revolution, however, "rigorously separated the events from its principles," insisting that the Terror was brought on by the peculiar and dire circumstances of the war and internal revolt. A third position, best represented by Michelet and Quinet, insisted that 1793 was in fact a second revolution overthrowing that of 1789.[5] Within these three positions, Louis Blanc clearly belongs to the second, invoking the "theory of circumstances" to explain the Terror. But while many historians have recognized this interpretation as one of the dominant currents in explaining the origins of the Terror, they have missed the central fact that the notion of exceptional circumstances itself, as well as the theory of the state it was founded upon, also had an eventful history in the nineteenth century.[6]

Tracing the history of invoking and using exceptional circumstances to explain state action in the Terror requires moving, once again, beyond the boundaries of the French metropole. Indeed, the Terror was decidedly not only a "French" problem in the nineteenth century or beyond. Outside the Hexagon, conceptualizing and interpreting the Terror as integral to the modern democratic state and not as a specter of the old regime was decisive in negotiating the relationship between a democratic state and a modern liberal imperialism. Indeed, Louis Blanc's interpretation of the Terror must be read in precisely such a context, for he spent twenty-two years in exile, writing and studying in London, participating in its intellectual milieu in the mid-nineteenth century.[7]

Pushing beyond the Hexagon to understand interpretations of the Terror also forces us to come to grips with unexpected influences on Louis Blanc's theory of the state.[8] Blanc has been considered an apologist for an overwhelming Jacobin state with the total power to assert social equality at the expense of any notion of individual liberty.[9] However, when we follow Blanc across the Channel and back, we see that it was neither Blanc's democratic socialism nor his supposed Jacobinism that furnished him with the ideological foundations of his theory of exceptional circumstances and the state in the 1860s and thus his reading of the Terror, but his post-1848 interactions with J. S. Mill, Ralph Waldo Emerson, and Thomas Carlyle, especially concerning their theories of popular revolt, representation, the imperial state and the question of martial law that accompanied it.[10] Through these influences, Blanc recognized that when the problem of the Terror was framed within a robust theory of exceptional circumstances, it shifted from being one of the greatest burdens of democracy to a resource; a power that only Bonapartist authoritarianism had been able to wield up to present. Combining his republicanism, his democratic socialism, and his condemnation of liberal imperialism, Blanc generated a sophisticated theory of the liberal democratic state in which the Terror was no longer the necessary outcome of a democratic state and therefore its great indictment, but one, extreme and juridifiable example of what a liberal democracy could sustain.

Beyond Virtue: Louis Blanc's Republican Critique of Classical Republicanism

Louis Blanc's place in the pantheon of nineteenth-century French republicanism has never been contested. Analyses of his work have tended overwhelmingly to focus on his *Organization of Labor*. And yet, this was a period of tremendous intellectual activity for Blanc, during which he treated many of the most important themes of modern republicanism and outlined ideas that would find their way into his theory of democracy and history of the French Revolution in the Second Empire and early Third Republic. In particular, like many of his contemporaries, Blanc took issue with the main tenets of classical republicanism.

The Terror has loomed large in work on classical republicanism in France, generating a consensus that the period 1793–94 made the classical republican paradigm problematic in France, pushing many toward the more stable and reliable climes of liberalism, which in its diverse forms became a dominant political paradigm of post-Terror politics. While classical republicanism remained a vital reference for some after the Terror, undiluted forms of the classical paradigm of virtue and civic commitment were seen as problematic because they unleashed uncontrollable civic passion which ran counter to the essential foundations of a modern society based on commerce, consumption, and industrial production.[11]

Of course, in spite of their relative triumph, early nineteenth-century liberals did recognize a potentially (deep) flaw in their political ideology: its emphasis on the private over the public and ambivalence on the importance of public engagement and political participation left the door wide open to the dominant (and dominating) forms of the early nineteenth-century French liberal polity, liberal authoritarianism. Out of this tension between the depoliticizing ambitions of postrevolutionary liberalism and the emphasis on the political within the civic republican tradition has emerged the larger question of whether or not liberalism had the resources within itself to overcome its depoliticizing tendencies or whether it was necessary to return to classical republicanism to reinforce civic spirit.[12] But while liberals probed this question, there were also committed republicans, like Blanc, who took on this question. Blanc also challenged classical republican themes, but he did not do so from a postrevolutionary liberal perspective. Instead, he critiqued classical republicanism from the perspective of the need to redefine a modern democratic state.[13]

Within the liberal critique of classical republicanism emanating from the Terror, the ideology of virtue and ancient liberty had been one of the most consistently derided themes. Classical republicanism's emphasis on the role of virtue in promoting participation in public affairs and its de-emphasis on private rights had been key ingredients, liberals believed, in unleashing the political passions behind the Terror. Among those who had framed this position most clearly were Germaine de Staël and Benjamin Constant, who insisted that virtue had been the keystone of a displaced ancient liberty that was dangerous in a modern age. Constant provided perhaps the most canonical statement when he wrote: "Previously, liberty could be supported by privation; now anywhere one finds privation, slavery is necessary to maintain it. It would be as impossible to turn an enslaved peoples into Spartans, as it would be to create Spartans for liberty."[14] In Constant's view, the modern age required a dismissal of the notion of virtue and self-abnegation in favor of a regime that protected the individual right to pursue his or her own interests.[15]

And yet, the critique of ancient liberty and classical republicanism was not the sole reserve of liberals. Louis Blanc crafted a modern republican theory that responded directly to liberals for whom French republicanism in the period 1793–94 had been a liberty of the ancients in the modern world. At the same time, he refused the liberal celebration of "negative liberty" as a response to the crises of the modern governance. Blanc was therefore caught between an interpretation of the republican Terror that had been the logical consequence of the pursuit of ancient liberty in modern times and the need to secure the centrality of democratic participation in the heart of the political regime. His critique took issue with the liberal assessment of modern liberty as *freedom from*, without proposing a return to the reign of classical virtue, which he too considered entirely inappropriate for a modern republic.

Blanc's article "On Virtue as a Principle of Government" specifically targeted the classical republicanism presented in Montesquieu's study of the republic. The originality of his argument in the early 1830s is startling. Even Tocqueville was not yet ready to entirely abandon the notion of virtue, choosing to reinterpret Montesquieu himself on this issue: "In America, it is not virtue that is great, it is temptation that is small, which amounts to the same thing. It is not disinterestedness that is great, it is interest that is well understood, which amounts to almost the same thing. Montesquieu was therefore right, although he spoke of ancient virtue, and what he said of the Greeks and Romans applies as well to the Americans."[16] Thus, as Jainchill notes, Tocqueville was more interested in the effects of virtue than in virtue as a cause—a people's motives did not need to be virtuous for their ultimate impact to be so. But, according to the perspective outlined by Blanc, Tocqueville may have recognized the problem of virtue in a modern age by looking at American democracy, but he remained unable to explain *why* it was a problem. In other words, why could virtuous acts be accomplished in a democracy when they were not presented as such? Blanc responded that it was because there was not yet a proper understanding of the democratic state and the role of virtue within it. Such a state, he insisted, should be based on what he called the principle of "admissibility" (*admissibilité*): "it admits, without any distinction, all the interests of society" (86). Thus, a republic did not require virtue, self-abnegation, or sacrifice: "Yes, it is in a monarchy that one needs abnegation above all, because the crowd stirs impatiently on land whose harvest is inaccessible to them" (86). It was only in a despotic regime that one needed the overarching influence of virtue. Republican government was dedicated to allowing each individual to realize one's full ambitions and, as a result, Blanc argued, virtue and abnegation ran counter to its very foundations.

With this critique, Blanc provided a novel reading of the place of virtue in modern politics: "What do they mean by the word virtue, those who consider virtue to be the keystone of any republican government? They repeat that egoism eats away at society, that ambition generates torment. For them, political virtue requires disinterest and resignation. Disinterest! Oh! Well, if it is necessary in certain circumstances, it is precisely in those cases where institutions push the interests of a suffering majority into desperate isolation. If resignation is necessary anywhere, it is in those places where the wounds of plebs is washed in political silence" (85). Under a Republican regime, pursuing one's individual interest actually reinforced democracy because it was the only regime that guaranteed each individual's access to the resources necessary to pursue his interest. The individual was not an isolated figure but was inherently social because his right to pursue his freedom depended on the cooperation of society as a whole. Such a *social individual* did not require virtue, but rather the simple pursuit of self-interest socially understood—that is, by pursuing one's own interests, one necessarily demonstrated one's support for the idea that every other individual should have the right to do the same. The opposition between virtue and egoism thus dissipated in a modern republican context. This redefinition of the relationship between the individual and the republic became a pillar of Blanc's social theory of democracy and contributed to later formulations of liberal socialism and new liberalism in the nineteenth and twentieth centuries.[17]

So while many of his most important writings remained to be written in 1848, by the time of the 1848 revolution, Louis Blanc had already provided an original conception of the relationship between the individual, civil society, and the state that took issue with the fundamentals of postrevolutionary liberalism and early modern classical republicanism. It was precisely by pursuing these ideas that he would engage in a long friendship with J. S. Mill and ultimately carve out a new theory of the democratic state that could accommodate the Terror on the eve of the Third Republic.

Toward a Theory of the Democratic State

The revolution of 1848 was a transformative moment for Louis Blanc. The opportunity finally to put a Republican constitution in place and the spread of revolution across Europe and beyond lent tremendous weight to this moment as a coming of age for a modern French republicanism. At the same time, it also put the early democratic socialist ideas of figures like Louis Blanc to the test. Thus, in spite of Louis Blanc's consistent critiques of the design of the national workshops (ultimately organized as a branch of the state, not as free associations overseen and encouraged by the state) and his insistence that they were, in fact, put in place to prevent the implementation of his real plan in the *Organization of Labor*, he would largely be held responsible for their creation and their failure. His experience at the head of the national workshops in 1848 and the ideological battles that plagued them during their early months left him with an ambiguous relationship to the dominant paradigms that had guided his republicanism since the revolution. As committed as always to the republican, democratic, and socialist cause, Blanc found the short months of the revolution between late February and the June Days ultimately marking a watershed in his intellectual biography, a break that would only be reinforced by his intellectual exchanges during his exile in London from the summer of 1848 until the declaration of the republic in 1870.

During these twenty-two years of exile, Blanc continued to write at a feverish pace, producing pamphlets, publishing in newspapers across Europe, completing his *History of the French Revolution*, and annotating and prefacing his previous works. Over the more than two decades he spent in England, British liberal ideas and the intellectual milieu around him had a profound impact on his political and historical theory of a modern republicanism and the democratic state. During his exile, Blanc bridged the gap between his democratic socialism of the 1840s and his post-1848 liberal democracy by constructing a historical theory of the state along two arcs. First, he continued to elaborate and refine his theory of the social power of the *democratic* state by elaborating his theory of the social individual. Second, building on his reading of J. S. Mill, Blanc conceptualized a regulatory and interventionist state as a permanent feature of modern democratic society. These two elements of his theory of the liberal democratic state later became the foundations for shifting the terrain around the Terror: no longer seeing it as the great threat to be avoided at all costs—one of the fundamental justifications for the authoritarian regimes that had followed throughout much of the nineteenth century—Blanc carved out a space even for the extremes of the Terror within his theory of the modern liberal democratic state.

In November 1849, more than a year after his departure and the collapse of the national workshops, Blanc wrote an article entitled "The State in Democracy" in which he elaborated the foundations of his new *historical* theory of the state. Written as a polemic against Proudhon, Blanc's article argued in favor a state that could increase liberty instead of limiting it: "The State in a democratic regime is the power of all the people, served by the elected officials; it is the reign of liberty."[18] For Blanc, then, the state was not opposed to individual liberty but was rather its guarantee. "Yes, the State *and* Liberty! These two terms are corollary. Of what does liberty consist, the complete development of each individual's faculties."[19] Blanc's claim assumed a natural inequality among individuals. Since each individual had different capacities, abilities, and strengths, without the power of the state, the strong would always control the weak. The state, in his view, should guarantee that each individual could take advantage of his or her strengths and not be victim to his or her weaknesses. As in his pre-1848 writings, Blanc's conception of the state as guarantor of nondomination broke down the opposition between the individual and society.[20] In his view, individual liberty was not opposed to the state but rather ensured by it.

His renewed interest in the social individual demonstrated a more sustained dialogue between his liberalism and socialism that would become a hallmark of his years in London. Specifically, he rejected the liberal hypothesis that the individual was an isolated subject who sought the satisfaction of his own private desires.

We have heard many speak of the rights of the individual, and this is a good thing, as long as we do not give it a meaning it does not contain. In truth, there is no such thing as a society of *individuals* that is only a society of individuals. The individual cannot be understood outside the milieu within which he is thrown, the relations that form a network around him, the moral atmosphere in which he breathes. Within, the individual being and the social being are fused to such an extent that the rights, which are often called upon as individual rights, are only real because of the identification of the individual with the social being.[21]

Through the social individual, Blanc was able to conceive of a state that did not intervene at the expense of the individual and on behalf of society, but which, to the contrary, preserved every individual's right to develop his or her own capacities, whether weak or strong, through its intervention. The democratic state, then, was not a group of elites asserting their authority over society; rather, it was a social power acting on behalf of the social individual. "There is no opposition between the state and the individual. If by the word state we mean the organization of society as a body on the one hand and the free development of the individual, not to the benefit of the few, but for all, the two ideas are difficult to oppose to each other and are in fact so far from contrary as to be correlated. *The second expresses the aim and the first explains the means*."[22] Setting aside the question of specific institutional alignments or policies, which had been at the heart of his reflections in the *Organization of Labor*, in this article Blanc shifted toward a pragmatic theory of the state in which state intervention pursued the ideal ends of individual liberty.[23]

The influence of Mill within this theory of the state became clear over the course of Blanc's stay in London.[24] Mill and Blanc had known each other since before the revolution of 1848. Mill's increasing openness to early socialist ideas led to his developing an interest in Blanc's work and in particular in his *Organization of Labor*. Even in the heart of the revolution of 1848, Mill supported Blanc and the Luxembourg Commission.[25] This support of Blanc's cause in the 1848 revolution was part of Mill's broader transition out of a utilitarian model of liberalism and toward an early form of his "amended socialism" that would blossom by the late nineteenth century in an English "New Liberalism," driven by what Serge Audier refers to as Mill's "social turn."[26] A soft turn toward strands of socialism was thus at the heart of Mill's liberal theory in the years following the 1848 revolution.[27] In this Blanc and Mill met halfway because Blanc too injected key elements of Mill's liberalism into his republicanism and theory of the democratic state.[28]

Mill's influence on Blanc's theory of the state could be seen most prominently in a re-edition of the pamphlet entitled *The Commune* that had originally appeared in the 1840s, and that Blanc subsequently republished with a new title, *The State and the Commune*, in 1865. The addition of the *The State* to the title was essential, because it was followed by a new first chapter on "The

State" as well as a preface dedicated to J. S. Mill.[29] It was precisely J. S. Mill, he argued, who demonstrated that state power could not be categorically defined as either entirely good or bad. State intervention, Blanc argued following Mill, needed to be based on particular circumstances: "The great thinker and honest man by the name of John Stuart Mill," wrote Blanc, "has taken the time to show us in his *Principles of Political Economy* that this question of *state intervention*, which is rightly of such great interest to us, cannot be clearly resolved once and for all in any absolute or exclusive sense. Following his ideas, there are moments when intervention is not only legitimate, but required and there are others when it is harmful."[30] It was not a question of moving toward a future point of social democratic equality in which the state would no longer have a place, but rather of the state's intervening occasionally and permanently toward the ideal ends of preserving a society of free individuals. Mill's liberalism therefore contributed to Blanc's concept of the state, by suggesting that public power would be a constant but variable force in organizing political life.

In keeping with this idea, he argued that the state could only ever be a partial representation of the society it served. "State intervention, even according to this hypothesis, must be controlled with care and limited, because unfortunately, there is no regime in which the state can be seen as a faithful and exact representation of society. You argue that this is what exists within the democratic regime? Alas, as superior as it may be to all the others, its power cannot represent the unanimity of all citizens."[31]

No regime, not even a democratic one, was a perfect representation of the entire society—a just regime worked toward the ideal of a society in which all individuals could realize their full capacities; however, as an ideal, this social condition remained unrealizable. As a result, the state was by nature historical because it was without an essence or a singular task that could ever be fully achieved.

A consequence of Blanc's historical theory of the state was that there could not be an absolute rule or principle to guide state intervention because the need and nature of government intervention necessarily changed according to the situation in which the state was called to act. Reminiscent of Laboulaye's argument on state power—he had also turned to Mill—there could be no hard and fast rules, or even absolute limits to state intervention, because the true measure of where, when and how a state was to intervene could only be determined by the need to serve the polity and protect the individual in specific circumstances.

We may ask if the principle of state intervention should be denounced or condemned. . . . But what is the point of insisting on such issues? The most sound

conclusion that we may draw on such an important subject is that of J. S. Mill
who formulated it in the following terms: "It is hardly possible to find any
ground of justification common to them all, except the comprehensive one of
general expediency; nor to limit the interference of government by any universal rule, save the simple and vague one, that it should never be admitted
but when the case of expediency is strong" [*Principles of political economy*,
t. II, p. 378].[32]

Adapting Mill's argument, Blanc presented a principle of government intervention: "With this insight we may discover all the cases when state intervention is legitimate and when it is not. Every time it is in opposition to the
free development of human faculties, it is negative; to the contrary, every time
it helps in the development or sets aside such obstacles, it is positive."[33]

This statement is doubly significant. First, it captured Mill's full influence
on Blanc's theory of the state and especially his attempt to define a broad pragmatic rule of state action. Second, and perhaps more importantly, it suggests
that French republicanism, even in its most ostensibly Jacobin and radical
democratic form, rooted a new and potent theory of the state in the rich soil
of a democratized English liberalism.

This state, captured in Blanc's synthesis of Mill's liberalism and his democratic republicanism, and his idea of the social individual formed the foundation of Blanc's *liberal democratic state*. Again, I employ this term to suggest in
a specifically historical sense to suggest that Blanc crafted a theory that was
at once liberal because it sought the defense of individual liberty and focused
on the development of individual human faculties and democratic because it
made democratic society and state the condition for any true realization of
individual capacity. Blanc developed this theory because he was confronted
with a series of what he perceived as problems including the limits of the early
liberal critique of classical republican civic engagement, the overwhelming
influence on individualism, and the need to develop a more thorough principle for when and how states could act to preserve individual liberty.

This new formulation of liberal democratic power offered a powerful
model for cultivating modern state power through its democratic foundations: in Blanc's view, individual liberty, civil society, and the state enriched
one another. Furthermore, Blanc's liberal democratic state was understood as
a means, a process, for achieving social justice, but never as a goal in itself. In
short, the political did not constitute the social any more than society could
be democratized by a withered state. A democratic state provided the conditions for social justice, that is, for society to construct itself as democratic.
And it was precisely through his theory of modern state power that he was
able to overcome the stain of the Terror on the liberal democratic polity.

The Social Individual and the Terror

Blanc combined liberal, democratic, and socialist influences to craft an original theory of the liberal democratic state. This theory relied on a conception of the social individual and a powerful and flexible state capacity to intervene toward positive social ends. However, while Blanc dedicated many hours to writing articles and pamphlets, the bulk of his intellectual energy during this period was dedicated to completing his *History of the French Revolution*. Key elements of the theoretical work discussed above—his principle of the interventionist state and the social individual—informed his interpretation and examination of the Terror. Drawing on his theory, he reinterpreted the Terror to explain the legitimacy of exceptional governance to save the polity in a time of crisis, applying his theory of the social individual to reconsider the legitimacy of Robespierre as a "representative man"—that is *socially* instead of *institutionally* representative during a period of institutional crisis.

On February 22, 1866, Louis Blanc published a letter on the Terror in *Le Temps* that would become the preface to the new edition of his *History of the French Revolution* in 1868. The letter recapitulated his key arguments on the Terror originally published in his *History*. "Revolutionary France," he argued, "assaulted on all sides from all of Europe, sapped by plots, harassed by tremendous riots, reduced to a life of death, so to speak, gave in to the necessity of multiplying its force and its energy by concentrating it."[34] The Revolution lacked money, gunpowder, iron, and bread and yet it defeated the English, the Dutch, the Austrians and the Spanish, just as it put down the revolt in Lyon, took Toulon and control of the Vendee. But, central to his reading of this period was that in spite of such successes it was impossible to simply condone all actions. Rather, he insisted: "Deplore the Terror to the depths of your soul. Condemn with all of your force the principle of dictatorship. Berate the excesses and punish the crimes, but do not argue that it was a popular delirium reduced into an effective system by a few men when it was in fact the fatal product of a horribly exceptional situation."[35]

Inherent in this analysis was a critique of the leading republican critics of the Terror, Edgar Quinet and Jules Ferry. While both were republicans, both also attempted to take the Terror out of the democratic impulse that had guided the Revolution up to year I. For Quinet, the Terror was a return to the methods and spirit of the old regime. Far from having introduced the definitive break with the past, it had been its last gasp: "The Terror was the fatal inheritance of French history. The arms of the past were taken up to defend the present. The iron cages and the Tristan l'Hermite of Louis XI, the scaffolds of Richelieu, the mass proscriptions of Louis XIV, such was the arsenal of the

Revolution. Through the Terror, new men suddenly became men of old."[36] While Ferry was also convinced that the Terror had destroyed the Republic, he looked in the opposite direction arguing that the Terror opened the path to modern dictatorship. "In the nineteenth century, there are no more tyrants, there are only dictators . . . Napoleon I . . . subordinated liberty to victory . . . Call me a heretic, but I would dare to say that in suspending the Constitution until peace was achieved, the Convention did exactly the same thing."[37] In both cases, there was a complete incompatibility between the Terror and the democratic state. It was as a *system*, in Quinet and Ferry's view, that the Terror operated according to its own logic and was therefore necessarily external to the principles of a democratic republic.

Blanc, however, was deeply convinced that the machine of the Terror was not external to its democratic impulse. The Terror, he readily admitted, had been a disastrous and devastating moment, but, in spite of Quinet and Ferry's arguments, it had never been an organized political structure; it was not the work of a few men who had taken the nation hostage, with a fixed plan, in order to establish a regime of dictatorship. Robespierre had acted to save the Republic and the Revolution, not systematize his own power. For Blanc, this was the very meaning of the Constitution of 1793:

> No one would argue that the Constitution of 1793, in which Robespierre had played such an important part and which had given him much of his influence, organized dictatorship or left the Terror the means of prolonging its morbid empire. Liberty, security, property, public debt, freedom of religion, popular education, public aid, unlimited liberty of the press, the right to petition, the right to assemble in popular associations: such were the guarantees that article 222 of the Constitution of 1793 guaranteed to all Frenchmen. I restate my question. Was this laying the foundations of dictatorship? Was this a systematization of the Terror?[38]

The essence of Blanc's disagreement with Quinet depended, then, on his fundamental claim that the Terror, to the very end, had been an instrument designed to save the constitution and the Revolution itself. "The dictatorship, of which terrorism was only the bloody side, was desired, accepted and put into place during the Revolution as a brief and desperate means of national defense, but never as a doctrine of government? Never!"[39] To be sure, exceptional circumstances had forced the suspension of the constitution as well as extreme and even excessive actions, but even at its height, the Terror did not betray the Revolutionary principles that animated it by attempting to establish a dictatorship: "The idea of dictatorship as a system was so directly opposed to the genius of the Revolution, and the mistrust was excessive and ferocious."[40] No matter how bloody, Blanc argued, the aim had always been to serve the republican constitution and the revolution.

Invoking exceptional circumstances, however, raised the fundamental problem of legitimacy. Specifically, how was it possible to explain Robespierre's legitimacy after the suspension of what Blanc considered the most democratic of all constitutions—1793? To explain the legitimacy of Robespierre in exceptional circumstances, Blanc drew on his theory of the social individual: "I am not one of those who places the entire life of a people in the life of an individual. . . . I know that among historic figures, the most illustrious were no more than ephemeral actors in a drama created by the society that enveloped them."[41] Blanc's argument for the social individual that had been at the heart of his theory of the democratic state helped him frame Robespierre as a social being whose actions could only be understood in the context of a democratic society that had given full expression to its anger. Robespierre was acting as a social force from within society itself, and not as a force exerted upon it from the outside. Indeed, he employed a reference that merits particular attention: "It is impossible to play a great role in history unless one is what I would willingly call a *representative man* [ce que j'appellerais volontiers *un homme représentatif*]. The force possessed by powerful individuals is only taken from themselves to a small degree: they take in principally from those who surround them. Their life is nothing more than a concentration of the collective lives within which they are plunged."[42] With the notion of representative man, Blanc introduced the idea that Robespierre could be representative, serve the people and the social norms captured by the Revolution at the same time that he outstripped the institutions of the government. Through the idea of representative men, Blanc was able to separate the means employed by the regime from the social norms that created and animated the revolution itself.

Blanc's analysis of Robespierre as representative man was also part of the larger set of international influences he explored during his time in London and in particular the debate between Carlyle's theory of the *Hero* and Emerson's response in *Representative Men*, both of which had given special importance to the French Revolution.[43] Though both had focused on the Revolution, Carlyle had focused on "modern revolutionists" and the Terror, while Emerson's essay included a chapter on Napoleon. Carlyle shared Blanc's conviction that the French Revolution had been a social phenomenon— when his *French Revolution*[44] was translated into French for the first time by one of Louis Blanc's former republican collaborators, Elias Regnault in 1866 wrote: "Nowhere, among none of our French writers, do we encounter such a profound insight into the causes of this great social movement."[45] He then concluded, "If it were possible to introduce such an original spirit into our contemporary political classifications, he would be placed first among those we call socialists."[46] It should be kept in mind that Mill had also congratulated Blanc on his "socialist" history of the French Revolution.[47] By suggesting in the 1860s that Blanc's and Carlyle's histories were "socialist," Regnault and Mill were arguing that they revealed the importance of the people and popular movements in the revolution.

Carlyle's "socialist" reading of the "Hero" in the French Revolution therefore also focused on the excesses of the Revolution although he profoundly disagreed with Blanc on its origins and management. One of the essential problems that had led to the Terror during the French Revolution, according to Carlyle, was a lack of heroic leadership. The Revolution had turned violent because it had been run by "quacks," or men who were precisely not heroes: "This is the history of all rebellions, French Revolutions, social explosions in ancient or modern times. You have put the too *Unable* man at the head of affairs! The too ignoble, unvaliant, fatuous man. You have forgotten that there is any rule, or natural necessity whatever, of putting the Able Man there."[48] Carlyle's theory of the French revolution was therefore grounded on the idea that a truly popular revolution required an extraordinary individual to channel social explosions— and a hero was exactly what had been missing in the reign of the Terror.

This embrace of the hero as representative marked a core difference with his friend and longtime interlocutor Ralph Waldo Emerson and the latter's theory of the "representative man." While Carlyle as Romantic unhesitatingly gave history over to heroes, such heroism was more problematic in the context of the United States for Emerson just as it was for Blanc in France. Emerson chose instead to focus on the very humanity of exceptional historical figures, even in the French Revolution. Turning away from the Terror to focus on Napoleon, Emerson did not celebrate his heroic superhuman as much as his extraordinarily human qualities. "Every one of the million readers of anecdotes or memoirs or lives of Napoleon, delights in the page, because he studies in it his own history. Napoleon is thoroughly modern, and, at the highest point of his fortunes, has the very spirit of the newspapers. He is no saint, to use his own word, 'no capuchin,' and he is no hero, in the high sense. The man in the street finds in him the qualities and powers of other men in the street."[49] Napoleon, for Emerson, was a *modern* representative man, and not a hero, precisely because he was a man who was both like and unlike everyday Frenchmen, because he was both exemplary and exceptional: "Bonaparte was the idol of common men because he had in transcendent degree the qualities and powers of common men."[50]

Emerson also portrayed the role of great men through the juxtaposition of democratic norms and institutions. Always wary of institutions and ever-fascinated with union, he used the notion of representation to celebrate norms at the expense of institutions, without, through his semantic slipperiness, undermining the "representative" norms of a democratic regime. As Shklar points out, the ambiguity of the term "representation" was fundamental. "The great person serves them. And that service is described in the language of democratic politics," she argues. "Nothing could illustrate more vividly the hold that democratic norms had on Emerson's intellectual imagination."[51] Though they outstretched the norm, "Representative Men" remained within the lexicon of democratic thought. It is through this capacity to *represent* norms that representative men could generate unity and mobilize social forces. In fact, it was impossible to separate a representative man from his social milieu because he drew his exceptionality from his ability to express the unity of his moment.

Emerson's representative man and Carlyle's hero shared fundamental traits with Blanc's interpretation of Robespierre as representative man and martyr for the revolutionary cause: "The impulse that they [representative men] impose on society," Blanc argued, "is in fact quite small compared to the impulse that they receive from it."[52] Similarly, though he was convinced, like Carlyle, that the Terror was a moment of truth, he was not at all convinced by the notion of a hero as natural king.[53] As Leo Loubère suggests, "this does not in any way mean that Blanc's representative man was identical to Carlyle's. Blanc emphasized the dependence of the great man on his milieu, the source of his ideas and of his strength. He refused to elevate this thinker above 'humanity.'"[54] It is therefore unsurprising that he used Emerson's notion of the "representative man" at the same time that he rejected the idea that Napoleon could serve in this capacity: Napoleon had been a dictator who imposed his will *onto* society; Robespierre was the representative man who *expressed* the will of the people.

So for all their differences, Blanc, Carlyle, and Emerson's readings of the hero or representative man in the French Revolution shared one essential trait. They all agreed that the hero and the representative man were products of their social milieu, and that while they necessarily captured and acted upon the reigning social norms, they were not necessarily limited to operating within specific government institutions. As Carlyle articulated it in the most extreme terms: "Find in any country the Ablest Man that exists there; raise him to the supreme place, and loyally reverence him: you have a perfect government for that country; no ballot box, parliamentary eloquence, voting, constitution-building, or other machinery whatsoever can improve it a whit. It is the perfect state; an ideal country."[55] Institutions, ballot boxes, parliaments, and constitutions were all secondary to the definition of the state—those who could effectively capture and exemplify society best served the state. For Louis Blanc, as for Emerson, it was only within a democratic regime that such figures could still fill the democratic contract.

Thus, paradoxically, for Blanc, the Terror was both the darkest moment of republican democratic rule at the same time that the democratic republic was its condition of possibility. Only under a democratic state were representative men carried to power. According to Blanc's historical democratic theory, only a democratic republic could be exposed to exceptional circumstances because it was only in the context of a democratic society that representative men could come forth and employ whatever means necessary to ensure social norms. A dictator, like Napoleon, in Blanc's view, was by necessity not a reflection of social norms and therefore would formalize a permanent exception, or exception as rule. In this context, dictatorship was, *a fortiori*, not exceptional but a system of arbitrary authority.

In this sense, the question of whether or not the Terror was internal or external to the Revolutionary dynamic misses the fundamental insight of Blanc's construction of a liberal democratic state. Once defined as a state of exception, the Terror was indeed neither; or rather it was both inside and outside the revolution. The Terror was neither the unfolding of a revolutionary logic nor the necessary result of the conception of a unified sovereignty. Even if the Terror suspended democratic norms, it did not destroy them; and it was not indifferent to the democratic order that it was ensuring by violent means. Blanc's theory of an exceptional government of "representative men" was in one sense the barest form of the democratic regime. It was, as Carlyle argued, "the nakedest haggard fact."[56] The Terror evacuated the Revolution of all institutional residue to reveal the purest, and most brutal, form of "democratic" as opposed to "dictatorial" expression.

Terror and the Pragmatic Principle of the Liberal Democratic State

So Blanc attempted to integrate the Terror into his theory of the liberal democratic state (instead of seeing it purely as a threat) by applying his notion of the social individual. With this key element of his theory of the liberal democratic state he expanded state legitimacy from a focus on institutional representation toward a theory of social representation. But this was only one aspect of his integrating the problem of the Terror through his new theory of the liberal democratic state. The second leg of his reading of the Terror depended on his application of the theory of state intervention he had adapted from Mill—that is, the incapacity to predetermine how much and to what extent the state could intervene because such action could only be determined by the specific circumstances within which the state was called to act. From this perspective, state actions could only be judged according to the principle presented above which determined "the cases when state intervention is legitimate and when it is not. Every time it is in opposition to the free development of human faculties, it is negative; to the contrary, every time it helps in the development or sets aside such obstacles, it is positive."[57] Blanc was therefore equipped with a vision of the state that was flexible enough to manage any situation.

But of course the Terror was not just any situation, civil war, foreign war with almost every neighbor, a newly minted (though suspended) constitution pushed this maxim to the limit. Interrogating the legitimacy of this moment therefore also required thinking about the legitimacy of state response under the specific circumstances of emergency situations. To begin, then, it is worth noting that Blanc's interpretation of the Terror shared key elements with many of the broader principles animating theories of emergency government in the nineteenth century. First, the insistence that the Terror was not designed as a system but as a period of transition, as discussed above, was central to all theories of exceptional powers: "The men of the Revolution always considered themselves in a purely transitory state,"[58] Blanc argued, "It was of the utmost importance that the revolutionary dictatorship end as quickly as possible. [il importait que la dictature révolutionnaire cessât le plus tôt possible]."[59] Emphasis on temporal limitation was in keeping with the leading theories of legitimate crisis government that had been outlined by eighteenth-century liberals like Montesquieu and Blackstone. As Bernard Manin has shown, establishing temporal limitations had been fundamental to the legitimacy of exceptional powers in the works of these theorists: "By casting the issue in temporal terms and by stating that parting with liberty for a while was justified as long as it served to preserve liberty for the future, the two writers were in effect making an argument that conformed to a key liberal principle, namely the principle that liberty may be restricted only for the sake of liberty."[60]

Similarly, in keeping with liberal theories of crisis government, Blanc argued that the regime needed to be subject to retroactive justice. Robespierre, Blanc insisted, had been judged and paid the price for his actions, and this in spite of the fact that he had consistently served the republic. The fact that Robespierre had ultimately been put to death for the Terror's excesses was a sign of the strength of the democratic impulse behind the Terror and proof that it had never been extinguished: "the very day that Robespierre was accused even of ruling through his speech, he was lost."[61] As Manin notes, such a conception of punishment after the end of temporary crisis government marked an essential tenet of emergency government between the eighteenth and the late nineteenth century. "Dicey," Manin argues, "saw another merit in the temporal limit: at the end of the suspension officials could be held accountable for what they had done under it."[62] Blanc justified the exceptional acts of Robespierre along similar lines. It was precisely because Robespierre's actions were necessary but ultimately unacceptable that the system brought him down, punishing him with death, "it triumphed and had the glory of dying enveloped in its own defeat."[63] It was, therefore, Robespierre's execution that both confirmed the legitimacy of the Terror and the fact that it had not betrayed the democracy that supported it.

But beyond the broader context of legal thought on emergency government, Blanc's ideas on this key question of how far the state could legitimately intervene in a time of emergency were also nurtured by the intellectual milieu in which he was writing. London in the 1860s provided a particularly fertile terrain for thinking through the legal issues surrounding martial law and crisis government in a time of military engagement. As Rande Kostal has shown, law was central to the worldview of the English political class in the 1860s: "This is an important point," writes Kostal; "the intense discussion of the law of martial law stimulated by the Jamaica affair [Morant Bay] did not take place only among lawyers. The burgeoning literature on martial law was often commissioned by or reprinted in the general political press."[64] The English political class, including Louis Blanc's milieu in London, was particularly engaged in these questions during the time of the Sepoy Rebellion in India in 1857 and the Morant Bay rebellion in 1865—the period when Louis Blanc completed his *History*, including the sections on the Terror, and then his *Letter on the Terror*.

The two events marked the British elites for their brutality as well as the lack of a clear legal framework for defending or denouncing the repressions that followed. The Sepoy Rebellion took place in May 1857 as Indian regiments, known as Sepoys, led a mutiny against the British military hierarchy. After days of revolt, the Sepoys led a massacre against the British residents of Cawnpore, including civilians, in June 1867. The British military response was ruthless, including torture, summary judgment, and mass executions. Nonetheless, as Kostal points out, "Even in the face of a pervasive and dangerous revolt, the authorities did not dispense with the pretence of law."[65] Lord Canning, governor general of India, insisting that all movements against the rebellion respect military law, sent numerous declarations. But the exact legal ramifications and procedures for establishing martial law remained in question.

The legal ambiguity remained when the Morant Bay rebellion was ignited on October 13, 1865, and Governor Eyre of the Colony of Jamaica declared martial law in response to a rebellion of Jamaican blacks, inaugurating what has been referred to as "a protracted and calculated reign of terror."[66] Under this declaration of martial law, between four and five hundred Jamaicans were shot. Eyre also called for the arrest of the black leader George Gordon, who was transferred to a county that had been placed under martial law, where he was summarily tried by a military commission and hanged six days later.

In part because Gordon was a well-known figure among London liberals, but also because this affair took place only eight years after the previous bloody colonial repression, the Morant Bay case became a *cause célèbre* in London known as the Eyre affair. As a result, Governor Eyre's actions and the acts committed in Morant Bay took on proportions similar that of the Dreyfus affair in *fin de siècle* France: "Ranged on either side of the debate were the major intellectuals of the day, Thomas Carlyle led the committee established to defend Eyre, while John Stuart Mill led the committee which aimed to prosecute him. Behind them were lined up many of the best known writers, philosophers and scientists."[67] On the side of Eyre and Carlyle were Charles Kingsley, Charles Dickens, John Ruskin, and Alfred Lord Tennyson, while Mill was seconded by Thomas Huxley, Leslie Stephen, Charles Lyall, Charles Darwin, and John Bright. Blanc sided with Mill, insisting that Eyre should be tried for his actions. Mill, for example, thanked Blanc for his support in the francophone press, after reading one of his articles on Morant Bay: "I cannot help but congratulate you on your admirable letters on the issues that have taken place in Jamaica, especially those which appeared on November 30," he wrote.[68]

Like his peers in London, Blanc took a particular interest in both cases using the popular legal discussions around them to gain perspective on the use of exceptional force during the Terror. In his *History of the French Revolution*, Blanc established a direct parallel between the Toulon siege of 1793 and those of the British Empire during the Sepoy Mutiny, insisting for example, that Toulon had not been nearly as horrible as the massacre performed by the British in the colonies:

> At this very moment, everyone is insisting on the necessity and the justice of the mass extermination of the Sepoy, who revolt in India; and there is applause from every direction for the energy of the English generals who attached their prisoners to mouths of cannons in front of shocked natives before giving the signal. . . . I'll stop there. These accounts make one's hair stand on end. It is true that among the Sepoy, unnamable horrors were committed; but not everyone participated, even among the rebels. And it will not be argued, I hope, that the Sepoys who, after all, were fighting for their country, were any more guilty than the French in 1793 who joined the enemy and called upon the enemy to put them in an even stronger position to strangle France from within France itself.[69]

Similarly, in November 1865, just a few months before he published his letter on the Terror in *Les Temps* on February 22, 1866, Blanc wrote an article on
Morant Bay that appeared in the *Sydney Morning Herald*, where he explained
why he was convinced that Eyre's behavior had been inappropriate. He employed many of the modes of argumentation that he would use in his *Letter on
the Terror*. Insisting on the horrors of Morant Bay, specifically those committed by the officials against the black uprising, he argued that the uprising had
in part been justified because of the horrible conditions of blacks in Jamaica.
He then continued, insisting that the British response had been inappropriate
in this context: "You will perhaps think that this inexorable severity, this cruel
precipitation, this brutal disdain of all the forms of justice, are explained by the
formidable character of the outbreak in question," wrote Blanc, "and by the im-
minence of the danger with which the colony was threatened by it. This, in fact,
is what is maintained by the instigators of these barbarities, and by those who
feel it necessary to veil their horrors."[70] He continued, citing the report, "I have
before me the official report of the governor of Jamaica, and in that attempted
justification of the measures adopted there is not a single line, not a single word
from which the reality of these abominable plans can possibly be deduced."[71]

In his *Letter* written a few months later, he once again drew a direct com-
parison between these two events and the Terror.

> The English are an enlightened, free and humane people, and we pride our-
> selves on living in a century that is not bloodthirsty. Well, what did the English
> do in India when their domination was threatened by the Sepoys a few years
> ago? One's hair stands on end just thinking of it. Can you imagine those mis-
> erable prisoners driven before their compatriots who were forced to come see
> them attached to the mouth of cannons with their fuses lit, and receive the
> shock of their scattered corpses, drenched in blood, all of it done to inspire
> a salutary fright among the indigenous populations! The Revolution never
> imagined anything comparable. And the horrors that have just taken place in
> Jamaica, horrors that so many in England are ready to applaud as long as the
> white population can be seen to have been in danger? Thus, today, by men
> who belong to the most humane peoples on the earth, a people who detest
> dictatorship and anything resembling it, the Orient has been placed under the
> regime of the Terror, Jamaica has become subject to the regime of the Terror.[72]

Mill himself was convinced by these parallels between the exceptional powers
of the Revolution and the events in Morant Bay. In a letter to Blanc, he wrote:
"If they [the Minister and the Parliament] allow for such extraordinary events
in the name of England, they will have nothing with which to reproach the
Russians in Poland—who never did as much—nor Carrier or Collot during
the French Revolution."[73]

The Terror therefore pushed Blanc's theory of state action to the furthest possible extent. How was it possible to determine whether or not the Terror was "in opposition to the free development of human faculties?" If one considered the circumstances under which it took place, as Blanc so painstakingly did, the question became almost impossible to answer. Or at least it was certainly impossible to answer at the moment it was taking place. This however did not mean that the question could not be asked subsequently. What was required, however, to do so was a legal and historical frame for making such judgments.

Blanc's and Mill's rapprochement between the Terror and invocations of martial law in India and Jamaica reveals the influence of the highly charged legal atmosphere, especially around issues of martial law and emergency powers. Rande Kostal's account of the political and intellectual climate surrounding the legal issues of the 1860s among political elites in London, has suggested that, in spite of the deep disagreements over how to interpret the regulations around martial law, an important result of the Eyre affair for the English governing class—that Blanc was frequenting—was a renewed commitment to treating even the most violent expressions of state power through legal debate. "The great virtue of law, it seemed, was its capacity to constitute and reconstitute the British constitutional community even as it provided a mechanism for articulating differences within that community."[74]

Blanc, living in London and participating in this debate directly through his political journalism and historical writing, was influenced by this milieu in his attempt to solve the problem of the Terror. Blanc too faced the fundamental problem of determining the legitimacy of state action under the cover of invocations of emergency government. And his references to the Sepoy and Morant Bay rebellions suggest that he too was searching for a language within which to discuss such issues without calling into question the possibilities of a liberal democratic state. Writing in a context when the very validity of a democratic and liberal government was still profoundly in question, Blanc used this legal language to interrogate the question of whether or not state action during Terror had been justified according to his own normative principles.

Blanc's discussion of the siege of Toulon offers a prime example. As he did throughout his discussion of the Terror, he attempted to reestablish the circumstances within which the acts were committed. Recognizing that they were excessive, he felt that it was nonetheless important to understand why. Attempting to explain the motivations behind the Toulon massacre he wrote: "Patriots hunted like wild beasts; republican corpses suspended here and there with pieces of meat in front of butcher shops—was any thing more necessary, especially in the drunkenness of a universal and desperate struggle to push the indignation of the victors to delirium?"[75] He therefore determined that the acts had been driven by folly. Furthermore, he judged that the justice put forth was excessive and was motivated by vengeance: "Such a mass execution was no doubt horrible; and it is obvious that to judge the royalists by the same men who were persecuted was to create the possibility, in spite of their oaths, and to confuse justice and vengeance."[76] But this guilt, in Blanc's view, did not mean that the case should be dismissed. It was still necessary to analyze and accurately account for what had happened. In other words, in order to judge appropriately, it was necessary to restore the truth of the incident, without prejudice, based on the facts and the most careful examination of the documents. Blanc's aim was to recount historical truth as closely as possible without hiding the horrors of Louis Fréron's actions, insisting that the accusations against him had been systematically exaggerated.[77] There were not eight hundred killed but rather no more than 150, he argued. Moreover, they were not killed without a hearing because there had in fact been an examination, interrogation, and an initial "*triage* by men who vowed to be just."[78] Likewise, they were not spared the guillotine in order to kill more effectively and less humanely, but rather because the Royalists had burned the only guillotine available. Lastly, Fréron had not maliciously announced a pardon for all in order to encourage those who might pretend to be dead to stand and be truly condemned to death. This had been impossible because he and Barras had recused themselves from the spectacle. Once again, this did not mean, Blanc insisted, that the acts had been justifiable; it did mean, however, that Fréron should be judged based on the truth and not lies and exaggerations.

In other words, Blanc refused merely to suggest that the acts were morally bankrupt or violent and therefore antithetical to just liberal democratic rule. Rather, he looked to dissect the motivations, the actions, and the horrors in order to present the appropriate diagnosis and determine whether or not the acts had been in the service of the ultimate ends of the democratic republic or not. The very fact that excessive force was used was not sufficient in itself to condemn the regime, because it was impossible to predetermine what circumstances could require. It was necessary, however, to determine who had participated, their motivation, to what degree they had participated, and whether or not the punishment was appropriate.

Blanc's *History* was full of references to historians of the Revolution: Michelet, Thiers, de Barante, Bouchez and Roux, Carlyle, and many others fill the footnotes and historiographical notes at the end of key chapters. Such notes argue systematically that these historians used the wrong sources, or did not properly read them, or even left out essential references. Blanc's adoption of a legal mode of analysis to plead his case through what he considered an inordinately rigorous use of sources was essential to his attempt to litigate the legitimacy of exceptional actions. By making the case that the Terror was brought on by exceptional circumstances, he insisted that one could, as long as proper rigor and documentation were provided, defend, and therefore judge, the Terror by writing its history.[79] In this sense, it was less important whether one agreed with all of Blanc's arguments. Instead, he was attempting to bring forward an irrefutable method that juridified the relationship between the circumstances, the Terror, and the state. As opposed to the philosophical history of Quinet, which sought the structural undercurrents of the Revolution that had generated the Terror, Blanc's use of evidence, his comparisons to contemporary invocations of martial law, and his legal argumentation introduced a new field for articulating profound political divisions emerging out of the French past—one in which the conclusions remained open, but the foundations remained uncontestable. The liberal democratic state was no longer to be accepted or refused based on an interpretation of the Terror. Instead, what was to emerge was a regime in which to build on Claude Lefort's statement of democracy, one was "to replace a regime regulated by laws, a legitimate power, with a regime founded on *the legitimacy of a debate on the legitimate and the illegitimate.*"[80] This was made possible through a combination of Blanc's concept of the democratic state, the increasingly elaborate discussions on emergency powers, and an increasing commitment among political and intellectual elites in London to solving even the most divisive issues through a commitment to legal debate.

Blanc left London for France immediately upon declaration of the republic, arriving on September 8, 1870. He was not called upon to participate in the Government of National Defense, though he supported the government wholeheartedly. In the February 1871 elections, he was elected to the Assembly with the impressive number of more than 216,000 votes, acquiring more votes than any of his long-standing republican friends and colleagues including Victor Hugo and Ledru Rollin. This extraordinary number of votes suggests the extent to which Blanc had become synonymous with the idea of the republic in France even amidst his exile. As a member of the Assembly, Blanc gave impassioned speeches on the peace treaty with Germany (insisting that France resist) and in support of returning the republican government to Paris. However, his intransigence confronted its limits in the Commune. He was conciliatory with the Commune's demands for municipal elections, but he refused any calls for communal independence. Thus, while he had attempted to play the role of mediator in the early moments of the conflict between the Commune and the Assembly, once the decision to lay siege upon the capital was taken, Blanc grudgingly accepted.

Blanc's relative silence during the siege was surprising enough to some that he offered an explanation. His response came on the front page of the *Figaro* on June 8, 1871: "Do not forget, dear sirs, that in the courts, the silence of the audience is of the greatest necessity because it is the duty of each individual to remain silent when the judge speaks." Blanc's ambivalence reduced his lyricism to metaphor, but in the context of his analysis on state-sponsored violence in the years leading up to the Third Republic, the trial metaphor was significant. Blanc pleaded his case to the Communards and to the Assembly: he had pushed for compromise, but he was convinced that the republic was in danger. Blanc's support for Thiers and his "civil" silence during the Bloody Week was therefore born of his conviction that only Thiers could save the republic against its enemies on both the left and right. One could argue one's case to the end, but the republican authority ultimately held the capacity to decide.

Like Laboulaye's, Blanc's thinking on the state and the state of emergency in the Second Empire were not just ideas on a page, but became essential to the actual foundation of the Third Republic. His emphasis on juridification found its way into the heart of the tumultuous establishment of the Third Republic in the wake of the Franco-Prussian War and the Commune as a series of parliamentary commissions were created to provide documents and judge state actions during the *année terrible* of 1870–71. It was Blanc himself who called for the creation of a parliamentary commission on the Government of National Defense. In his appeal for the commission he invoked the same reasoning that had driven his letter on the Terror. Suggesting that the actions of the Government of National Defense in Paris were little known, he insisted that "this has created not only a strange lacuna in the history of our country, but also misunderstandings and a great confusion of ideas, a lamentable conflict of sentiments. This menace must be dissipated. When the facts are enveloped in obscurity in the name of the *salut* of the people, it furnishes an arm of discontent. It is not by prolonging the obscurity that the agitation will cease."[81] By insisting that the Assembly itself investigate the actions of the government, Blanc was calling upon a higher order of state authority— a state authority that could judge the specific acts of any given government. Although Blanc had been an essential contributor to this new reason of state, he was not alone. Some months later, when the parliamentary commission on the insurrection of March 18 was established, they asserted a position that clearly set aside the philosophical method of Quinet in favor of the positivist approach captured by Blanc: "You do not expect of us a profound discussion of philosophical, political or social question raised by the insurrection of Paris," they stated. "All of the depositions that we have heard have been stenographed; we ask that you organize them as you will. . . . Nothing for the politician or the historian can replace original documents; you must be able to control assertions and judge for yourselves the results of the inquiry that you have called for."[82]

In the years that followed, Louis Blanc embraced wholeheartedly his political career serving as one of the leaders of the leftist current of republicanism, the *Republican Union*—a position that afforded him an important role in shaping the most radical republican position within the constitutional debates of the Third Republic. Among his most intransigent positions was his resistance to Edouard Laboulaye's amendment, which, as we have seen, attempted to found the republic definitively by instituting a president and two chambers. On Laboulaye's amendment, he wrote: "Supporting his proposition: 'the government of the Republic is made up of two houses and a president.' He [Laboulaye] gave a well-prepared speech in which it was hardly question of the presidency or the two houses. However, and in spite of the fact that he began by stating that we lived in a Republic, he insisted at length on the necessity of ensuring everyone's security by establishing it."[83] Blanc explained his resistance to this logic before an impatient assembly. He declared:

> If the authors of the present amendment hope to affirm the Republic, as I am sure they do, I wonder why they did not pose the question in the following terms: 'Art. 1. The French government is a Republic.' 'Art. 2. It is composed of two Houses.' In that case, everyone's conscience would be put to ease. Those who, like us, think that the Republic must not be put to a vote, because it must not be called into question, have no choice but to express their profound conviction. But they have the right to claim that these two ideas should be have been separated one from the other.[84]

As Blanc's speech revealed, it was not the republic that divided Blanc from liberals like Laboulaye. The variety of institutional alignments possible under the heading of the republic made this the one thing upon which they could all agree. Rather, it was precisely on the relationship between the institutions and the republic that they disagreed. This disagreement was profound, for not only was it the question of the institutional matrix itself, but the very relationship between the republic and any institutional structure. As he revealed in his amendment, for Laboulaye the republic required institutions at almost any cost; to vote for the republic was to vote for a president and a bicameral legislative branch. To the contrary, for Louis Blanc the republic was indisputable and, most importantly, was independent of any particular institutional structure or government—to bind the two was to undermine the republic itself. "The Republic," he wrote in a letter to the *Temps*, "is a fact, and consequently, does not need to be recognized."[85] Blanc insisted repeatedly within the debates that the republic had already been declared and that therefore there was no reason to vote on the republic within the laws of the Constitution that established any particular institutional structure. Here, he found a rare occasion to agree even with the president of the republic, Adolphe Thiers: "M. Thiers has made clear," Louis Blanc insisted, "it is impossible to deny that the Republic was the legal government of the country long before the vote on the constitutional laws."[86] The republic, in Blanc's view, existed outside of any particular institutional structure. Or, in other words, Blanc debated and voted within the National Assembly as a republican before the republic had a constitution precisely because he was able to conceive of a republic, worthy of the name, which remained free of any specific institutional organization.

Thus, in this early dawn of the new republic, "Jacobin" republicans of the most radical sort and dyed-in-the-wool liberals such as Laboulaye and Thiers were able to agree on a regime and the measures necessary to save it, even while the most fundamental question of its institutions remained unresolved. Any agreement whatsoever (and even the possibility of a search for compromise) between "Jacobins," centrist republicans, and liberals required nothing less than the capacity to accept the "fact" of the republic while debating its very institutional foundations. They were, in short, debating the institutional architecture under the miraculously suspended roof of the republic (which threatened collapse at any moment). And, it was precisely under such exceptional conditions, Blanc argued, that the republic could be legitimately founded.

CONCLUSION

DEMOCRATIC ENDS OF STATE

The history of the idea of the state in nineteenth-century France leads, as it just has, to results that may not provide a solution to all problems contained in this single word, but at least put the mind on the proper path for finding one.

HENRY MICHEL[1]

The forty-year period explored in this book represents a relatively short moment in the long history of democracy. Its brevity, however, is disproportionate to its importance. One struggles to imagine the profound discredit of democratic politics in Europe in the wake of Napoleon's defeat—both in spite of and because of the intensity of the revolutionary experience. If the notion slowly made its way into the vocabulary of politicians, journalists, activists, theorists, and even rulers in the years that followed, it was not until 1848 that democracy as a political ideal found itself squarely in the heart of European politics. No doubt, what happened in the three decades that followed marked one of the most extraordinary moments in the history of the very old set of ideas and practices assembled under this title. Across Europe a new democratic experiment—rooted in the idea of universal suffrage, representative parliamentary government, and modern administration—found a home in large territorial states. By the last decades of the nineteenth century, democracy definitively entered European and American political vocabularies and practices as a structural feature of their political future. France's long and complex historical relationship to democracy from the Enlightenment through the Revolution, and beyond, ensured it would play a central role in integrating these practices and ideas.

This new attachment to democracy pushed the state once again into the center of European politics, thought, history, and, ultimately, political science. For this new generation of theorists and politicians, the state—and its attendant popular foundations, responsibilities, and accountabilities—became the centerpiece of political life. Slowly, the liberal critique of the state inherited from the eighteenth century and the relentless wariness of organized popular power that so marked the postrevolutionary generation was on the defensive. A new, more widespread—and necessarily ambiguous—conception of the modern state was formed in the second half of the nineteenth century. Upstream of the moment discussed in this book was a fear of democracy and the state shrouded in the dark shadow of absolutism, terror, and Napoleonic centralization; downstream was the emergence of a new social progressivism rooted in democracy that placed the modern state at its heart.

Traversing these upheavals and challenges, the figures discussed here were sentinels in a massive transition that only fully gained steam in the final decades of the nineteenth century and the early twentieth century, a period when the state became an unchallenged and central feature of daily political life. I have not chosen these figures because they were representative of a singular movement in French, European, or Atlantic democracy—though many of their ideas found their way into modern political thought, constitutions, and institutional structures. Rather, I have focused on their work because they all lived in this moment and had an untiring concern for coming to grips with what it meant to live in a democratic age. While they largely disagreed with the form that their democracies had taken, especially between 1849 and 1870, none of them turned their backs on democracy, even as they critiqued the democracies within which they lived in an effort to find other, more compelling democratic arrangements.

During this key period, no distinct definition of democracy emerged. Or rather, it would seem that there were as many definitions as there were people seriously interested in the question. As a result, this historical investigation offers no normative or prescriptive definition of democracy, just as it provides few insights into the precise origins of today's democratic crisis—and certainly not in the form of some hidden problem or conundrum that these individuals understood which may solve today's challenges. Its ambition is at once more and less lofty. It has uncovered a moment when democracy's unsettling triumph sparked a desire to interrogate the very foundations of their democratic present. And it is through this interrogation that they remain our contemporaries.

At the center of this project was an attempt to redefine the foundations for a modern democratic state. It is difficult to exaggerate Tocqueville's importance in shaping modern political inquiry into democracy during these years. Of course, since the mid-twentieth century, his significance has been documented again and again. But beyond an overwhelming tendency to read Tocqueville as a nineteenth-century liberal, given Tocqueville's discussion of the role of regulatory police powers, it would appear that democracy and political liberty had a much deeper relationship to democratic governance: the fact that a government that operates on the people must thoroughly issue from it. Democratic government must be "of the people" or, in Tocqueville's words, "it is a government that instead of reducing human liberty, comes to its rescue in a thousand different ways, which instead of limiting it on all sides, opens all sorts of new perspectives."[2] To this extent, Tocqueville's is not a sociologically defined "liberty from"; it is democratic and pragmatic politics "for."

Of course, as this book and Tocqueville scholarship have emphasized, historically such calls for the democratic also played a key role in promoting colonial as well as gender domination. This *is* part of the critical legacy of these nineteenth-century thinkers and politicians. Indeed, it is also in their very insufficiencies that they were disciples of the democratic. They challenged the liberal economic ideals of laissez-faire and free trade that dominated the Second Empire; they provided novel substantive approaches that combined political liberty—in the form of democratic government—and economic liberty—in the form of economic self-sufficiency and substantive equality (especially in the form of antipauperism); just as they promoted an unjust politics along racial, gender, and imperial lines. For some of the people discussed here, like Tocqueville, these were two parts of the same larger project. The individuals explored in this book (and many others who are not) were students of the democratic—in the sense that they thought and acted on their understanding of the implications of a new democracy all the way down through its political, social, and economic implications as they understood them. Therefore, recognizing their limitations (and ours), this book suggests, is essential to elaborating a more robust conception of the democratic as a historical practice.

For all of its potency for understanding modern French political history, republicanism (like liberalism) has also had trouble coming to terms with democracy's critical history. Certainly a revived republicanism may have helped us break out of some of the sterilities of a liberal-socialist debate that thrived in the postwar era.[3] But to read an ideal republican tradition into nineteenth-century politics, to use a reified republican discourse as an explanatory mechanism for the transformation of the modern state obscures the tremendous novelty and internationalism of the democratic question in the nineteenth century. Recounting these thinkers as republican (or not) thus has the dangerous effect of securing their place within an embattled relationship to other political traditions while solidifying a French *Sonderweg*. In this view, France's liberal and socialist "failures" send us running back to the republic, while democracy languishes, hidden behind its transparency.

And yet, it was during this moment that many French did systematically confront problems of democratic governance, opening a kind of questioning and practice that remains with us today. First, they jettisoned an inherited notion of democracy as a key feature of a mixed regime and thus a mere political antidote. Instead, they understood democracy to be as social as it was political.

Following on his predecessor Royer-Collard, Tocqueville no doubt captured it in the most complex and appropriate language when he spoke of the decline of the aristocratic orders as a matter of social equalization and the increasing equality of condition as the salient factor in postrevolutionary social life. In the years that followed the July Monarchy, figures such as Prévost-Paradol grasped this idea when they posited democracy as a social form.

Second, as all the figures in this book show, the concept of political liberty properly understood revealed the political capacity of democracy: the people as constituent of political power, authors of their own laws, and government issuing from people. And, finally, in the realm of the economic, democracy was driven by an (all-too-often unrealized) ambition to preserve the general welfare through provision, utility, antipauperism, and regulation. From this perspective, the economy was in sync with the equalization of condition as well as the egalitarian prerequisites of the democratic polity, or the priority of democracy over economy. The economy could become a tool for democratic progress, instead of an autonomous, naturalized limit on democracy. A demos assembled comprehensively engaged its social, political, and economic capacities.

Each of the figures discussed here (and many others that weren't) encountered these problems of the new democratic order and theorized a democratic state power to come to terms with them. These theories of the modern state emerged out of attempts to reckon with the changing traditions of republicanism, liberalism, and socialism. Political thinkers of the early and mid-nineteenth century had bequeathed them a complex set of problems. But all of those present here reconsidered the politically saturated character of society and culture and therefore confronted the problem of defining politics as government.[4] Recognizing this problem, the generation rediscovered the state to develop a more ambitious theory of democratic politics. They discarded key elements of aristocratic liberalism, the classical republican tradition, a doctrinaire suspicion of democracy, and the illiberal, plebiscatory democracy of Napoleon III at the same time that they built their theories out of the society-centered approach of Tocqueville and the statism of Guizot. But they also looked abroad to find models of a robust liberal democratic state in the United States and Britain. In so doing, by the end of the Second Empire, they had gathered an original conception of the relationship between the individual, civil society, and the state that was increasingly distinct from the earlier fundamentals of a postrevolutionary politics. It was precisely by pursuing these ideas that they engaged with their colleagues and theories of state in the United States and Britain and ultimately carved out a new notion of the democratic across the decades surrounding the foundation of the Third Republic.

But again it is clear that the legacy of this group was not unambiguous. Dividing lines emerged within the competing responses to this new investment in state power. There were those who saw in the colonial experience an opportunity to build an effective liberal democratic state and those who didn't. Tocqueville, Prévost-Paradol, Laboulaye, and Thiers each in their own way saw the colonial experience as a means of reinforcing the liberal democratic ambitions of the metropole. Paradol did so by crafting a theory of equality among Frenchmen that solidified the national interest and thus turned the native Algerians into an other, or foe, that provided the opportunity to both reinforce the democratic ideal within the metropole and make it that much easier for France to impose itself on conquered subjects. Laboulaye retheorized the limits of the state by conceiving of "French" sovereignty as the only legitimate mode of expressing individual will. In this way, it was only by being under the control of France that Algerians could have access to the national sovereignty that was to guide a new international system. Engaged in the pragmatics of governance and the history of modern France, Thiers insisted that Algeria was a space of necessity in which French glory could once again be found.

Louis Blanc did of course show an interest in the question of imperialism, especially that of Britain, but it quickly became an antimodel used to gain perspective on the horrors of the Terror. D'Héricourt showed little interest in the colonial question, but it is worth noting that had her agonistic vision of the state been applied there, it would have provided the means for colonial subjects to challenge the dominance of the metropole. No matter what the ambitions, the problems of the liberal democratic state were not solved, but remained for many and only increased as European imperialism took hold in the late nineteenth century. Such a legacy is a central feature of this book. For, as long as the ways in which a democratized liberalism accommodated colonial ambitions remains under cover, democracy will continue to appear a utopian ideal on some distant horizon that may be used to defend supposed "freedom" at home and brutal action abroad.

Another divide appeared in managing the problems of the democratic: how to integrate popular power. There were those who sought a means of thinking about exceptional or necessary powers as a response to democratization and the growth of the state. That is, while increasingly fewer liberals on the eve of the Third Republic and especially after its establishment denied what they perceived as the inevitability of democracy and the need for a more robust state, some sought to bolster state power by focusing on how the state could intervene in specific moments of civil unrest or military conflict. Laboulaye developed this logic by emphasizing the essential problem of how a liberal democratic state could effectively respond to crisis while remaining

committed to liberty in moments of non-emergency. The difficulty with Laboulaye's reflections was that while he paid greater attention to the state, its
new powers were largely conceived as responses to emergency. Thiers developed a more holistic theory, similar to the police powers, in which necessity
played a role in even the most everyday modes of governance from fiscal
power to foreign policy. But while Thiers's theory opened a far wider path
for state intervention in the early Third Republic, it also generated the fundamental problem of how and when necessity was to be reined in.

Both of these innovations were important. Through the focus on exceptional and necessary state intervention, it was possible to consider a society
that was in the deepest sense politically constituted. This new conception
shed the abstract ideals of human liberty to foster new practices of social intervention, and economic regulation, as well as carve out a place for the state
to ensure political liberty. They were able to theorize the possibility of a democratic polity that could take governance into its own hands. However, their
embrace of democracy remained tepid to the extent that they remained reluctant to give the state entirely over to the demos. From this perspective, exception was an indication of what the democratic polity was capable of while the
conception of emergency and necessity remained to keep it in check. There
were no utopic lines cutting through the polity; there was the demos, and
the demos, in the view of Laboulaye and Thiers, needed to be contained. In
many ways, the turn toward a theorization of necessity and emergency may
be understood then as an escape valve that allowed them to embark on the
full range of capacities afforded by a democratic state while avoiding the very
real question of how to create a state that constantly responded to democratic
pressures in return. To that extent, this response was equally problematic: try
as they might to put the genie back into the box, using exceptional powers or
a theory of necessity to bring the state back in raised the fundamental question of when and who could put an end to such powers. This question would
hover over the next generation of state theorists and even feed some of the
most dangerous ideas of state in the early decades of the twentieth century.

There was, however, another response to the political nature of democracy, the social individual. Both Louis Blanc and Jenny d'Héricourt elaborated this position, breaking down the perceived opposition between the
collective order and individual development. In so doing, the state became
a means of ensuring the liberty of the individual by guaranteeing relative
equality among its members. Though it has been largely forgotten, this vision would also have an extensive following in the decades to come, especially among social progressives in France, Britain, and the United States. It
is worth noting that for both Blanc and d'Héricourt, only by overcoming the

basic inequalities in modern society would a liberal democratic polity be able to thrive. From this perspective, Blanc and d'Héricourt would have agreed with Philip Pettit's assertion that "the notion of the solitary individual is essentially bogus."[5] But if Blanc and d'Héricourt were clearly republicans, it was their desire to democratize a modern polity without falling into the depths of an overbearing regulatory state that nourished them. To do so, they did not return to Machiavelli or early modern states. They had no need to. The Enlightenment, modern democracy, and the legacy of eighteenth-century democratic revolutions had freed the state to act with the demos to confront quotidian problems of governance.

The bequest of these two responses—the turn to exception on the one hand and the social individual on the other—no doubt merits further attention. For all of the juridical investigations into exceptional powers, we need more empirical histories that show how emergency powers have been both depended upon and used to combat innovative forms of democratic engagement. It goes without saying that necessity and emergency may be used in a changing democratic environment to ensure the order of the few against the many and to this extent, the other response discussed in this book, the social individual, offered a promising legacy.[6]

The book has also opened a small window into the thorny question of equality and the democratic state. In his support of racism and colonization, Prevost-Paradol was unfortunately not alone. Indeed, racist theories abounded across the Third Republic and yet the regime *was* a democracy, for some. Many have used this basic fact as a means to challenge the very existence of a democratic state—if a state maintains inequalities, colonizes, incarcerates large numbers of its citizens, disenfranchises them, uses violence against them, or imposes its will upon them, then, they argue, it must not be a democracy. Through a more nuanced history of regimes of equality, it becomes clear that in Paradol's conception of liberal democracy and colonization, unfortunately, quite the contrary may be true. Instead of serving as a mode of "freeing" individuals from the power of the state, he argued, democratic government was a means of organizing the power among those who were equal (white men within the metropole) and generating new modes of violent power over those individuals who were not. It also suggests that if defined entirely without a theory of natural rights—or some guarantee of individual or human rights—it becomes extremely difficult to establish the limits of a state democratically empowered.

This was precisely what Jenny d'Héricourt's theory of agonistic democracy attempted to remedy. In her theory of equality, French men and women were not equal in that they were all "the same." By deconstructing what many of her day perceived as the most natural social distinction, gender, and politicizing it, she reinvented a new and capacious notion of equality that did not rigidify the boundaries between friends and enemies, but attempted to turn all political conflict into a struggle between adversaries. It was not an attempt to maintain equality through the imposition of general rules that could be applied to everyone equally or uniform offerings that ensured everyone the same amount of a given unit. Rather, it was a theory of equality rooted in access to a common subject position from which one could express all aspects of one's self and ambition individually. It therefore established a more intimate connection between individual and collective action—collective action ensuring the opportunity to express individual singularity.

Of course, the balance between a concept of democracy that empowers the demos and a reliance on natural rights to defend against despotism is not a problem that was solved by Paradol, d'Héricourt, or anyone else in this book. To this extent, the exploration of this question may serve best as a reminder of Chantal Mouffe's claim that "no final resolution or equilibrium between those two conflicting logics is ever possible, and there can be only temporary, pragmatic, unstable and precarious negotiations of the tension between them."[7]

Another way of making this point would be to say that democracies are saturated with power and therefore must self-define the limits of this power. But as long as we assume that democracies are stateless in their ideal form, we remain incapable of coming to terms with the consequences of a properly democratic organization. Whether it comes from our human condition or elsewhere, it is only through a historical grasp of democratization that we may garner the capacity to govern ourselves. And, it is not by understanding democracy as an ephemeral moment, in opposition to the state, that we will come to terms with this fundamental tension. Democracy, it would seem, is as vexing as it is vital.

Notes

Introduction

1. "C'est que, poser un problème, c'est précisément le commencement et la fin de toute histoire," Lucien Febvre, "Vivre l'histoire," *Combats pour l'histoire* (Paris: Armand Colin, 1992), 21.

2. "Le difficile avait été de poser, comme elle l'avait fait, les termes du problème, non de le résoudre, " Alexis de Tocqueville, *Études Économiques, Politiques et Littéraires* (Paris: Michel Levy, 1866), 73.

3. John Dewey, *The Public and Its Problems* (Columbus: Ohio University Press, 1988), 44.

4. For a more thorough discussion of the problem of the democratic state, see our (Stephen W. Sawyer, William J. Novak, and James T. Sparrow) "Beyond Stateless Democracy," *Tocqueville Review* 36, no. 1 (Spring 2015); "Toward a History of the Democratic State," *Tocqueville Review/ La Revue Tocqueville 33, no. 2 (2012)*; "Democratic States of Unexception: Toward a New Genealogy of the American Political," in *The Many Hands of the State*, ed. Ann Orloff and Kimberly Morgan (Cambridge: Cambridge University Press, 2017); and "Introduction: Boundaries of the State in US History," in *Boundaries of the State in U.S. History* (Chicago: University of Chicago Press, 2015). For a review of this project, see Claire Lemercier, "L'État vu de ses marges," *La vie des idées* (Septembre 2016).

5. Quentin Skinner, *The Foundations of Modern Political Thought*, vol. 1 (Cambridge: Cambridge University Press, 1978), ixn.

6. Richard Tuck has highlighted Hobbes's role in redefining the relationship between sovereignty and government in a democracy. See his *Sleeping Sovereign: The Invention of Modern Democracy* (Cambridge: Cambridge University Press, 2015).

7. Jean-Jacques Rousseau, *The Social Contract*, Book III, chap. 3, "The Division of Governments" (1762).

8. Louis Blanc, *Pages d'histoire de la Révoluion de février 1848* (Paris: Nouveau Monde, 1850).

9. Pierre Rosanvallon, "The History of the Word 'Democracy' in France" (P. J. Costopoulos, trans.), *Journal of Democracy* 6, no. 4 (1995): 140–54.

10. John Dunn, whose work has been among the most important contributions to this field, has noted on the history of "democracy's global ascent,": "A serious intellectual history, . . . still needs to be done, country by country, language by language, decade by decade and done by those already sufficiently at ease with the context in question to fathom just what has occurred

within them. This huge and barely initiated collaborative task is as urgent politically as it is intellectually." John Dunn, *Breaking Democracy's Spell* (New Haven, CT: Yale University Press, 2014). There have been some important steps in this direction, including James Kloppenberg's towering history of democracy, *Toward Democracy: The Struggle for Self-Rule in European and American Thought* (New York: Oxford University Press, 2016), as well as the collection of essays edited by Joanna Innes and Mark Philp, *Re-imagining Democracy in the Age of Revolutions: America, France, Britain* (Oxford: Oxford University Press, 2013). Wim Weymans has also recently suggested that we are currently witnessing the creation of "no less than a new genre, the history of democracy": "Radical Democracy's Past and Future: Histories of the Symbolic," *Modern Intellectual History* 13, no. 3 (2016): 841–51, 851. One of the most sustained historical reflections on the history of modern democracy in recent decades has been those of the Paris School of political history, and in particular Pierre Rosanvallon and Marcel Gauchet. We will return to the importance of Rosanvallon's work further on. As for Gauchet, his four-volume history on the "Advent of Democracy" [*l'Avènement de la démocratie*] offers a history of democracy from the early modern period to present.

11. Though covering a much larger period, James Kloppenberg has also identified the last decades of the nineteenth century as a key moment in the widespread acceptance of democracy: "Swept forward by waves of popular passion, democracy has buried all alternatives to become the world's governing ideal. It was not always so. . . . "Democracy" was a term of abuse, usually yoked with labels such as "rabble," "herd," or "mob." By the end of the nineteenth century, however, things had changed." *Toward Democracy*, 1.

12. Perhaps one of the clearest statements of this approach during the period under study came in 1868 by Jules Barni: "There is indeed democracy and democracy: there is true democracy and false democracy." He continued, arguing that the supposedly democratic foundations of the Second Empire fell under the latter: "There is a different type of so-called democracy . . . that which gives itself over to a master." Jules-Romain Barni, *La morale dans la démocratie* (Paris: Germer Baillière, 1868), 3. For a discussion and genealogy of "critical democracy," see Stephen W. Sawyer, "Neoliberalism and the Crisis of Democratic Theory," in *In Search of the Liberal Moment*, ed. S. Sawyer and I. Stewart (New York: Palgrave, 2016), and "What is Critical Democracy?" *La Revue Tocqueville*, 2016.

13. These conceptions run deep. Mathew Arnold famously argued of the British in 1869: "We have not the notion, so familiar on the Continent and to antiquity, of the State" [*Culture and Anarchy* (Cambridge: Cambridge University Press, 1963), p 75]. Recent specialists have continued to echo this opposition. In his book *The French State in Question*, H. S. Jones writes: "In the light of this contrast, it makes sense to think of England and the United States as instances of 'stateless societies.'" He then turns to the French state and concludes: "How can we plausibly pin down the distinction between state cultures and stateless cultures?" [*The French State in Question: Public Law and Political Argument in the Third Republic* (Cambridge: Cambridge University Press, 1993), 8]. Likewise, in a recent attempt to compare American and French liberal political traditions, Mark Hulliung summarizes: "It is one thing to emancipate civil society in France, a nation with an overblown state; it is quite another matter to do the same in America where the battle fought by the New Dealers was an uphill struggle against a powerful tradition of populist laissez-faire and anti-government rhetoric" [*Citizens and Citoyens* (Cambridge, MA: Harvard University Press, 2002), 91].

14. The appraisal of the French state as an unmanageable anachronism is so widespread as to form a kind of popular contemporary wisdom. In the form of a small contemporary sample, it

is sufficient to explore the press at any given moment. See, for example, an article in the *Economist*: "France has resorted to public spending and debt. Even as other EU countries have curbed the reach of the state" ("France and the Euro: The Time-Bomb at the Heart of Europe," *Economist*, November 17, 2012). A *New York Times* editorial similarly argued that the S&P lowered France's rating "for not being sufficiently committed to dismantling the welfare state" ("Non-Crisis France, *NYT*, November 8, 2013). *New York Times* editorialist Roger Cohen claimed to be restating the obvious when he remarked, "Now, it is true that France . . . is chronically divided between a world-class private sector and vast state sector of grumpy functionaries; that its universalist illusions have faded as its power diminishes; and that its welfare state is unaffordable" ("France's Glorious Malaise," *New York Times*, July 10, 2013). In France, the arguments for an untamable, "Jacobin" centralized state are equally common. Again just as examples of how widespread these assumptions are, the debate over the autonomy of universities in 2012 was presented as a question of overcoming the Jacobin state by the president of the Université de Strasbourg: "Moreover, autonomy directly confronts the Jacobin and centralized conception of elite administration as well as many elected officials by calling their vision of the state into question" ("L'autonomie est une chance pour nos établissements," *Le Monde*, January 20, 2012). While on the left, Daniel Cohn Bendit criticized the positions of Jean-Luc Mélenchon, "The emergence of this new Jacobin, centralized and caricatured left is a blessing for Nicolas Sarkozy," *Le Monde*, April 10, 2012.

15. Capturing this distinction and what it owes to Weberian sociology, Pierre Birnbaum has noted that "the theory of the state is undergoing a profound reinterpretation." The result has been an increasing attack on "the idea that the state is stronger the more it resembles the Weberian ideal-type." Pierre Birnbaum, "Défense de l'État 'fort.' Réflexions sur la place du religieux en France et aux États-Unis," *Revue française de sociologie* 52, no. 3 (2011): 559–78, 559.

16. Larry Siedentop, "Two Liberal Traditions," *French Liberalism from Montesquieu to the Present Day*, ed. Raf Geenens and Helena Rosenblatt (Cambridge: Cambridge University Press, 2012), 15–35.

17. "One of the overriding aims of this volume is thus to convey a sense of the richness, variety and longevity of French liberalism from Montesquieu to Lefort and Gauchet. Another goal is to interrogate the internal consistency and uniqueness of this tradition. . . . A strong case can be made, then, for the distinctiveness of the French liberal school of thought." Raf Geenens and Helena Rosenblatt, "French Liberalism, an Overlooked Tradition?" *French Liberalism from Montesquieu to the Present Day*, ed, Geenens and Rosenblatt (Cambridge: Cambridge University Press, 2012), 2–3.

18. In the realm of bureaucracy, King and Lieberman have referred to an anti-Weberian process of state building in the United States, but elsewhere as well, as "capacity without bureaucracy." See Desmond King and Robert Lieberman, "Ironies of State Building: A Comparative Perspective on the American State," *World Politics* 61, no. 3 (July 2009): 570.

19. "While studies of the state proliferate in the historical and social sciences, most restrict themselves to rearguard actions—stealthily sneaking up on the state through empirical and inductive investigations of 'state effects.' . . . Studies pursued in this vein have contributed to a helpful and burgeoning accumulation of information on and thick descriptions of state institutions, state policies, state officials, state resistance, and other assorted state effects. But the hoped for grand achievement of an ultimately better appreciation of the abstract conception of the state itself has been ineluctably postponed." William J. Novak: "Beyond Max Weber: The Need for a Democratic (not Aristocratic) Theory of the Modern State," *Tocqueville Review/La Revue Tocqueville* 36, no. 1 (2015): 43–91, 45.

20. Michael Behrent has noted, "The story of French liberalism is, we are often told, one of exceptions, eccentricities, and enigmas. Compared to their British counterparts, French liberals seem more reluctant to embrace individualism. . . . A new wave of scholarship seems, however, to be emerging, in which the paradigm of exceptionalism takes a back seat to considerations that, at first glance, would seem to be more conventional and less polemical in their approach to the history of French liberal thought. . . . Generally speaking, they are less impressed with French liberalism's peculiarities than with the insights it provides into the nature of the liberal experience as such." "Liberal Dispositions: Recent Scholarship on French Liberalism," *Modern Intellectual History*, February 2015, 1–31, 1–2.

21. Stephen W. Sawyer and Iain Stewart, "Introduction, New Perspectives on France's Liberal Moment," in *In Search of the Liberal Moment: Democracy, Anti-totalitarianism and Intellectual Politics in France since 1950* (New York: Palgrave, 2016).

22. "The development of institutionalized public power—'the government,' or 'the state'— has once again become an important subject of inquiry in the history of the United States, preoccupying an ever-growing number of theorists, historians, and social scientists. American historians now routinely invoke the concept of 'the state' when discussing governmental power, particularly within the precincts of political history. Social scientists working in the fields of comparative politics and American political development (APD) continue to devote much effort to accounting for the defining features of the American state." James T. Sparrow, William J. Novak, and Stephen W. Sawyer, "Introduction," *Boundaries of the State in US History* (Chicago: University of Chicago Press, 2015), 1.

23. See in particular John Brewer, *The Sinews of Power: War, Money, and the English State, 1688–1783* (Cambridge, MA: Harvard University Press, 1990); Max Edling, *A Revolution in Favor of Government* (Oxford: Oxford University Press, 2003); William Novak, *The People's Welfare: Law and Regulation in Nineteenth-Century America* (Chapel Hill: University of North Carolina Press, 1996) and "The Myth of the Weak American State," *American Historical Review* 113 (June 2008): 752–72; Ira Katznelson, "Flexible Capacity: The Military and Early American Statebuilding," in *Shaped by War and Trade: International Influences on American Political Development,* ed. Ira Katznelson and Martin Shefter (Princeton, NJ: Princeton University Press, 2002); James T. Sparrow, *The Warfare State: Americans and the Age of Big Government* (Oxford: Oxford University Press, 2011); Peter Baldwin, *Contagion and the State in Europe, 1830–1930* (Cambridge: Cambridge University Press, 2004); Gary Gerstle, "The Resilient Power of the States across the Long Nineteenth Century: An Inquiry into a Pattern of American Governance," in *The Unsustainable American State*, ed. Jacobs and King (Oxford: Oxford University Press, 2009), 61–87.

24. Max Edling, *A Hercules in the Cradle: War, Money, and the American State, 1783–1867* (Chicago: University of Chicago Press, 2014), 219.

25. Ibid., 179.

26. George M. Fredrickson, *The Inner Civil War: Northern Intellectuals and the Crisis of the Union* (Urbana: University of Illinois Press, 1993 [1965]), ix.

27. William J. Novak, *The New Democracy*, chap. 1, "Intellectual Foundations of the Modern Democratic State," in manuscript.

28. Peter J. Gurney, "The Democratic Idiom: Languages of Democracy in the Chartist Movement," *Journal of Modern History* 86 (September 2014).

29. Joanna Innes and Mark Philp, "Introduction," *Re-Imagining Democracy in the Age of Revolutions: American, France, Britain, Ireland 1750–1850* (Oxford: Oxford University Press, 2013).

30. Nadia Urbinati, *Mill on Democracy: From the Athenian Polis to Representative Government* (Chicago: University of Chicago Press, 2002), 15.

31. *L'État et la Commune* (Paris: Librairie Internationale, 1866), 7.

32. " 'In the last years,' noted the German Campe in 1813, 'the friends of absolutism and the nobility have made the word Democrat into an insult.' " Charles S. Maier, "After the Revolution: Political Dangers and Social Trends," in *Democracy: The Unfinished Journey, 508 BC to AD 1993*, ed. John Dunn (Oxford: Oxford University Press, 1992), 125.

33. This group is no doubt the most well-known, including such figures as Germaine de Staël, Constant, and Tocqueville. See Lucien Jaume, *L'individu effacé ou le paradoxe du libéralisme français* (Paris: Fayard, 1997).

34. Annelien de Dijn, *French Political Thought from Montesquieu to Tocqueville: Liberty in a Levelled Society?* (Cambridge: Cambridge University Press, 2008), 5; Alan S. Kahan, *Aristocratic Liberalism: The Social and Political Thought of Jacob Burckhardt, John Stuart Mill, and Alexis de Tocqueville* (New York: Oxford University Press, 1992).

35. The most coherent among them was the tradition of Catholic liberals described by Lucien Jaume in *L'individu effacé*; for an example of the Protestant response, see Helena Rosenblatt, *Liberal Values: Benjamin Constant and the Politics of Religion* (Cambridge; Cambridge University Press, 2008).

36. Lucien Jaume refers to this group as the "libéralisme notabiliaire" (*L'individu effacé*); On this tradition, see in particular Aurelian Craiutu, *Liberalism under Siege: The Political Thought of the French Doctrinaires* (Lanham: Lexington Books, 2003); Pierre Rosanvallon, *Le Moment Guizot* (Paris: Gallimard, 1985); Vincent Starzinger, *The Politics of the Center: The Juste Milieu in Theory and Practice, France and England, 1815–1848* (Edison: Transaction, 1965).

37. Although his book is not explicitly about French liberalism, I am employing the term "liberal authoritarianism" as developed by Howard Brown, *Ending the French Revolution: Violence, Justice and Repression from the Terror to Napoleon* (Charlottesville: University of Virginia Press, 2006). On the peculiarities of French liberalism in an international context during the Restoration and July Monarchy, see J. A. W. Gunn, *When the French Tried to Be British: Party, Opposition and the Quest for Civil Disagreement, 1814–1848* (Montreal: McGill-Queens University Press, 2009).

38. On this movement, see Andrew Jainchill's *Reimagining Politics after the Terror: The Republican Origins of French Liberalism* (Ithaca, NY: Cornell University Press, 2008), 236.

39. On the discredit and then new interest in the word democracy from the late eighteenth-century revolutions through 1848, see Innes and Philp, *Re-imagining Democracy in the Age of Revolutions*, especially the introduction; see also Peter J. Gurney, "The Democratic Idiom: Languages of Democracy in the Chartist Movement," *Journal of Modern History* 86 (September 2014); and Pierre Rosanvallon, "The History of the Word 'Democracy' in France," Philip J. Costopoulos, trans., *Journal of Democracy* 6, no. 4 (October 1995): 140–54.

40. For an example of a massive expansion of the democratic debate beyond elites following 1848, see Samuel Hayat, *Quand la République était révolutionnaire: Citoyenneté et représentation en 1848* (Paris: Seuil, 2014).

41. For a discussion of Napoleon III's Second Empire as an illiberal democracy, see Pierre Rosanvallon, *La démocratie inachevée*, especially chap. 5, "La démocratie illibéral (césarisme)"; and Quentin Deluermoz, *Le crepuscule des revolutions 1848–1871* (Paris: Seuil, 2012), especially chap. 3, "Le Second Empire ou la démocratie illibérale."

42. Brown, *Ending the French Revolution* . . . , 16.

43. Etienne Vacherot, *La Démocratie* (Bruxelles: Lacroix, 1860), iii.

44. For liberalism, this argument has been made most clearly by Lucien Jaume in his *L'individu effacé*. For republicanism, this argument has been made most effectively by Sudhir Hazareesingh, *From Subject to Citizen;* and Philip Nord, *The Republican Moment*.

45. For thorough analyses of five other figures from this pivotal generation including Charles Dupont-White, see Sudhir Hazareesingh, *Intellectual Founders of the Republic: Five Studies in Nineteenth-Century French Republican Political Thought* (Oxford: Oxford University Press, 2001). While he emphasizes the foundations of the republic more than the democratic question, he too suggests that it was democracy that brought this generation together: "Daniel Stern's salon attracted much of the elite of French intellectual life, both present and future: leading figures such as Jules Michelet, Alexis de Tocqueville, Hippolyte Carnot, and Jules Grévy discussed the prospects for a republican Europe with younger luminaries such as Ernest Renan, Jules Simon, Émile Ollivier, and Lucien Prévost-Paradol. So intense and passionate were these discussions that the Maison Rose became known in republican circles as 'the abbey in the Woods of Democracy'" (1).

46. The convergences in political thought on these themes between the United States and Europe have been noted in James T. Kloppenberg's classic study of social democracy and progressivism, culminating in the conversation between the French solidarists, the British new liberals, and the American pragmatists from the 1880s through the 1920s. What follows suggests that attempts to reconsider the relationship between liberalism, democracy, and the state which were essential to this later collaboration were prepared across the Atlantic and beyond in the previous generation. James T. Kloppenberg, *Uncertain Victory: Social Democracy and Progressivism in European and American Thought, 1870–1920* (New York: Oxford University Press, 1986).

47. Hanotaux, *Histoire Contemporaine*, 3:365.

48. Michel, *L'idée de l'État*, 401.

49. Ibid., 665.

50. L. T. Hobhouse, *Liberalism* (London: Oxford University Press, 1911), 19–20.

51. Ibid., 213.

52. Dewey, *Liberalism and Social Action*, 60.

53. F. A. Hayek, *The Fortunes of Liberalism: Essays on Austrian Economics and the Ideal of Freedom*, in *The Collected Works of F. A. Hayek*, vol. 4, ed. Peter G. Klein (London: Routledge, 1992), 216.

54. Carl Friedrich, "The Political Thought of Neo-Liberalism," *APSR* 49, no 2 (1955): 510.

55. "There can be no doubt that most of those in the democracies who demand a central direction of all economic activity still believe that socialism and individual freedom can be combined. Yet socialism was early recognized by many thinkers as the gravest threat to freedom. . . . Nobody saw more clearly than the great political thinker de Tocqueville that democracy stands in an irreconcilable conflict with socialism." Friedrich Hayek, *The Road to Serfdom*, in *The Collected Works of F.A. Hayek*, vol. 2, ed. Bruce Caldwell (New York: Routledge, 2008), 77.

56. Writing in the 1940s and resurrecting a specific reading of Tocqueville and early nineteenth-century liberalism became a central ambition in defining Hayekian neoliberalism. On this question, see Serge Audier, *Tocqueville retrouvé: Genèse et enjeux du renouveau tocquevillien français* (Paris: VRIN/EHESS, 2004).

57. "The first half of the nineteenth century arguably represented the golden era of French liberalism." Raf Geenens and Helena Rosenblatt, "French Liberalism, an Overlooked Tradition?" *French Liberalism from Montesquieu to the Present Day*, ed. Geenens and Rosenblatt (Cambridge: Cambridge University Press, 2012), 7.

58. Katznelson, *Desolation and Enlightenment* . . . , 24–25.

59. See, for example, Mona Ozouf's very Arendtian observation in the Critical Dictionary of the French Revolution, "We touch here on the here on the heart of the relation between the French Revolution and totalitarianism, both of which seek to create a new man." François Furet and Mona Ozouf, *A Critical Dictionary of the French Revolution* (Cambridge: Belknap Press, 1989), 789.

60. While a whole generation of Second Empire historians placed the history of democracy at the center of their histories of the Revolution—Tocqueville and Louis Blanc central among them—the full impact of this approach was perhaps best captured by the following generation in Alphonse Aulard, who wrote: "I wish to write the political history of the Revolution from the point of view of the origin and development of Democracy and Republicanism."(Alphonse Aulard, *Histoire Politique de la Révolution Française. Origines et développement de la démocratie et de la République, 1789–1804 (Paris: Armand Colin, 1901), v.*

61. Foucault has described this distinction as one of the essential techniques of governmentality in the postwar period. It is an underlying argument of this book that one of the key modes of a democratic art of government as it was posited in the nineteenth century was precisely to deny the cordoning off of the social and the political. On the question of Foucault and the state, see Stephen W. Sawyer, "Foucault and the State," *Tocqueville Review* 36, no. 1 (2015): 135–64; and Arnaud Skornicki, *La grande soif de l'État. Michel Foucault avec les sciences sociales* (Paris: Les Prairies ordinaires, 2015).

62. On the role of antitotalitarianism in this moment, see S. Moyn, "Introduction" to Pierre Rosanvallon, *Democracy Past and Future* (New York: Columbia University Press, 2006), 1–28, 4; Michael Scott Christofferson, *French Intellectuals against the Left.*

63. Warren Breckman has captured this moment well in his suggestion that "the same widespread skepticism about the foundational discourses of modern politics that shook Marxism to its core makes it impossible to return to a naïve conception of democracy." *Adventures of the Symbolic: Post-Marxism and Radical Democracy* (New York: Columbia University Press, 2013), 6. Beyond those discussed in this introduction, this movement is also captured by such figures as Pierre Clastres, Jacques Rancière, Etienne Balibar, and later Miguel Abensour or Chantal Mouffe. On these figures as radical democratic thinkers, see Martin Breaugh, Christopher Holman, Rachel Magnusson, Paul Mazzocchi, Devin Penner, *Thinking Radical Democracy: The Return to Politics in Post-War France* (Toronto: University of Toronto Press, 2015).

64. Andrew Jainchill and Samuel Moyn, "French Democracy between Totalitarianism and Solidarity: Pierre Rosanvallon and Revisionist Historiography," *Journal of Modern History* 76, no. 1 (March 2004): 107–54.

65. Stephen W. Sawyer, "Epilogue. Neoliberalism and Crisis of Democratic Theory," in *In Search of the Liberal Moment.*

66. Pierre Rosanvallon, "Inaugural lecture. Collège de France," in *Democracy Past and Future: Selected Essays,* ed. Samuel Moyn (New York: Columbia University Press, 2006), 36–37.

67. Pierre Rosanvallon, *Le sacre du citoyen. Histoire du suffrage universel en France* (Paris: Gallimard, 1992), 20.

68. Though it differs in the architecture and content of its response, this conception of Rosanvallon's work shares the ambition of Samuel Moyn and Andrew Jainchill's assessment that future histories of democracy must leave the fear of democracy permanently behind: "All future interventions on the history of French democracy will have to take [Rosanvallon's] formidable oeuvre as their starting point. . . . Rosanvallon's project raises the question of . . .

whether, in the name of democracy, the exaggerated fear of democracy has to be permanently left behind." Jainchill and Moyn, "French Democracy between Totalitarianism and Solidarity, 107–54, 154.

69. In his comment on Warren Breckman's *Adventures of the Symbolic*, Wim Weymans underlines the importance of the state in Lefort's thinking: "For Lefort—and this is important—it is the state that prevents society from occupying these symbolic entities like the 'people': no contestation and radical democracy without the modern state." "Radical Democracy's Past and Future: Histories of the Symbolic," 847.

70. The best examples may be found in his *L'État en France de 1789 à nos jours* (Paris: Seuil, 1990); *Le modèle politique français: La société civile contre le jacobinisme de 1789 à nos jours* (Paris: Seuil, 2004); *Le Bon Gouvernement* (Paris: Seuil, 2015).

71. On the problem of the symbolic in rethinking the foundations of democracy, see Warren Breckman, *Adventures of the Symbolic: Postmarxism and Democratic Theory* (New York: Columbia University Press, 2013).

72. While this project builds on Sheldon Wolin's path-breaking work to elaborate a more robust conception of democracy in response to liberalism as well as the idea that "democracy eludes definition because it has a protean nature." It ultimately moves in a different direction to explore a historical moment when democracy was perceived as a more robust and lasting set of engagements. In this process, the state and democracy were aligned in a radical new way that at once challenged the autonomy of the state and instituted democracy as a sustained historical practice. See for example, Sheldon S. Wolin, "Fugitive Democracy," *Constellations* 1 no. 1: 1994. On Wolin's legacy see Aryeh Botwinick and William E. Connolly, *Democracy and Vision: Sheldon Wolin and the Vicissitudes of the Political* (Princeton, NJ: Princeton University Press, 2001); the quotation is from chap. 2, Nicholas Xenos, "Momentary Democracy," 36.

73. Michel Foucault, *Fearless Speech* (Los Angeles: Semiotext(e), 2001), 172.

74. Lucien Febvre, "Contre le vain tournois des idées: Une étude sur l'esprit politique de la réforme," in *Combats pour l'histoire* (Paris: Armand Colin, 1992), 75.

75. Bloch writes: "The very names we use to characterize the concerns of those long disappeared, or social forms that have evanesced, what sense would these things have we had not already seen living men?" Marc Bloch, *Apologie pour l'Histoire ou Métier d'Historien, Cahier des Annales*, 3 (Paris: Librairie Armand Colin, 1952 [1949]), 28.

76. The pragmatic current of sociology has provided important insights for this historical approach to the democratic state, especially the way it foregrounds reflexivity as a mode of indetermination: "action cannot be simply or mechanically deduced from the past, to the extent that it always introduces, with respect to the latter, an indetermination. Such a position hardly refuses historical perspective or a rejection of genealogical inquiry, but rather suggests another means of practicing them." Yannick Barthe, Damien de Blic, Jean-Philippe Heurtin, Éric Lagneau, Cyril Lemieux, Dominique Linhardt, Cédric Moreau de Bellaing, Catherine Rémy, Danny Trom, "Sociologie Pragmatique: mode d'emploi" *Politix* 3, no. 103 (2013): 175– 204, 184.

77. It therefore attempts a history that builds on, but ultimately is distinct from, previous "postfoundational" political approaches. On these thinkers and their investment in the distinction between politics and the political, see Oliver Marchart, *Post-Foundational Political Thought: Political Difference in Nancy, Lefort, Badiou and Laclau: Political Difference in Nancy, Lefort, Badiou and Laclau* (Edinburgh: Edinburgh University Press, 2007).

78. In this sense, it builds from the "pragmatic turn" of the Annales, led by Bernard Lepetit, and the argument that: "On proposait donc [. . .] de considérer que les identités sociales ou les

liens sociaux n'ont pas de nature, mais seulement des usages" [Bernard Lepetit, *Les formes de l'expérience: une autre histoire sociale* (Paris: Albin Michel, 1995), 13].

79. On the political as episodic, see Wolin, "Fugitive Democracy," *Constellations*, p. 11.

80. Building on work in Science Studies, John Tresch has elaborated a similar position noting: "actors may spend time in labs, offices, or lecture halls, while involved in religious, governmental, or artitistic activities, all of which are underwritten by distinct concepts and principles of value. To reckon with the tensions between the phenomenological and the pragmatic worlds of complex societies . . ." John Tresch, "Cosmologies Materialized: History of Science and History of Ideas," in *Rethinking Modern European Intellectual History*, ed. Darrin M. McMahon and Samuel Moyn (New York: Oxford University Press, 2014), 163.

81. Reinhart Koselleck, "Transformations of Experience," *The Practice of Conceptual History: Timing History, Spacing Concepts* (Palo Alto, CA: Stanford University Press, 2002), 49.

82. Chantal Mouffe has highlighted the problem of democratic equality as one of the essential challenges posed by Schmitt: "If a state attempted to realize the universal equality of individuals in the political realm without concern for national or any other form of homogeneity, the consequence would be a complete devaluation of political equality, and of politics itself." Chantal Mouffe, ed., *The Challenge of Carl Schmitt* (London: Verso, 1999), 41.

83. A question that sits in the background of this book is: Does constructing a democratic state on the terrain of the political run the risk of turning back upon itself? Without the formal protections of liberalism— however phantasmatic they may be—is there any means of preventing the modern demos from descending into a permanent state of exception? It is an argument of this investigation that such characterizations of the potential danger of the modern democratic state rest on an insufficiently historical rendering of democratic rule. This book attempts to open a new path by exploring a historical, nonformalist account of the democratic state that consistently confronted the problem of exceptional powers inherent in democracy. For an elaboration of this historical approach, see William J. Novak, Stephen W. Sawyer, James T. Sparrow, "Democratic States of Unexception: Toward a New Genealogy of the American Political," in *The Many Hands of the State*, ed. Ann Orloff and Kimberly Morgan (Cambridge: Cambridge University Press, 2017).

Chapter One

1. Alexis de Tocqueville, "Rapport à l'Académie des sciences morales et politiques sur le cours administratif de M. Macarel," *Oeuvres complètes d'Alexis de Tocqueville, vol. IX, Études économiques, politiques et littéraires* (Paris: Michel Lévy, 1866), 60–75.

2. John Stuart Mill, "De Tocqueville on Democracy in America," in *Collected Works of John Stuart Mill*, vol. 188, ed. J. M. Robson (Toronto: University of Toronto Press, 1970), 156.

3. *Tocqueville between Two Worlds: The Making of a Political and Theoretical Life* (Princeton, NJ: Princeton University Press, 2001), 8.

4. Françoise Mélonio, *Tocqueville et les français* (Paris: Aubier, 1993); Audier, *Tocqueville retrouvé*.

5. Raymond Aron, *Main Currents in Sociological Thought: Montesquieu, Comte, Marx, Tocqueville, the sociologists and the Revolution of 1848* (New York: Penguin, 1990).

6. François Furet, *Penser la Révolution Française* (Paris: Gallimard), 226.

7. Wolin, *Tocqueville between Two Worlds*, 369.

8. Alan Kahan has suggested that because of his basic suspicion of democracy, Tocqueville did not have a political definition of democracy but rather understood it as "a social situation

in which everyone is presumed to be equal." Alan S. Kahan, *Aristocratic Liberalism: The Social and Political Thought of Jacob Burckhardt, John Stuart Mill, and Alexis de Tocqueville* (New York: Oxford University Press, 1992), p. 24. Lucien Jaume has specifically noted this point in his intellectual biography of Tocqueville, insisting that "we will better understand our contemporary situation by reading Tocqueville, he argues, because 'today, the rise of the power of civil society and the dissemination of identity groups have entered into competition of legitimacy with the traditional state. This force of opinion that has emerged as the great competitor with the state and its government—in short, the revenge of society on the state—is a question Tocqueville discusses incessantly.'" Lucien Jaume, *Tocqueville* (Paris: Fayard, 2008).

9. Daniel Ernst's book, *Tocqueville's Nightmare*, suggests like so many others that Tocqueville's observations in America led him to believe that "if the populace of a democratic republic like the United States ever habituated itself to centralized administration . . . 'a more insufferable despotism would prevail.'" And yet, Ernst insists, "by 1940, America . . . had acquired a great deal of centralized administration" (1). Ernst's book thus focuses on how the United States built a large central administration through a handful of lawyers who crafted administrative law and prevented it from attaining any institutional autonomy that would have prevailed otherwise. In so doing, he concludes, that what "Americans had built for themselves had confounded Tocqueville's expectations" (1). Daniel R. Ernst, *Tocqueville's Nightmare: The Administrative State Emerges in America, 1900–1940* (Oxford: Oxford University Press, 2014).

10. On the limits of these theories, see Stephen W. Sawyer, William J. Novak, and James T. Sparrow, "Beyond Stateless Democracy," *Tocqueville Review* 36, no. 2 (Spring 2015).

11. Michel, *L'idée de l'État*, 326.

12. Guido de Ruggiero, *The History of European Liberalism*, trans. R. G. Collingwood (Boston: Beacon Press, 1959 [1927]), 191.

13. Ruggiero, *The History of European Liberalism . . .* , 371.

14. Lamberti, *Tocqueville et les deux démocraties*, série Sociologie, éd. (Paris: Puf, 1983), 237.

15. Richard Swedberg, *Tocqueville's Political Economy* (Princeton, NJ: Princeton University Press, 2009), 143.

16. Alexis de Tocqueville, "Mémoire sur le paupérisme," in *Tocqueville Œuvres* (Paris : Gallimard, Pléaide, 1991), 1:1184.

17. Swedberg has noted that Tocqueville argued for "a development toward equality ('democracy') and, on the other, a development toward 'the cult of money' and a new type of inequality." (*Tocqueville's Political Economy*, 136).

18. Alexis de Tocqueville, "Influence de la démocratie sur les salaires," in *De la démocratie en Amérique II, Tocqueville Œuvres* (Paris : Gallimard, Pléaide, 1992), 2:704–5.

19. Tocqueville reiterated this point in his discussion of pauperism by arguing that "the industrial proletariat is subject to sudden crises that agriculture never encountered." (*Mémoire sur le paupérisme*, 1185).

20. Alexis de Tocqueville, "Inégalité croissante dans les institutions et dans les mœurs, a mesure qu'elle décroit dans les faits" [Esquisse du chapitre IX], *L'Ancien Régime et la Révolution*, in *Tocqueville Œuvres* (Paris: Gallimard, Pléaide, 2004), 3:420.

21. Ibid., 420–21.

22. Ibid.

23. Tocqueville also makes this point in his discussion of India. For example, poor tax policies, he argues, had also been responsible for bankrupting the indigenous landed aristocrats: the difficulty of collecting taxes from the "peasants" while it was very easy to collect the taxes from

the landed aristocrats. The only option therefore to meet the new demands was to sell off the lands that were supposed to provide the taxes in the first place. "Ce qu'il faut dire, c'est que la plus grande source du mal était dans le taux d'une taxe montant aux trois cinquièmes du revenu. Une pareille taxe (d'ailleurs mal établie et mal levée) était de telle nature que le cultivateur ne pouvait point ou du moins très difficilement acquérir un capital pour améliorer. C'était là la source première, non unique du mal. Mais on ne pouvait y toucher sans diminuer des revenus déjà insuffisants. L'établissement perpétuel ne s'est jamais étendu sur aucune portion de la présidence de Bombay" (Alexis de Tocqueville, "Dans l'Inde. Impôts. Etat de la propriété," in Tocqueville Œuvres, vol. 1 (Paris: Gallimard, Pléaide, 1991), 1058.

24. "En l'année 1776 on essaye de transformer la corvée en une taxe locale; l'inégalité se transforme aussitôt avec elle et la suit dans le nouvel impôt" ("La dégradation de la condition du paysan français," L'Ancien Régime et la Révolution, 162).

25. See, for example, Jean-Fabien Spitz, "On the Supposed Illiberalism of Republican Political Culture in France," in In Search of the Liberal Moment . . . , 111–29. For a discussion of neoliberal uses of Tocqueville's writings on social welfare, see Chad Alan Goldberg, "Social Citizenship and a Reconstructed Tocqueville," American Sociological Review 66, no. 2 (April 2001): 289–315.

26. Tocqueville, Mémoire sur le paupérisme, 1170.

27. Ibid., 1184.

28. Alexis de Tocqueville, De la démocratie en Amérique II, Tocqueville Œuvres, vol. 2 (Paris : Gallimard, Pléaide, 1992), 824.

29. Ibid., 77.

30. "Je ne connais point d'ami de la démocratie qui ait encore osé faire ressortir d'une manière aussi nette et aussi claire la distinction capitale entre délégation et représentation, ni qui ait mieux fixé le sens politique de ces deux mots . . . Il s'agit bien moins pour les partisans de la démocratie de trouver les moyens de faire gouverner le peuple, que de faire choisir au peuple les plus capables de gouverner, et de lui donner sur ceux-là un empire assez grand pour qu'il puisse diriger l'ensemble de leur conduite, et non le détail des actes ni les moyens d'exécution," Tocqueville, Oeuvres, 6:53.

31. Alexis de Tocqueville, L'Ancien Régime et la Révolution (Paris: Les Éditions Gallimard nrf, 1952 [1856]), 9.

32. These are translations of the terms "État social" and "Constitution politique."

33. L'Ancien Régime, 104 [trans., Alan S. Kahan, 138].

34. Ibid., 107 [trans., Alan S. Kahan, 141].

35. "Il me le fallait contemporain, et qui me fournît le moyen de mêler les faits aux idées, la philosophie de l'histoire à l'histoire même. Ce sont pour moi les conditions du problème. " L'Ancien Régime et la Révolution, 8.

36. L'Ancien Régime . . . [Pléaide], 246 [trans., Alan S. Kahan, 259].

37. Ibid., 45–46 [trans., Alan S. Kahan, 85].

38. Ibid., 101.

39. Ibid., 81.

40. Ibid., 218.

41. Ibid., 93.

42. "It seems difficult to say today precisely how cities were governed in the eighteenth century. For independently of the constant changes in municipal powers, as we just explained, each city conserved a few elements of its old constitution and customs." Ibid., 89.

43. Ibid., 88.

44. Ibid., 93.

45. *De la démocratie* . . . [Pleiade], 80.

46. Ibid., 79n.

47. *Mémoire sur le paupérisme*, 1178.

48. Michel Foucault, *Security, Territory, Population. Courses at the Collège de France*, 1977–78 (New York: Palgrave, 2009); Vincent Milliot, ed., *Les mémoires policiers: Écritures et pratiques policières du Siècle des Lumières au Second Empire, 1750–1850* (Rennes: PUR, 2006); Paolo Napoli, *Naissance de la police moderne: Pouvoir, normes, société* (Paris: La Découverte, 2003); William Novak, *The People's Welfare: Law and Regulation in Nineteenth-Century America* (Chapel Hill: University of North Carolina Press, 1996); Gary Gerstle, *Liberty and Coercion: The Paradox of American Government from the Founding to the Present* (Princeton, NJ: Princeton University Press, 2015).

49. Michel Foucault, *Security, Territory, Population. Courses at the Collège de France*, 1977–78 (New York: Palgrave, 2009), 320–22.

50. Paolo Napoli makes a similar argument: "A la fin du XVIIIe siècle, l'administration rationalise et unifie des pratiques de police jusqu'alors *dispersées*, favorisant ainsi le déplacement de la rationalité juridique d'un modèle casuistique à un régime classificatoire, de la solution des problèmes à l'étude de principes." (Paolo Napoli, *Naissance de la police moderne: Pouvoir, normes, société* (Paris: La Découverte, 2003), 181.

51. *L'Ancien Régime* . . . [Pléiade], 86.

52. Ibid., 86.

53. "Ce qu'elle saisit avant tout, c'est un ensemble de besoins primaires indispensables à la vie d'une communauté" (Napoli, *Naissance de la police* . . . , 23).

54. On Vacherot as an intellectual founder of the Third Republic, see Sudhir Hazareesingh, *Intellectual Founders of the Republic: Five Studies in Nineteenth-Century French Political Thought* (Oxford: Oxford University Press, 2001).

55. Etienne Vacherot, *La Démocratie* (Bruxelles: Lacroix, 1860), 294.

56. Maurice Block, *Dictionnaire de l'administration française* (Paris: Berger-Levrault, 1877–85), 17.

57. Ibid., 1305.

58. Ibid., 1306.

59. *L'Ancien Régime* . . . [Pléiade], 75.

60. Ibid., 71.

61. Ibid., 248.

62. Ibid., 247–48.

63. Ibid., 247–48.

64. Ibid., 251 [trans., Alan S. Kahan, 264].

65. Ibid., 251.

66. Ibid., 87.

67. William Novak, *The People's Welfare: Law and Regulation in Nineteenth-Century America* (Chapel Hill: University of North Carolina Press, 1996), 13. Building on Novak's work on police powers, Gary Gerstle has also argued for the importance of police powers on the state level as opposed to the scale of the federal government, Gary Gerstle, *Liberty and Coercion: The Paradox of American Government from the Founding to the Present* (Princeton, NJ: Princeton University Press, 2015).

68. *De la démocratie* . . . [Pléiade], 40.

69. Ibid., 45.

70. *L'Ancien Régime* . . . [Pléiade], 93.

71. "What hinders me the most, I admit, from understanding these different points in America is that I know almost nothing about what exists in France. You know that, in our country, administrative law and civil law form two distinct worlds that do not always peacefully co-exist, but which are neither friendly nor different enough to know each other well. I have always lived with one in complete ignorance of the other." Letter from the United States to Vicomte Ernest de Blosseville, October 10, 1831, *Nouvelle correspondance entièrement inédite d'Alexis de Tocqueville*, 66–68.

72. Letter from the United States to Vicomte Ernest de Blosseville, October 10, 1831, *Nouvelle correspondance entièrement inédite d'Alexis de Tocqueville*, 66–68.

73. *Rapport sur Macarel* . . . , 71–72.

74. *L'Ancien Régime* . . . [Pléiade], 81.

75. Ibid., 81.

76. Ibid., 76.

77. In his work on the police powers of the old regime, Paolo Napoli has argued that it was precisely as an ill-defined, pragmatic technology that police powers operated in the old regime: "the police was above all a pragmatic notion. Its approach confronted a reality that escaped any attempt to establish a predetermined form" (Napoli, *Naissance de la police moderne*, 58).

78. *L'Ancien Régime* . . . [Pléiade], 81.

79. Ibid., 280.

80. Ibid., 150. In a similar fashion, the local parliaments defended their interests through an active interpretation of the law. "Les parlements étaient sans doute plus préoccupés d'eux-mêmes que de la chose publique; mais il faut reconnaître que, dans la défense de leur propre indépendance et de leur honneur, ils se montraient toujours intrépides, et qu'ils communiquaient leur âme à tout ce qui les approchait." While Tocqueville had no illusions about the parliament's motivations, he was interested in how they used their old juridical power to resist the absolutist administration. In this sense, Tocqueville did not argue that the parliaments or former local authorities were hiding behind law; there was not some neutral legal defense that provided a protection from the absolutist state in this account. Rather, a specific form of legal practice became a place from which they could defend themselves against a new mode of administrative justice. "L'intervention irrégulière des cours dans le gouvernement, qui troublait souvent la bonne administration des affaires, servait ainsi parfois de sauvegarde à la liberté des hommes: c'est un grand mal qui limitait un plus grand" (ibid., 150).

81. Ibid., 150.

82. Ibid., 76.

83. Ibid., 97–98.

84. Ibid., 98.

85. Ibid., 97.

86. Ibid., 97.

87. Here too Hayek's reading of Tocqueville is deeply problematic when he writes: "The one thing which the Revolution did not touch and which, as Tocqueville has so well shown, survived all the vicissitudes of the following decades was the power of the administrative authorities" (*Constitution of Liberty*, 195).

88. "Révolution française, qui a introduit tant de nouveautés dans le monde, n'a rien créé de plus nouveau que cette partie de notre droit politique qui se rapporte à l'administration

proprement dite. La, rien ne ressemble à ce qui a précèdé; presque tout est de date récente: les fonctions aussi bien que les fonctionnaires, les obligations comme les garanties" (*Rapport sur Macarel...*).

89. "Quand on étudie l'histoire de notre Révolution, on voit ... [le] même mépris pour des faits existants; même confiance dans la théorie" (*L'Ancien Régime* ... [Pléiade], 177).

90. *Rapport sur Macarel* ..., 85.

91. *L'Ancien Régime* ... [Pléiade], 99.

92. "Une autre sorte de justice ordinaire devant laquelle doivent se vider tous les procès dans lesquels l'Etat est intéressé; celle-ci rendue par l'administration elle-même. . . . Ce sont la, messieurs, j'ose le dire, des axiomes de droit qu'aucun peuple libre, et j'ajouterai qu'aucun peuple civilisé n'admettra jamais dans la forme générale et absolue (*Rapport sur Macarel* ..., 67).

93. Ibid., 63.

94. Ibid., 63.

95. Ibid., 74.

96. J. S. Mill, *The Collected Works of John Stuart Mill, Volume I—Autobiography and Literary Essays*, ed. John M. Robson and Jack Stillinger, introduction by Lord Robbins (Toronto: University of Toronto Press; London: Routledge & Kegan Paul, 1981), 203.

97. Ibid., 204.

98. John Stuart Mill, *The Collected Works of John Stuart Mill*, Vol. XVIII - *Essays on Politics and Society Part I*, ed. John M. Robson, intro. Alexander Brady (Toronto: University of Toronto Press; London: Routledge & Kegan Paul, 1977). June 10, 2017. http://oll.libertyfund.org/titles/233 #Mill_0223-18_779

99. Edouard Laboulaye, *De l'enseignement du droit en France et des réformes dont il a besoin* (Paris: Durand, 1839), 589.

100. Mill, *Collected Works*, Vol. XVIII - *Essays on Politics and Society Part I*, http://oll.liberty fund.org/titles/233#Mill_0223-18_779

Chapter Two

1. Lucien-Anatole Prévost-Paradol, *La France nouvelle* (Paris: Lévy Frères, 1868), 296. [Hereafter *LFN*.]

2. "La démocratie s'impose presque partout comme un fait inévitable." Joseph Barthelemy et Paul Duez, *Traité de Droit Constitutionnel: Les rapports entre le Parlement et le Gouvernement* (Lille: Cogery, 1933), 60.

3. Alexis de Tocqueville, [Définition de la démocratie], "Écrits et Discours Politiques," *Oeuvres* vol. 3 (Paris: Gallimard, 1990), 196.

4. As one of his closest friends wrote after his death: "For Prévost-Paradol, as for Tocqueville, democracy was the inevitable and legitimate state of the modern world" (Octave Gréard, *Prévost-Paradol. Étude suivi d'un choix de lettres* (Paris : Hachette, 1894), 75).

5. The family included the musicians Fromental Halévy and Georges Bizet; a disciple of Saint Simon, Lucien Anatole's father, Léon Halévy; the librettist of *Carmen* and operettas by Offenbach; a model for Proust's Duchesse de Guermantes, Geneviève Halévy; and two prominent intellectuals of the early twentieth century, Daniel Halévy and Élie Halévy, who directly influenced Raymond Aron and later François Furet. (See Jacques Julliard, "Élie Halévy, le témoin engage," *Mil Neuf Cent* [1999] 17, no. 1: 27–44, here 27–28.)

6. Even Walter Bagehot in England praised Prévost-Paradol's work: "Lorsque M. Prévost-Paradol parle de l'Angleterre, ce qu'il en dit est toujours parfaitement exact" (*La Constitution Anglaise* [Paris: Baillière, 1869], 11). On this relationship, see Pierre-Xavier Boyer, *Angleterre et Amérique dans l'histoire institutionnelle française. Le poids des exemples anglais et américain dans la réflexion française 1789-1958* (Paris: CNRS, 2012).

7. Prévost-Paradol has been read almost entirely for his liberalism. There is no doubt that, like Tocqueville, he fits squarely within the European liberal tradition. However, like Tocqueville, his major book, *La France nouvelle*, is decidedly focused on democracy. What follows explicitly looks at his exploration of the democratic and its legacy for the foundation of a republic in France.

8. "The potential establishment of the Republic and its adjustment to the conditions at hand was studied," noted Esmein, in "*La France Nouvelle* by Prévost-Paradol which appeared in 1868." Adhémar Esmein, *Éléments de droit constitutionnel français et comparé* (Paris: Larose et Tenin, 1909), 566-67. "Nous aurons l'occasion de constater maintes fois, chemin faisant, la concordance qui existe entre les solutions adoptées par les lois constitutionnelles de 1875 et celles proposées dans les *Vues sur le Gouvernement de la France* ou dans *La France nouvelle.*"

9. "It was the Duc de Broglie and Prévost-Paradol, whose profound influence on the Constituents of 1875 I have showed. Both wanted in the Republic that they imagined to introduce a system of two Chambers; both also wanted an elected Senate. . . . Prévost-Paradol was even clearer. He was among those who, as we know, wanted to be the most precise about reinforcing the authority of the Chamber and the deputies of the Cabinet. He wanted it to be able to vote directly on the maintenance or confirmation of a minister. He wanted them to elect the President of the Council. But he refused any such right to the Senate that he did not want to intervene in any way in these questions." Esmein, *Éléments de droit constitutionnel . . .* , 567.

10. Joseph Barthélemy et Paul Duez, *Traité de Droit Constitutionnel*, 46.

11. Schmitt writes: "Who still remembers the time when Prévost-Paradol saw the value of parliamentarism over the 'personal regime' of Napoléon III in that through the transfer of real power it forced the true holders of power to reveal themselves, so that government, as a result of this, always represents the strongest power in a 'wonderful' coordination of appearance and reality? Who still believes in this kind of openness? And in parliament as its greatest 'platform'?" (*The Crisis of Parliamentary Democracy*, Ellen Kennedy, trans. (MIT Press, 1988), 7).

12. "Beyond a few technical divergencs, the imprint of *La France nouvelle* on the electoral modalities of the Senate in 1875 is undeniable." Jean-Éric Gicquel, "Les idées constitutionnelles de Prévost-Paradol," *La Revue administrative*, 53/316 (Juillet-Aout 2000), 395-407, 400.

13. "Bref, la vision de Prévost-Paradol a été déterminante et a plus fortement influencé le texte final que les idées défendues par Victor de Broglie, par Dufaure-Thiers dans leur projet du 19 mai 1873 et par Albert de Broglie avec son 'Grand conseil du 15 mai 1874'. En mettant sur pied des restrictions spécifiques touchant soit l'électorat, soit l'éligibilité, il s'agissait surtout de rompre avec la dynamique du suffrage universel même indirect et de s'opposer ainsi, sans détours, au 'principe brutal et démagogique de la souveraineté pure et absolue du nombre.' Nul doute qu'avec de tels obstacles, la reconquête du Sénat par les républicains, des le 5 janvier 1879, date capitale dans l'histoire de la République, eut été difficilement envisageable." Gicquel, "Les idées," p. 400.

14. Richard Tuck, *The Sleeping Sovereign: The Invention of Modern Democracy* (Cambridge: Cambridge University Press, 2015).

15. Prévost-Paradol was certainly not alone in posing this question anew. In France, others including his professor at the ENS, Etienne Vacherot, tackled the question directly in his "La

Démocratie." As we saw in the previous chapter, outside France, J. S. Mill's *Considerations on Representative Government* was also part of a new interest in this question.

16. "Même si son nom n'apparaît guère lors des travaux préparatoires et débats parlementaires, Prévost-Paradol est un des pères fondateurs de la IIIe République et les constituants ne cessèrent jamais de s'inspirer directement de l'esprit de *La France nouvelle* pour y puiser leurs idées politiques et institutionnelles." Jean-Éric Gicquel, "Les idées constitutionnelles de Prévost-Paradol," *La Revue administrative*, 53/316 (Juillet-Aout 2000), 395–407, 401.

17. M.A. Granier de Cassagnac, *L'Empereur et la démocratie moderne* (Paris: Dentu, 1860), 31.

18. Eugène Rouher, "Discours par S. Exc. Rouher ministre d'Etat dans la séance du Corps législatif du 11 janvier 1864," 7.

19. Napoléon III, *Des idées napoléoniennes* (Paris: Paulin, Paris, 1839), 52–53.

20. Granier de Cassagnac, *La révision de la Constitution (Paris: Plon, s.d.)*, 24.

21. Édouard Boinvilliers, *Catéchisme impérial* (Paris: Lachaud, 1874 [2nd ed]), 22.

22. Ibid., 22–23.

23. On the treaty and the debates around it, see David Todd, *L'identité économique de la France* (Paris: Grasset, 2008); see also Jean Walch, *Michel Chevalier: Économiste, Saint-Simonien, 1806–1879* (Paris: Vrin, 1975).

24. Lettre de M. Chevalier à Bonamy Price, "Historique de la négociation du traite de commerce entre la France et l'Angleterre," *Journal des économistes*, février 1869.

25. "Le problème théorique et pratique qui préoccupe les libéraux, c'est la démocratie. Comme nous l'avons vu dans le chapitre V, la démocratie devient le fondement du régime impérial. Pourtant les libéraux ne peuvent pas refuser la démocratie qui devient une institution solide par plusieurs fois d'exercice du suffrage universel. La solution de Guizot était, sous la Monarchie de Juillet, le libéralisme par le refus de la démocratie, et l'Empire est la démocratie contre le libéralisme. Par contre, le poids du réel demande aux libéraux d'accepter la démocratie" (Tai-Young Hong, *Les fondements libéraux de la IIIe République*. Thèse de doctorat, EHESS, 3 février 2001), 363–64).

26. *LFN*, 3–4.

27. *Ibid.*, 34.

28. "The people who apply it to such varied political situations confuse two very distinct things: society and government." Ibid., 6.

29. Ibid., 23.

30. In this sense, his work on democracy, like that of many of the thinkers in this period discussed in this book, departs from the approach outlined in Tuck's *Sleeping Sovereign*.

31. Speech of January 22, 1822, to the Chamber of Deputies, *Archives parlementaires*, 2nd series, vol. 34, 133.

32. Noting Prévost-Paradol's deeply shared sympathies with Tocqueville, his friend Octave Gréard recounted Prévost-Paradol's comment upon their reading his correspondence: "I too, must have said that. . . . In truth we must have had some kind of intimate discussion about that in another world" [Octave Gréard, *Prévost-Paradol. Étude suivi d'un choix de lettres* (Paris: Hachette, 1894), 75].

33. *LFN*, 22.

34. Gréard, *Prévost-Paradol . . .*, 86.

35. Vincent Duclert, "La pensée de Spinoza et la naissance de l'intellectuel démocratique dans la France du tournant du siècle," *Archives Juives* 36, no. 2 (2003): 20–42.

36. Pierre-François Moreau, "Spinoza's Reception and Influence," in *The Cambridge Companion to Spinoza*, ed. Don Garrett (Cambridge: Cambridge University Press, 1995), 422–23.

37. On the importance of Spinoza for the rebirth of western European democratic thought, see Jonathan Israel, *Radical Enlightenment: Philosophy and the Making of Modernity, 1650–1750* (Oxford: Oxford University Press, 2002). We do not yet have a good history of the return of Spinoza within democratic thought in the wake of 1848.

38. In a letter to Taine, he wrote: "You are my philosophical heart [sens]; you digested the Spinoza that I read and have given it back to me through every pore" (Gréard, *Prévost-Paradol* . . . , 196).

39. Victor Delbos, *Le problème moral dans la philosophie de Spinoza et dans l'histoire du Spinozisme* (Paris: Alcan, 1893), 516.

40. *LFN*, 81.

41. On the lack of a theory of ministerial responsibility in early nineteenth-century France, see Antonio Vazquez-Arroyo, *Political Responsibility: Responding to Predicaments of Power* (New York: Columbia University Press, 2016), chap. 2, "Responsibility in History"; Mary S. Hartman, "Benjamin Constant and the Question of Ministerial Responsibility in France, 1814–1815," *Journal of European Studies* 6 (1976): 248–61; Lucien Jaume, "Le concept de 'responsabilité des ministres' chez Benjamin Constant," *Revue française de droit constitutionnel* 42 (2000): 227–43; and Pierre Rosanvallon, *Le bon gouvernement* (Paris: Seuil, 2015), 182–84.

42. *LFN*, 121.

43. Ibid., 123.

44. Ibid., 124.

45. Ibid., 125.

46. *LFN*, 144.

47. Quoted in Pierre Guiral, *Prévost-Paradol (1829–1870). Pensée et action d'un libéral sous le Second Empire* (Paris: PUF, 1955), 519.

48. Lucien-Anatole Prévost-Paradol, *Quelques pages d'histoire contemporaine*, vol. 3 (Paris: Michel-Lévy frères, 1862–67), 183–84.

49. "Les charges que l'Etat impose aux chemins de fer français ne sont rien à cote de la protection éclairée qu'il leur a dès le début accordée en les préservant de ces concurrences et de ces exactions qui sont le fléau des Compagnies anglaises. L'établissements incessant de lignes rivales, la présence de double stations dans la plupart des grandes villes, la nécessité de soutenir des luttes ruineuses ou de les prévenir en achetant le désistement de ses adversaires, telles sont les causes principales qui empêchent la prospérité des chemins de fer anglais, et, selon le témoignage des hommes les plus compétents, elles agissent avec assez d'énergie pour décourager les capitaux et pour les détourner de cette grande industrie" (*Journal des Débats*, 27 mars 1858).

50. Ibid., 27 mars 1858.

51. Ibid., 9 avril 1861.

52. Ibid., 9 avril 1861.

53. Ibid., 9 avril 1861.

54. Ibid., 28 juillet 1869.

55. Ibid., 28 juin 1861.

56. Ibid., 21 décembre 1860.

57. Michael Mann, *Sources of Social Power, vol. 2: The Rise of Classes and Nation States, 1760–1914* (Cambridge: Cambridge University Press, 1993).

58. Ira Katznelson, "Flexible Capacity: The Military and Early American Statebuilding," in Ira Katznelson and Martin Shefter, eds., *Shaped by War and Trade: International Influences on American Political Development* (Princeton, NJ: Princeton University Press, 2002), 85.

59. John Hobson, *The Wealth of States: A Comparative Sociology of International Economic and Political Change* (Cambridge: Cambridge University Press, 1997), 207.

60. *LFN*, 40.

61. Ibid., 41.

62. *Journal des Débats*, 3 juillet 1858.

63. Ibid.

64. Ibid.

65. Ibid., 21 février 1862.

66. Ibid., 3 juillet 1858.

67. *Quelques pages d'histoire . . .* , vol. 3, 325–26.

68. *LFN*, 418.

69. *Quelques pages d'histoire . . .* , vol. 3, 328–29.

70. Ibid., 349.

71. Ibid., 352.

72. Ibid., 352–53.

73. Ibid., 352.

74. Ibid., 352–53.

75. Esmein, *Éléments de droit constitutionnel . . .* , 566.

76. Joseph Barthelemy et Paul Duez, *Traité de Droit Constitutionnel: Les Rapports Entre le Parlement et le Gouvernment* (Lille: Cogery, 1933), 47.

77. *LFN*, 129–30.

78. Ibid., vii-viii.

79. *Journal des Débats*, 21 décembre 1860. Paradol made this argument again and again. It may even be considered one of the most consistent aspects of his thinking. See, for example: "Quoi de plus étranger à l'esprit de parti? quoi de plus accommodant, disons mieux, de plus respectueux pour le pouvoir que de mettre tout d'abord la forme et le nom du gouvernement en dehors de ces recherches, que de les concentrer sur les institutions fondamentales qui peuvent également convenir à toutes les formes du gouvernement libre, et que de reprendre l'étude de la société politique à sa base?" (ibid., 9 avril 1861).

80. Pierre Rosanvallon has highlighted this important distinction in his book, diagnosing one of the maladies of our contemporary democracies in his *Le bon gouvernement* (Paris: Seuil, 2015). He writes: "Our regimes may be described as democratic, but we are not governed democratically. This is the tremendous gap that nourishes our present disenchantment and disarray." See the Introduction.

81. "January 2, 1870, will be among the most importante moments of our history," Paradol argued in a posthumously published letter. This was the day, he insisted, "that a new democratic government had finally been established under the same emperor without a coup d'état or revolutionary violence." "L'Empereur s'engage, de son côté, à pratiquer sincèrement le régime parlementaire, c'est à dire le gouvernement de la nation par un cabinet en accord avec la majorité d'un Parlement élu, tandis que, de leur cote, les amis de ce régime acceptent sans arrière pensée l'Empereur comme le chef de ce gouvernement, et sacrifient au bien public les ressentiments et les défiances qu'avaient suscités sa façon de s'emparer du pouvoir et l'usage qu'il en avait fait jusqu'à ce jour" *Lettres Posthumes de Prévost-Paradol* (Bruxelles: Lebegue), 43–44.

82. *Discours d'Adolphe Thiers*, Vol. XIII, p. 10.

83. Séance du 15 mai 1874 *Journal officiel* du 16 mai 1874, p 3286 . . . It is a principle that is not necessarily "en propre ni à la monarchie, ni à la republique. Toutes les republiques du nouveau monde ont deux assemblées, aussi bien que toutes les monarchies constitutionnelles de l'ancien" (ibid., 3268).

Chapter Three

1. Edouard Laboulaye, "Les États Unis" in *Études Morales et Politiques* (Paris: Charpentier, 1862), 153.

2. Edouard Laboulaye, "Préface," in *Le droit internationale codifié* by Johann Caspar Bluntschli (Paris: Guillaumin, 1870), vi.

3. On Laboulaye see in particular André Dauteribes, *Les idées politiques d'Édouard Laboulaye (1811-1883)* (Thèse de doctorat, Université de Montpellier, 1989); Walter Dennis Gray, *Interpreting American Democracy in France* (Associated University Press, 1994); and "Liberalism in the Second Empire and the Influence of America: Edouard Laboulaye and His Circle" in *Liberty/ Liberté, The French and American Experiences* (Washington: W. Wilson Center, 1991), 71-85. See also Vida Azimi, "Edouard Laboulaye: Vues sur l'Administration," *La Revue administrative* 47, no. 281 (1994): 521-27; Émile Boutmy, *Taine, Schere, Laboulaye* (Paris: Colin, 1901); Marc Lahmer, *La Constitution américaine dans le débat français: 1795-1848* (Paris: L'Harmattan, 2001), 367-79; Jean-Claude Lamberti, "Laboulaye and the Common Law of Free Peoples," in *Liberty, The French American Statue in Art and History* (New York: Harper & Row, 1986), 20-25; Pierre Legendre, "Méditation sur l'esprit libéral, la leçon d'Édouard de Laboulaye, juriste-témoin," *Revue de droit public* (1971); Eugène de Rozière, "Bibliographie des oeuvres de M. Ed. Laboulaye," *Nouvelle revue historique de droit français et étranger* 12 (1888): 771-821; Jean de Soto, "Edouard Laboulaye," *Revue internationale d'histoire politique et constitutionelle* 5 (1955): 114-50; Maike Thier, "In the Shadow of Tocqueville: French Liberals and the American 'Model Republic'," (paper presented at the *UCL Commonwealth Colloquium: Transatlantic Liberalism*, February 20, 2009); Henri Wallon, *Notice sur la vie et les travaux de M. Edouard Laboulaye* (Paris: Larose et Forcel, 1889).

4. Laboulaye, *Le parti libéral* . . . [6th ed., 1863], xi.

5. This emphasis on a powerful executive is not necessarily more evidence of the Bonapartist influence on French liberals in founding the Third Republic: the bulk of the intellectual contributions of this cohort were developed while they stood in opposition to the Second Empire until its last gasp in the "liberal empire" of 1870. Sudhir Hazareesingh has analyzed how Bonapartism established some of the key tenets of French Republicanism. However, he focuses primarily on the "paradox" that a dictatorship took democracy seriously especially in the sphere of decentralization ["Bonapartism as the Progenitor of Democracy: the Paradoxical Case of the French Second Empire," in Peter Bachr and Melvin Richter, eds., *Dictatorship in History and Theory: Bonapartism, Daesarism, and Totalitarianism* (Cambridge: Cambridge University Press, 2004)].

6. On the history of the executive power in France, see Paolo Colombo, "La question du pouvoir exécutif dans l'évolution institutionnelle et le débat politique révolutionnaire," *Annales Historique de la Revolution française*, 319 (mars 2000); François Furet, *Revolutionary France, 1770-1880*, Antonia Nevill, trans. (Oxford: Wiley Blackwell, 1995); Jean-Philippe Feldman, "Le constitutionalisme selon Benjamin Constant," *Revue Française de Droit Constitutionel* 76 (2008);

675–702; Bernard Gilson, *La découverte du régime présidentiel* (Paris: Librairie générale de droit et de jurisprudence, 1968); Lucien Jaume, "Tocqueville et le problème du pouvoir exécutif en 1848," *Revue française de science politique* 41, no. 6 (1991): 739–55; Jean-Paul Valette, *Le pouvoir exécutif en France de 1789 à nos jours* (Paris: Ellipses, 1999); Gordon Wright, *Raymond Poincaré and the French Presidency* (Palo Alto, CA: Stanford University Press, 1942).

7. Brown has highlighted the importance of a theory of exceptional circumstances for understanding the liberal political context of the Directory and its legacy for political liberalism into the nineteenth century. I would like to argue that Laboulaye, through his reading of Lincoln, attempted to respond to precisely this question in the context of the Second Empire as Napoleon III's illiberal democracy was increasingly perceived as bankrupt.

8. Laboulaye was already well integrated into powerful intellectual circles, having been sent by Victor Cousin to inspect schools throughout Germany in 1840. See Gray, *Interpreting American Democracy* . . . , 41.

9. Laboulaye's early writings were well received, having won prizes from the French academy. His three principal early works were *Histoire du droit et de propriété foncière en Occident* (1839); *Essai sur la vie et les doctrines de Savigny* (1842); *Recherches sur la condition civiles et politique des femmes depuis les Romains jusqu'à nos jours* (1843).

10. Ibid., 161.

11. Alexis de Tocqueville, *De la démocratie en Amérique* (Paris: Gallimard (folio), 1986), 199.

12. Ibid., 197.

13. Laboulaye, *L'Etat et ses limites* (Paris: Charpentier, 1865), 174.

14. Ibid., 195.

15. Ibid., 173.

16. Ibid., 171–73.

17. Ibid., 158.

18. On the role of Tocqueville and the executive in 1848 see Lucien Jaume, "Tocqueville et le problème du pouvoir exécutif en 1848."

19. Meetings of May 25–27, 1848, on the drafting of the Constitution. Reprinted in Aurelian Craiutu and Jeremy Jennings, *Tocqueville on America after 1840: Letters and Other Writings* (Cambridge: Cambridge University Press, 2009), 392.

20. Ibid., 392.

21. Alexis de Tocqueville, *Recollections*, 200.

22. It should be noted that this shift was not limited to Laboulaye. Tocqueville himself seems to have shifted his position after 1848. His correspondence during this period also looked toward increasingly different issues: "The tone and content of the letters written and received by Tocqueville from 1852 to the end of his life are strikingly different from those of his previous correspondence with the Americans. New themes appeared, such as immigration and economic crises, whereas older themes such as slavery gained new prominence during this period" (Craiutu and Jennings, *Tocqueville on America* . . . , 45). I would argue that this change in Tocqueville's writings was part of a broader shift in French liberalism after 1848 as it set out to cope with the increasingly new power wielded by the modern state.

23. Laboulaye, *L'Etat et ses limites*, 151.

24. Ibid., 186–87.

25. Ibid., 81.

26. Henry Michel, *L'idée de l'Etat* (Paris : Fayard, 2003 [1898]), 362.

27. On Laboulaye's relationship to Tocqueville's use of the United States in the 1850s and 1860s, see Grégoire Bigot, *L'Administration française: Politique, droit et société, 1789–1870*, vol. 1 (Paris: Litec, 2010), 234–41.

28. It is worth noting, as Frederick A. de Luna points out, that Cavaignac also made a strong impression on other liberals like Tocqueville and Rémusat. However, Tocqueville remained very skeptical of a strong executive power in spite of this positive impression (*The French Republic under Cavaignac 1848* [Princeton, NJ: Princeton University Press, 1969]).

29. Laboulaye, *Considérations sur la Constitution* (1848), 7.

30. Ibid., 7.

31. Ibid., 53.

32. *Questions Constitutionelles* (1872), 316.

33. Ibid., 68.

34. *De la Constitution Américaine* (1849), 21–22.

35. *Considérations sur la Constitution*, in *Questions Constitutionelles*, v.

36. Ibid., 41.

37. Ibid., 69.

38. On Tocqueville in Algeria, see Margaret Kohn, "Empire's Law: Alexis De Tocqueville on Colonialism and the State of Exception," *Canadian Journal of Political Science/Revue canadienne de science politique* 41, no. 2 (2008): 255–78; Jennifer Pitts, *A Turn to Empire: The Rise of Imperial Liberalism in Britain and France* (Princeton, NJ: Princeton University Press, 2005); and Alexis de Tocqueville, *Writings on Empire and Slavery*, ed. Jennifer Pitts (Baltimore: Johns Hopkins University Press, 2001); Melvin Richter, "Tocqueville on Algeria," *Review of Politics* 25 (1963): 362–98; Tzvetan Todorov, *De la colonie en Algérie* (Éditions Complexe, 1988).

39. Tocqueville, *Writings on Empire and Slavery*, 109.

40. On the question of martial law, Kohn writes: "despite the obvious need for a strong military presence, Tocqueville concluded that governing the French colonists in Algeria through martial law was not a viable long-term strategy because it was antithetical to French tradition." ("Empire's Law . . . ," 265).

41. Laboulaye's liberal theory of empire has not been discussed nor has its relationship to his analysis of the United States. On Tocqueville's analysis of American slavery and the Amerindians and Algeria, see Tocqueville, *Writings on Empire and Slavery*.

42. Edouard Laboulaye, *Histoire politique des Etats-Unis depuis les premiers essais de colonisation jusqu'à l'adoption de la constitution fédérale, 1620–1789* (Paris: Guillaumin, 1855).

43. As Augustin Bernard wrote in 1930, "Having completely pacified Algeria [by 1857], the war now over, the Governor General was left principally with the question of administration and colonization; his functions as chief general were increasingly second to those of director of the colony. It was either necessary to increase his civil capacities and make them more precise or put an end to the general form of government and concentrate all administration in Paris." Augustin Bernard, *L'Algérie*, in *Histoire des Colonies Françaises et de l'expansion de la France dans le monde*, ed. Gabriel Hanotaux and Alfred Martineau, vol. 2 (Paris: 1930), 325.on the importance of 1848 in the French colonization of Algeria, see Jennifer Sessions, *By Sword and Plow: France and the Conquest of Algeria* (Ithaca, NY: Cornell University Press, 2011).

44. Todorov, *De la colonie . . .* , 19.

45. Laboulaye, *Le parti libéral*, xi [6th ed].

46. Laboulaye, *Histoire des Etats-Unis*, vol. 1 [2nd ed.], 45–46.

47. On the friendship between Laboulaye, Bluntschli, and Lieber, an early biographer of Lieber wrote: "It was in 1860 that Lieber entered into relations with Bluntschli and Laboulaye, and bound himself to them in a close friendship; they were liberal, too; they also wanted to see progress. He used to like to say 'that he had formed with these illustrious publicists a "scientific clover-leaf" representing the international character of Anglo-American, German and French civilization'" (Ernest Nys, "Francis Lieber—His Life and His Work II," *American Journal of International Law* 5, no. 2 [1911]: 355).

48. Johann Kaspar Bluntschli, *Le droit international codifié* (précédé d'une preface par Édouard Laboulaye), trans. M. C. Lardy (Paris: Guillaumin, 1870). The importance of Lieber's code has been highlighted by John Witt. However, he does not discuss the extent to which the friendship between Lieber, Laboulaye, and Bluntschli was important for its development: "The code quickly spread around the world. European international lawyers translated it almost immediately into French, German and Spanish. . . . Traces of the code are visible in the Geneva Conventions of 1949 and the United States Army Field Manual on the Law of Land Warfare" (John Witt, "Lincoln's Code," Duffy Lecture, HLS draft, Yale University, February 21, 2011, 1–2). See also John Fabian Witt, *Lincoln's Code: The Laws of War in American History* (New York: Free Press, 2012).

49. Bluntschli, *Le droit internationale codifié*, 171.

50. See, for example, Quentin Deluermoz, *Le Crépuscule des Révolutions, 1848–1871,* 257; see also Laure Blévis, *Sociologie d'un droit colonial: Citoyenneté et nationalité en Algérie (1865–1947), une exception républicaine?* Doctoral thesis, University of Aix Marseille, 2004; and Kamel Kateb, *Européens, "indigenes" et juifs en Algérie (1830–1962)* (Paris: Ined/PUF, 2001).

51. Laboulaye, *Histoire des Etats-Unis: La Guerre de l'indépendance 1763–1782* (Paris: Charpentier, 1867 [2nd ed.]), "Première leçon, Les Causes de la Révolution," 3. This work appeared in 1866 (first edition). Such a claim is only to be comprehended within the context of the slowing of military expansion and the Second Empire's attempts to find a new model of imperial governance for the colonies.

52. This also marks a clear break from the radical distinction that historians have generally emphasized in the legal frames used to apprehend colonial versus metropolitan spaces since the Revolution. See, for example, Miranda Spieler, "The Legal Structure of Colonial Rule," *William and Mary Quarterly* 3, 66, no. 2 (April 2009): 365–408.

53. Laboulaye, "Alexis de Tocqueville," in *L'Etat et ses limites* (Paris: Charpentier, 1865 [3rd ed.]), 163.

54. Ibid., vi.

55. Ibid., vii-viii.

56. Laboulaye, *Les Etats Unis et la France* (Paris: Dentu, 1862), ix.

57. Laboulaye, *Le parti libéral* [6th ed., 1863], ix.

58. Ibid., ix.

59. Ibid., ix-x.

60. Ibid., x.

61. "Letter from MM. De Gasparin, Martin, Cochin, and Laboulaye to the Loyal Publication Society of New York," Mary L. Booth, trans. (New York: Westcott, 1866), 1. Francis Lieber was the chairman of this LPS of New York and this publication was no doubt aided by the close friendship between Lieber and Laboulaye.

62. Laboulaye, *La France et les Etats Unis*, 43. As Bernard Manin has noted, A. V. Dicey, the famous English jurist writing in 1885, offered a similar assessment of the suspension of *habeas corpus* in the English context. "Dicey," Manin writes by emphasizing to what extent the

suspension of *habeas corpus* differed from the general suspension of constitutional guarantees, "wanted to show that suspending *habeas corpus* was at least to some extent consistent with the rule of law." "The Emergency Paradigm and the New Terrorism" . . . , 12.

63. Laboulaye had a long political career and as Gray explains, he became one of the "founding fathers of the Third Republic" (*Interpreting American Democracy in France*, 114).

64. See ibid., chap. 6, "Senator for Life and the Statue of Liberty."

65. Laboulaye, *Questions constitutionnelles* (Paris: Charpentier, 1872).

66. "Souveraineté," in *Questions constitutionelles*, 413–14.

67. This emphasis on plebiscite in the Third Republic no doubt helps explain his decision to rally to Ollivier's liberal empire in what would prove to be the final moments of Napoleon III's reign. However, in a letter to John Bigelow, he noted, "I voted for the plebiscite [of 1870] and advised voting for it for two reasons . . . the second being that the plebiscite by restoring the constitutive power to the people, and by declaring that one can no longer make constitutions except by the will of the nation seemed to me in keeping with the democratic principles, such as they are understood and practiced in the United States."(Quoted in Gray, *Interpreting American Democracy* . . . , 108). It is noteworthy that while plebisciting a constitution was a Bonapartist idea, Laboulaye did not defend it as such, but rather as an approach worthy of the American political tradition.

68. *Questions constitutionelles*, 370.

69. "Souveraineté," in *Questions constitutionelles*, 416.

70. Ibid., 419.

71. Ibid., 419.

72. David Bates, "Political Unity and the Spirit of Law: Juridical Concepts of the State in the Late Third Republic," *French Historical Studies* 28, no. 1 (Winter 2005): 71.

73. "La République Constitutionelle," in *Questions constitutionnelles*, 317.

74. John Ferejohn and Pasquale Pasquino, "The Law of the Exception: A Typology of Emergency Powers," *International Journal of Constitutional Law* 2 (2004): 210–39 [here, page 7 of offprint available on Lexis-Nexis Academic].

75. "La République Constitutionelle," in *Questions constitutionnelles*, 314.

76. This interpretation of the Convention differed greatly from that of others who saw in 1793 a model for emergency powers such as Adolphe Thiers, Louis Blanc, or, later, Mirkine-Guetzévitch. On Mirkine-Guetzévitch's interwar analysis of the Convention as "a new parliamentary structure that linked the legislative and executive in a way that superseded the ineffectual division of powers," see Bates, "Political Unity . . . ," 96.

77. Laboulaye, *Le parti libérale*, XIV–XV.

78. Adhémar Esmein, *Éléments de droit constitutionnel française et comparé* (Paris: L. Larose & Forcel, 1903), 460.

79. As Gray points out, Laboulaye "considered it a personal triumph that France, in his view, incorporated a bicameral legislature with a president as chief executive in its Constitutional Laws of 1875. For Laboulaye, France, thereby, followed the American example" (*Interpreting American Democracy* . . . , 32).

80. Léon Duguit, *Manuel de droit constitutionnel: théorie générale de l'État* (Paris: Fontenoing & cie, E. de Boccard, successeur, 1918), 512.

81. Duguit, *Manuel de droit constitutionnel* . . . , 926.

82. Esmein, *Éléments de droit constitutionnel française* . . . , 554.

83. Ibid., 554.

84. On these jurists see in particular H. S. Jones, *The French State in Question: Public Law and Political Argument in the Third Republic* (Cambridge: Cambridge University Press, 2002).

85. Esmein recognized Laboulaye's influence in thinking about the separation of powers in the republican constitution throughout his discussion on the relationship between the executive and the legislative power. For example, he emphasized Laboulaye's role in inserting certain tenets of the constitutional monarchy within the republican constitution (ibid., 464 and 464 n1).

Chapter Four

1. Letter from Thiers to le Comte de Saint-Vallier Versailles, January 29, 1872 [*Correspondances: Occupation et libération du territoire, 1871–1875*, tome I (Paris: Calman-Levy, 1903), 146].

2. On Adolphe Thiers see René Albrecht-Carrié, *Adolphe Thiers, or The Triumph of the Bourgeoisie* (G. K. Hall, 1977); J. P. T. Bury and R. P. Tombs. *Thiers, 1797–1877: A Political Life* (Harper Collins, 1986); François Charles-Roux, *Thiers et Méhémet-Ali* (Plon, 1951); Robert Dreyfus, *La république de Monsieur Thiers, 1871–1873* (Gallimard, 1930) and *Monsieur Thiers contre l'empire, la guerre, la commune, 1869–1871* (B. Grasset, 1928); Didier Fischer, *L'homme Providentiel de Thiers à de Gaulle: Un Mythe Politique en République* (Editions L'Harmattan, 2009); Achille Gastaldy, *Adolphe Thiers: origine, naissance, jeunesse du premier Président de la République française : détails authentiques publiés par le chef unique de la famille paternelle de M. Thiers* (M. Dreyfus, 1878); Pierre Guiral, *Adolphe Thiers, ou, De la nécessité en politique* (Fayard, 1986); Sudhir Hazareesingh, "Napoleonic Memory in Nineteenth-Century France: The Making of a Liberal Legend," *MLN* 120, no. 4 (2005): 747–73 : Académie des Sciences, lettre et arts de Marseille, *Monsieur Thiers: d'une République à l'autre : colloque tenu à l'Académie des sciences, lettres et arts de Marseille, le 14 novembre 1997* (Publised, 1998); Alain Laquièze, "Adolphe Thiers, théoricien du régime parlementaire. Ses articles dans Le National en 1830," *Revue Française d'Histoire des Idées Politiques* 5 (1997): 59–88; Allan Mitchell, "Thiers, MacMahon, and the Conseil supérieur de la Guerre," *French Historical Studies* 6, n° 2 (October 1, 1969): 232–52; Paul de Rémusat, *Adolphe Thiers* (Hachette, 1889); Robert Tombs, "The Thiers Government and the Outbreak of Civil War in France, February-April 1871," *The Historical Journal* 23, no. 4 (December 1, 1980): 813–31.

3. Cited in "La libération du territoire, correspondence de M. Thiers 3 mai 1871 au 27 septembre 1873," *La Revue des Deux Mondes*, March 1903, 25.

4. Oddly, Agamben suggests that the state of necessity or *notstand* did not exist in French thinking on the state of exception. A careful reading of Thiers suggests that though this may have been the case in formal legal discussion, it certainly was not the case when it came to managing the everyday matters of governance. "This term," Agamben writes, "which is common in German theory (*Ausnahmezustand*, but also *Notstand*, "state of necessity"), is foreign to Italian and French theory, which prefer to speak of emergency decrees and state of siege." Agamben, *State of Exception . . .* , 4.

5. Stephen W. Sawyer, William J. Novak, James T. Sparrow, "Democratic States of Unexception: Towards a New Genealogy of the American Political," in *The Many Hands of the State*, ed. Kimberly Morgan and Ann Orloff (Cambridge: Cambridge University Press, 2017).

6. On this point, see in particular Laquièze, "Adolphe Thiers . . ."

7. Adolphe Thiers, *Discours parlementaires de M. Thiers*, ed. Marc Calmon (Paris: Calmann Lévy, 1879), IX, 104–6 (hereafter *Discours de Thiers*).

8. Alexis de Tocqueville, *De la démocratie en Amérique*, vol. 2, 107.

9. *Discours de Thiers*, 1834, 257–58.

10. *Discours de Thiers*, VIII, 546.

11. Ibid., VIII, 548–49.

12. Recent work on mutual aid societies in France suggests that Thiers's reflections on state power and associations spread far beyond the realm of ideas. For example, Christine Adams's work on "dames de charité" has revealed the key role that national and municipal authorities played in helping and funding "sociétés de bienfaisance" led by women. However, she also shows that the government's contributions to the societies often remained out of public view. Christine Adams, "In the Public Interest: Charitable Association, the State, and the Status of *utilité publique* in Nineteenth-Century France," *Law and History Review* 25 (2007): 283–321.

13. *Discours de Thiers*, VIII, 510.

14. Elisabeth Clemens, "The Encounter of Civil Society and the States: Legislation, Law and Association, 1900–1920," American Political Development Workshop, 6. Claire Lemercier has noted similar modes of state intervention in her recent work on the French state and civil society.

15. *Discours de Thiers*, II, 267–68.

16. William J. Novak, "The American Law of Association: The Legal-Political Construction of Civil Society," *Studies in American Political Development* 15 (Fall 2001): 163–88.

17. For a different reading of the Coppet group and the French state, see Lucien Jaume, *L'individu effacé ou la paradoxe du libéralisme français* (Fayard, 1998).

18. *Discours de Thiers*, II, 272–73.

19. Novak, "The American Law of Association: The Legal-Political Construction of Civil Society."

20. Quoted in Hugh Brogan, *Alexis de Tocqueville: Prophet of Democracy in the Age of Revolution* (London: Profile Books, 2009), 85. Tocqueville was not the only one to find fault in Thiers' seeming unwillingness to judge even the Convention. "Dès le début, *l'Histoire de la Révolution* a irrité parce qu'elle ne prenait pas parti et mettait sur un même pied les victimes et les bourreaux." (Guiral, 530).

21. Blanc, then, was not the first to employ "the theory of circumstances" to explain the Terror "Ainsi le critère qui met à part l'historiographie jacobine [Blanc], au XIXe siècle, n'est pas la théorie des circonstances, sous-produit de celle de la nécéssité, puisque les Jacobins l'ont en commun avec les libéraux. Ce qui la caracterise est de mettre 1793 au centre de la Révolution comme le vrai patrimoine du peuple. Il s'agit d'arracher à la bourgeoisie ses titres à l'héritage révolutionnaire, qu'elle a irrémédiablement renié par le tour de passe-passe de juillet-aout 1830." François Furet, *La gauche et la révolution francaise au milieu du XIXe siècle: Edgar Quinet et la question du Jacobinisme . . .* , 16–17.

22. See, for example, Knibiehler, "Une révolution « nécessaire » : Thiers, Mignet et l'école fataliste," *Romantisme* 10 no. 28 (1980): 279–88; François Furet, *Penser la révolution française;* . . .

23. Explaining the Terror according to its exceptional circumstances had been an essential part of Thiers's attempt to overcome the fundamental conundrum facing the regime of 1830, which had also been born of a revolution. Furet argues that Thiers faced a fundamental problem: if 1789 was such a great revolution for France, and if it inaugurated what should have been a period of peace and good governance brought forth by the rule of the bourgeois elites, then why did it end in the Terror and by extension, what would prevent the regime born of 1830 from doing the same?

24. *L'histoire de la révolution* . . . , Vol. VI, 135.

25. *L'histoire de la révolution* . . . , Vol. V, 240.

26. Ibid., Vol. VI, 135.

27. Ibid., Vol. VI, 135.

28. Bernard Manin, "The Emergency Paradigm and the New Terrorism, in Sandrine Baume and Biancamaria Fontana, eds., *Les usages de la séparation des pouvoirs–The Uses of the Separation of Powers* (Paris, Michel Houdiard, 2008), 135–71. This quotation is taken from a version available on Manin's website on the internet, p. 9.

29. Jack M. Balkin and Sanford Levinson, "Constitutional Dictatorship: Its Dangers and Its Design," *Yale Law School Legal Scholarship Repository* 1, no. 1 (2010): 1804.

30. Saint Bonnet, *L'État d'exception*. Saint Bonnet provides a very insightful reading of Guizot's interpretation of the revolution of 1830 which has been essential for my understanding in this section. However, he does not discuss Thiers in his work.

31. Adolphe Thiers, *La Monarchie de 1830* (Paris: Mesnier, 1831), ii.

32. Ibid., 21–22.

33. Kohn, "Empire's Law . . ."

34. J. B. Duvergier, *Collection complète des lois, décrets, ordonnances, règlements et avis du Conseil d'État* (Paris: Guyot, 1827) vol. 19, 80.

35. Thiers wrote a series of articles on the abuses of Article 14 in *Le National* on May 2, 3, and 5. On Article 14, see Agamben, *The State of Exception*, 11–12, Saint-Bonnet, *L'État d'exception*, 31–324, Stéphane Rials, *Révolution et contre-révolution aux XIXe siècle* (Paris: DUC-Albatros, 1987), 88–125.

36. Adolphe Thiers, *La Monarchie de 1830* (Paris: Mesnier, 1831), 71.

37. Ibid., 38.

38. Ibid., 71–72.

39. Ibid., 58.

40. Ibid., 74.

41. Ibid., 78.

42. Ibid., 74–75.

43. Ibid., 55.

44. Ibid., 57–58.

45. Ibid., 83.

46. Ibid., 83.

47. Ibid., 83–84.

48. Ibid., 92.

49. Ibid., 91.

50. *Discours de Thiers*, Vol. III, 503.

51. Ibid., 503.

52. Ibid., 545.

53. Ibid., 525.

54. Ibid., III, 546.

55. *Discours de Thiers*, IV [1837], 154.

56. *Discours de Thiers*, III, 544.

57. Ibid., III, 505.

58. Ibid., III, 534.

59. Ibid., III, 535.

60. *Discours de Thiers*, IV [1837],

61. *Discours de Thiers*, IV, [1837], 128–29).

62. *Discours de Thiers*, VIII, 393.

63. "Above all, the crystallization of this 'Napoleonic liberalism' reflected the emergence of a new and powerful constellation of intellectual forces in France during the 1860s and 1870s, a loose coalition that would hold together—under the political leadership of Thiers and Léon Gambetta—to create the Third Republic, a regime which would unhesitatingly retain Napoleon's administrative and territorial organization." Sudhir Hazareesingh, *The Legend of Napoleon* (London: Granta, 2004), 182–83.

64. Adolphe Thiers, *Histoire du Consulat et de l'Empire*, vol. 1, 20.

65. Ibid., vol. 1.

66. Ibid., vol. 1.

67. Ibid., vol. 12, 639.

68. Ibid., vol. 16, 438.

69. *Discours de Thiers*, VIII, 194.

70. *Correspondance, Occupation et libération du territoire*, 379.

71. *Histoire du Consulat . . .* , vol. 14, 297.

72. *Discours de Thiers*, IX, 367.

73. Ibid., 365.

74. *Discours de Thiers*, XV, 684.

75. Ibid., XV, 210.

76. *Discours de Thiers*, XIII, 128.

77. Ibid., XIII, 203.

78. Ibid., XIII, 204.

79. Journal Officiel, 12 avril 1871, 525.

80. Journal Officiel, 12 avril 1871, 525.

81. *Discours de Thiers*, XIII, 283.

82. Ibid., XIII, 266.

83. Ibid., XIII, 278.

84. *Discours de Thiers*, XV, 220.

85. "Mon père, qui avait déjà passé environ sept années aux Etats Unis et qui était intimement lié avec plusieurs des hommes dont le rôle dans les crises politiques de la ait été considérable, commença à rédiger ce volume vers 1872 lorsque la IIIe République s'établissait en France. Une correspondance suivie avec M. Thiers lui avait fait songer à l'utilité qu'il y aurait peut-être à exposer au public français la théorie du pouvoir exécutif américain, à l'époque où le pouvoir présidentiel tel qu'il s'implantait chez nous allait débuter. » (Chambrun, Le pouvoir exécutif aux Etats-Unis" (Adolphe de Chambrun, *Le pouvoir exécutif aux États-Unis: Étude de droit constitutionnel* [Paris: Fontemoiing, 1873 [1896, 2nd ed.], x).

86. For a more thorough investigation of the larger transformations of public law during this period and their impact on the construction of the modern state in France and the United States, see Stephen Sawyer and William Novak, "Emancipation and the Creation of Modern Liberal States in America and France," *Journal of the Civil War Era*, 3, no. 4, December 2013: 467–500.

87. *Journal Officiel*, 12 avril 1871, 528.

88. *Discours de Thiers*, XIII, 201–2.

89. Ibid., 210.

90. "Toute tentative de sécession essayée par une partie quelconque du territoire sera éner-giquement réprimée en France, ainsi qu'elle l'a été en Amérique" (*Journal Officiel*, 14 avril1871, 566).

91. Richard Bonney, "The Apogee and Fall . . ." in *Paying for the Liberal State*, 92.

92. *Journal Officiel*, 1871/08/05 (A3,N217), 2459.

93. *Journal Officiel*, 27 juillet 1871, 2266.

94. *Journal Officiel*, 1871/08/26 (A3,N237).

95. *Journal Officiel*, 1872/02/02 (A4,N32), 750–51).

96. *Journal Officiel*, 1872/01/30 (A4,N29). Ministre des finances [PQ?]: 665).

97. *Discours de Thiers*, XIII, 149–50.

Chapter Five

1. Jenny d'Héricourt *La Femme Affranchie* (Paris: Bohné, 1860), 132.

2. Bonnie Anderson has noted that d'Héricourt was a lynchpin in the international women's movement of the 1850s.

3. This new republicanism that called upon both the liberal and socialist tradition came into its own in the second half of the nineteenth and early twentieth century before being sent into the waste bin of republican historiography as French socialism fell under the mantle of German materialism. See Vincent Peillon, *La Révolution n'est pas terminé* (Paris: Seuil, 2008).

4. It is a key argument of this chapter that Jenny d'Héricourt was one of the most original members of this tradition. This movement has enjoyed a tremendous field of intellectual and political scholarship over the last ten years. Vincent Peillon has launched a series called the "Re-publican Library" that is reediting classics of this tradition including such figures as Pierre Le-roux, Louis Blanc, Benoît Malon, as well as many others. At the same time, Monique Canto Sperber has explored these themes beginning with her book *Les règles de la liberté* and then the reader that followed on *Le Socialisme Libéral*. The recent synthesis by Serge Audier on *Le Social-isme Libéral* has also been essential to laying out the foundations of this tradition. Jean-Fabien Spitz. *Le moment républicain en France* (Paris: Gallimard [NRF], 2005), has revealed the extent to which this tradition came of age at the turn of the century in the work of Henry Michel, Al-fred Fouillée, Célestin Bouglé, and Emile Durkheim.

5. See Caroline Arni and Claudia Honegger. "The Modernity of Women." *Journal of Classi-cal Sociology* 8, no. 1 (1 février 2008): 45–65; and Caroline Arni, "'La toute-puissance de la barbe' Jenny P. d'Héricourt et les novateurs modernes," ed. Mathilde Dubesset and Florence Rochefort. *CLIO. Histoire, femmes et sociétés*, no. 13. Intellectuelles (1 avril 2001): 145–54.

6. Pierre Rosanvallon, "The Republic of Universal Suffrage," in *The Invention of the Modern Republic*, ed. Biancamaria Fontana (Cambridge: Cambridge University Press, 1994).

7. Rosanvallon, "Republic of Universal Suffrage," 192.

8. For a more detailed explanation of this process and its final resolution in the Third Re-public, see Rosanvallon, *Le sacre du citoyen. Histoire du suffrage universel en France* (Paris: Gal-limard, 2001).

9. As Alice Primi has shown, the French feminist movement in the July Monarchy was closely wedded to Saint-Simonian and other utopian ideas. Alice Primi, "Women's History (2006): 150–59; see also Michèle Riot-Sarcey, *La démocratie à l'épreuve des femmes*. Karen Offen also notes, "These 'utopian socialist' groups would be among the most significant in terms of their long-term impact on the formulation of issues and on subsequent empancipatory projects" (*European Feminisms, 1700–1950* [Stanford, CA: Stanford University Press, 2000], 99).

10. Quoted in *Women, the Family and Freedom*, 144.

11. Ibid., 145.

12. Karen Offen refers to this moment as "Birthing the 'Woman Question,'" *European Feminisms*; Michèle Riot-Sarcey suggests that 1848 was a watershed moment for revealing the tremendous development of French feminism during the July Monarchy in *La Démocratie à l'épreuve des femmes: Trois figures critiques du pouvoir, 1830–1848* (Paris: Albin Michel, 1994). Only Offen discusses Jenny d'Héricourt in this context.

13. *La Revue Sociale*, 91. This article was not written by Pierre Leroux, but by his son-in-law, Luc Desages, who wrote for the *Revue Sociale* and worked with the feminist Pauline Roland and George Sand on the local newspaper *L'éclaireur de l'Indre*.

14. Mona Ozouf, *Women's Words . . .* , 258.

15. Pierre Leroux, *D'une religion nationale*, chap. XIII, 127.

16. Letter reprinted in P. Félix Thomas, *Pierre Leroux: sa vie, son oeuvre, sa doctrine. Contribution à l'histoire des idées au XIX siècle* (F. Alcan, 1904), 113.

17. For an analysis of d'Héricourt's contribution to Cabet's newspaper see Diana M. Garno, "Gender Dilemmas: 'Equality' and 'Rights' for Icarian Women," *Utopian Studies* 6, no. 2 (December 1995).

18. In her chapter on Pierre Leroux, d'Héricourt wrote, "Pierre Leroux, l'homme le plus doux, le meilleur et le plus simple que je connaisse, écrit." (*Femme Affranchie*, 30).

19. See Michèle Riot-Sarcey, "Emancipation des femmes, 1848," *Geneses* 7 (1992): 194–200.

20. The document is reproduced in Riot-Sarcey, "Emancipation des femmes . . ."

21. *La Ragione*, n 5, p 161.

22. *Femme Affranchie (FA)*, 185.

23. "The only other former participant in 1848 who discussed the subject was Eugénie Niboyet, who was in great jeopardy as the president of the Club des Femmes. In her attempt to regain favour with the authorities, she subscribed to the prevailing version of events: in Le vrai livre des femmes, she presented the women in her entourage in 1848 as an anonymous, fanatical mass by which she was manipulated. However, brief they may be, d'Héricourt's reminders are thus precious for the 'feminists' of the next generation: they inherited in turn a terribly incomplete collective memory of the struggles, not only neglected by historians but also truncated b the protagonists themselves."(Primi, *Women's History according . . .* , 153).

24. D'Hericourt, *Woman Affranchised*, 219.

25. *FA*, I, 13.

26. Offen, "Femmes et suffrage 'universel': une comparaison transatlantique," 507.

27. *FA*, 219.

28. Bonnie S. Anderson, *Joyous Greetings: The First International Women's Movement, 1830–1860 (Oxford: Oxford University Press, 2000)*, 20.

29. Alice Primi, "Women's History according to . . . , 152.

30. J. S. Mill, in the letter he had written to Leroux, noted that the American women's movement was developing quickly. "Il existe aux États-Unis nombreux associations de femmes et d'hommes pour revendiquer les droits politiques et industriels des femmes," he explained, F. Thomas, *Pierre Leroux: sa vie, son oeuvre, sa doctrine. Contribution à l'histoire des idées au XIX siècle* (Paris: Alcan, 1904), 113.

31. "Madame Rose: A Life of Ernestine L. Rose as told to Jenny P. d'Héricourt," *Journal of Women's History* 15, no. 1 (Spring 2003): 183–201, 186.

32. "*Madame Rose: A Life of Ernestine L. Rose*," 196–97.

33. On Proudhon she noted: "What is the result of all this? Your ideas are false because the facts destroy them. How did you form them? This is worth examining. You have chosen a few remarkable men; and through a process of commodious abstraction, you have seen all men, even cretins; . . . What a strange way to reason, in truth. You have fallen into the mania of imposing rules on nature instead of studying them and you merit that apply your own ideas to you" (*FA*, 156).

34. Ibid.

35. Ibid., 197.

36. Joan Scott writes, "The answer requires reading the repetitions and conflicts of feminism as symptoms of contradictions in the political discourses that produced feminism and that it appealed to and challenged at the same time. These were the discourses of individualism, individual rights, and social obligation as used by republicans (and by some socialists) to organize the institutions of democratic citizenship."(3) Joan Wallach Scott. *Only Paradoxes to Offer: French Feminists and the Rights of Man* (Cambridge, MA: Harvard University Press, 1997), 168–69; Mona Ozouf has provided a similar argument in *Women's Words: Essays on French Singularity* (Chicago: University of Chicago Press, 1997).

37. *FA*, 175.

38. Ibid., 177.

39. Ibid., 212–13.

40. Ibid., 243.

41. Ibid., 247.

42. Ibid., 276.

43. As one of the few articles on d'Héricourt argues: "Individuality . . . does not coincide with egoism and thus does not, per se, threaten social cohesion."Arni and Honneger, "The Modernity of Women," 56.

44. *La Ragione*, n 5, p 157.

45. This position on the social individual also built on key elements of Charles Renouvier's work as described by Jean-Fabien Spitz: "L'individualisme de Renouvier récuse en effet la contrainte égalisatrice exercée par un Etat central qui est la conséquence logique de l'évolution pervertie du socialisme. . . . S'il doit y avoir égalité, ce ne peut être que celles des droits et des ressources c'est-à-dire *l'égalité compatible avec l'exercice des responsabilités personnelles*—et qui est même nécessaire à un authentique exercice de ces responsabilités—, et non pas l'égalité des situations, des conditions ou des jouissances." [Spitz, *Le Moment Républicain*, 96.]

46. *FA*, 243.

47. This vision shared a striking resemblance to the work of Durkheim some decades later. In one of the few articles on d'Héricourt's work, Arni and Honneger noted this similarity: "The very same idea operates in d'Héricourt's elaboration of what we now call the 'functional integration' of what she called 'l'organisme social' (d'Héricourt, 1860: II, 102), building on the analogy between a biological organism and society which informs her sociological fragments as well as Durkheim's sociology. From this, she derives the positive evaluation of individualization that distinguishes her from Comte: individuality does not equal egoism and makes modern society possible rather than posing a threat to its cohesion" Arni and Honneger, "The Modernity of Women," 57.

48. *FA*, 194.

49. This idea would also find itself at the heart of Durkheim's republican theory of the individual in society in the heart of the Third Republic. "Ce que critique Durkheim, c'est précisément la

thèse selon laquelle la société moderne serait caractérisée par un 'développement progressif de l'individualisme, dont l'action de l'Etat ne pourrait prévenir que pour un temps et par des procédés artificiels les effets dispersifs.' Et sa critique ne porte pas sur l'impuissance de l'Etat à contenir ces effets de dispersion mais bien sur la réalité de ces derniers: pour Durkheim, la société moderne n'est pas un agrégat mécanique de parties séparées, d'individus sans portes ni fenêtres; tout au contraire, dit-il, cette société est animée d'une vie organique interne, endogène, qui n'est pas produite par l'action extérieure de l'Etat même si l'action de ce cerveau central est nécessaire pour l'articuler et la soutenir" (Spitz, *Le Moment Républicain*, 237).

50. *FA*, 115.

51. For example, after arguing against the position of Étienne Cabet, with whom she disagreed on key points, she wrote: "we are pleased to note that though modern Communists are divided on the question of marriage, the family and morality in the relations between genders, they speak with one voice when they refer to women's liberty and equality of the sexes before the law and society."(*FA*, 22).

52. Ibid., 11.

53. Ibid., 11.

54. Ibid., 223.

55. Ibid., 123–24.

56. Ibid., 126–27.

57. Ibid., 148.

58. Ibid., 132.

59. Ibid., 145.

60. Ibid., 146.

61. Ibid., 136.

62. Ibid., 149.

63. Ibid., 162.

64. Ibid., 166.

65. Ibid., 213–14.

66. Ibid., 218.

67. Ibid., 220.

68. For just a few examples, see Elna C. Green, "From Antisuffragism to Anti-Communism: The Conservative Career of Ida M. Darden," *Journal of Southern History* 65, no. 2 (May 1999): 287–316; Susan E. Marshall, "In Defense of Separate Spheres: Class and Status Politics in the Antisuffrage Movement," *Social Forces* 65, no. 2 (December 1986): 327–51; Susan E. Marshall, "Ladies against Women: Mobilization Dilemmas of Antifeminist Movements," *Social Problems* 32, no. 4 (April 1985): 348–62; Elizabeth Gillespie McRae, "Caretakers of Southern Civilization: Georgia Women and the Anti-Suffrage Campaign, 1914–1920," *Georgia Historical Quarterly* 82, no. 4, GEORGIA WOMEN: PERSPECTIVES ON CLASS, RACE, AND ETHNICITY (Winter 1998): 801–28.

69. See David Van Reybrouck, *Contre les élections . . .*

70. *FA*, 305–6.

71. Jenny d'Héricourt, "Comparaison entre les institutions américaines et les futures institutions françaises," in Maria Deraismes, *France et progrès* (Paris: Librairie de la Société des Gens de Lettres, 1873), 437–55.

72. Deraismes, *France et progrès*, 255–56.

73. Ibid., 255.

74. Ibid., 254.

75. Ibid., 259.

76. Ibid., 254.

77. Ibid., 262.

78. Ibid., 266.

Chapter Six

1. Ralph Waldo Emerson, "Heroism," *Essays and Lectures* (New York: Library of America Edition, 1983), 380.

2. Quoted in Claude Lefort, "Préface," Edgar Quinet, *La Révolution* (Paris: Belin, 1987), 5.

3. See, in particular, François Furet, *La Gauche et la révolution au milieu du XIXe siècle: Edgar Quinet et la question du Jacobinisme 1865–1870* (Paris: Hachette, 1996). See also Mona Ozouf et François Furet, "Interprètes et historiens," *Dictionnaire Critique de la Révolution française* (Paris: Flammarion, 2007).

4. Keith Michael Baker, ed. *The French Revolution and the Creation of Modern Political Culture: The Terror*, Vol IV (Bingley: Emerald Press, 1994); Howard Brown, *Ending the French Revolution: Violence, Justice and Repression from the Terror to Napoleon* (Charlottesville: University of Virginia Press, 2006); Andrew Jainchill, *Reimagining Politics after the Terror: The Republican Origins of French Liberalism* (Ithaca, NY: Cornell University Press, 2008).

5. Patrice Gueniffey, "Violence et Terreur dans la Révolution Française," in *Histoire de la Révolution et de l'Empire* (Paris : Perrin, 2011), 159–60.

6. Gueniffey suggests that such an explanation can be easily dismissed because "en France, la Terreur a précédé les circonstances qui sont supposés l'expliquer—notamment le déclenchement de la guerre en 1792." ("Violences et Terreur . . . ," 160). Furet argues that it is doubly wrong because it takes the discourse of the Revolutionaries at face value and because it places the Terror outside of the logic of the Revolution itself. (*Interpreting the French Revolution*, trans. Elborg Forster (Cambridge: Cambridge University Press, 1981), 62). On the history of exceptional circumstances and its relationship to the French Revolution, see Giorgio Agamben's *State of Exception* (Chicago: University of Chicago Press, 2005); Bernard Manin, "The Emergency Paradigm and the New Terrorism," in Sandrine Baume and Biancamaria Fontana, eds., *Les Usages de la Séparation des Pouvoirs–The Uses of the Separation of Powers* (Paris, Michel Houdiard, 2008); Clinton Lawrence Rossiter, *Constitutional Dictatorship: Crisis Government in the Modern Democracies* (Princeton, NJ: Princeton University Press, 1948); François Saint Bonnet, *L'Etat d'exception* (Paris: PUF, 2001).

7. On Louis Blanc's reading of the Terror, see David Amar, *Lettre sur la Terreur* (2009); Benoît Charraud, *Louis Blanc, La République au service du socialisme. Droit au travail et perception démocratique de l'État*, thèse de doctorat, Université de Strasbourg III-Robert Schuman-Faculté de Droit, 2008; François Furet, *La Gauche et la révolution au milieu du XIXe siècle: Edgar Quinet et la question du Jacobinisme 1865–1870* (Paris: Hachette, 1996), and "Louis Blanc," in *Dictionnaire Critique de la Révolution Française*; Jean-François Jacouty, "Louis Blanc et la construction de l'histoire, " *Louis Blanc, un socialiste en république*, ed. F. Demier (Paris: CREAPHIS, 2005), 51–65 ; and J. F. Jacouty, "Robespierre selon Louis Blanc. Le prophète christique de la Révolution française," *Annales historiques de la Révolution française*, n 331, (janvier-mars 2003).

8. Blanc's *History of the French Revolution*, written between 1847 and 1862, and his *Letter on the Terror* written in 1866 have been among the most famous (and maligned) interpretations of

the Terror, marking as they did the "Jacobin" democratic socialist position. Historiography has made Blanc a proponent of an unstable mid-nineteenth century Jacobin French republicanism. Perhaps the most influential and canonical vision was provided by Marx himself when he opened his 18th Brumaire with: "Hegel remarks somewhere that all great world-historic facts and personages appear, so to speak, twice. He forgot to add: the first time as tragedy, the second time as farce. Caussidière for Danton, Louis Blanc for Robespierre. . . ." In his history of theories of the state in France, Henry Michel summarized Louis Blanc's theory of the state in the *Organization of Labor,* writing: "What is the state? What must it do in this system? One is tempted to respond: everything. . . . Is there some small portion or domain where individual activity can escape it? No." In this vein, François Furet offered a penetrating and cogent analysis of Blanc, arguing that Blanc's reading of the Revolution was inspired by a Catholic tradition that, while different from Buchez in fundamental ways, confirmed many of his basic ideas on the dangers of bourgeois individualism and the principle of authority. Echoing Furet, Miriam Revault d'Allones has argued that Blanc's political theory of the Revolution was incomplete, if not dangerous.

9. Lucien Jaume, *Le discours Jacobin* . . .

10. Spitz's preface to a recent reedition of some of Louis Blanc's political writings does not continue into the Second Empire. See Jean-fabien Spitz, "Louis Blanc: La république démocratique et sociale," in *Louis Blanc Textes Politiques, 1839–1882* (Paris: Editions le Bord de l'eau, 2011).

11. While early work on classical republicanism focused on the Anglo-American political context, recent historiography has since broadened its geographical reach by tracing the role of classical republican themes into the French Revolution and the early nineteenth century, particularly its role in informing the dominant currents of political thought during this period. See in particular Keith Baker, "Transformations of Classical Republicanism in Eighteenth-Century France," *Journal of Modern History* 73, no. 1 (2001): 32–53; Andrew Jainchill, *Reimagining Politics After the Terror: The Republican Origins of French Liberalism* (Ithaca, NY: Cornell University Press, 2008); Lucien Jaume, *L'individu effacé* (Paris: Fayard, 1997); Ira Katznelson and Andreas Kalyvas, *Liberal Beginnings: Making a Republic for the Moderns* (Cambridge: Cambridge University Press, 2008); John Kent Wright, *A Classical Republican in Eighteenth-Century France: The Political Thought of Mably* (Palo Alto, CA: Stanford University Press, 1997).

12. Katznelson and Kalyvas as well as Lucien Jaume have argued that liberalism had the resources within itself to overcome these limitations, while Jainchill claims that some liberals, like de Staël, Théremin, and ultimately, Constant and Tocqueville, returned to classical republicanism to recuperate a moderate dose of civic spirit.

13. From this perspective, Kent Wright's suggestion that nineteenth-century Jacobinism owed a large debt to the classical republican tradition would seem to have fallen on deaf ears. "Defeated in the short term, Jacobinism helped to effect a permanent delegitimizing of monarchism in France, and no doubt paved the way for the emergence of the decisive French contribution to *modern* republicanism, the political culture of the Third Republic"(Wright, *A Classical Republican* . . . , 209).

14. Benjamin Constant, "De la liberté des anciens comparée à celle des modernes" in Charles Louandre, ed., *Oeuvres politiques de Benjamin Constant* (Paris: Charpentier, 1874), 273.

15. This, of course, is not to suggest that Constant completely turned his back on the republican themes of democratic participation. For, as many have shown, his vision of modern liberty was influenced by key elements of republicanism—in the last formulation of his liberty of the moderns in 1819, Constant did insist that such liberal individualism could not come at the expense of democratic participation.

16. Alexis de Tocqueville, *Manuscripts*, quoted in Jainchill, *Reimagining Politics* . . . , 300.

17. Although he does not discuss Louis Blanc, on the legacy of liberal socialism see Serge Audier, *Socialisme Libéral* . . .

18. Louis Blanc, *Questions d'aujourd'hui et demain*, Vol. III (Paris: Dentu, 1874), 143.

19. Blanc, *Questions* . . . , Vol. III, 144.

20. Nondomination is the term borrowed from Philip Pettit by Jean-Fabien Spitz in his preface to the *Textes Politiques de Louis Blanc*.

21. Louis Blanc, *L'Etat et la commune* (Paris: Librairie Internationale, 1866), 7.

22. *Ibid.*, 26.

23. As Jean-Fabien Spitz argues on the normative theory of the state that came of age in the Third Republic, "any form of state legitimacy comes from the essential contribution that it brings to guarantee and defend an ideal." The similarities between Blanc's theory of the state and this characterization suggest that he was already developing one of the core principles that would later emerge within liberal republican thought of the Third Republic, especially with the jurist Henry Michel and his work on the state, as well as key ideas of Hobhouse in England and Dewey in the United States. See Jean-Fabien Spitz, *Le moment républicain en France*, chap. 2, "Le républicanisme idéaliste d'Henry Michel: la réhabilitation de l'Etat."

24. Historians have largely missed that Mill was one of the dominant influences on Blanc during his exile. Outside of their correspondence, Blanc's obituary of Mill reveals his tremendous debt to Mill. The obituary is particularly praiseworthy, "John Stuart Mill est mort. Ceux-là seuls mesureront toute l'éntendue de ce malheur à qui il fut donné de connaître personnellement John Stuart Mill, de subir la douce et fortifiante influence de son amitié, de l'entendre, de le voir agir; et c'est bien en vain qu'à ceux-là, pour adoucir l'amertume de leur douleur, on dirait: il est mort, mais ses livres vivent; un grand flambeau vient de s'éteindre, mais non sans avoir allumé sur son passage des milliers d'autres flambeaux qui ne s'éteindront à leur tour qu'après avoir communiqué de proche en proche ce qu'ils avaient reçu de chaleur et de lumière!" ("John Stuart Mill," *Questions d'aujourd'hui et demain*, Vol. III, 329).

25. "I feel an entireness of sympathy with the [the Provisional Government]," he wrote, "which I never expected to have with any government. . . . I also sympathize very strongly with such socialists as Louis, who seems to be sincere, enthusiastic, straightforward, and with a great foundation of good sense and good feeling, though precipitate and *raw* in his practical views." Letter to John Pringle Nichol, 30 septembre 1848, quoted in Fabrice Bensimon, "Louis Blanc en Angleterre," *Louis Blanc Socialiste en République*, note 14.

26. "While rejecting the tyranny of society over the individual, they [Mill and his wife, Harriet Taylor] projected a new social state that would no longer be 'divided' between 'the leisure and industrial classes' and that would resolve the social problem of the future: uniting the greatest degree of individual action to the common property of primary resources on the planet' and the 'equal participation of all from the profits associated with work." (Serge Audier, *Le socialisme libéral* [Paris: La Découverte, 2006], 9).

27. Audier, *Le socialisme libéral*, 9.

28. Mill's correspondence is filled with letters to Louis Blanc inviting him to dinner or engaging in intellectual debate. There are at least nineteen letters addressed to Louis Blanc personally and many others that discuss his works or recommend him to others. See *The Collected Works of John Stuart Mill, Volume XVI—The Later Letters of John Stuart Mill 1849–1873*, ed. Francis E. Mineka and Dwight N. Lindley (Toronto: University of Toronto Press; London: Routledge & Kegan Paul, 1972).

29. The book consists of four chapters: L'Etat (written in septembre 1865), La Commune (octobre 1840), La Commune.–Ce qu'elle est (1840), La Commune.–Ce qu'elle devrait être (1840). Published as *L'État et la Commune* (Paris: Librairie Internationale, 1866).

30. *Ibid.*, 7.

31. *Ibid.*, 10.

32. *Ibid.*, 12–13.

33. *Ibid.*, 7.

34. Louis Blanc, *Lettre sur la Terreur* (Paris: Editions Manucius, 2010), 46.

35. *Lettre sur la Terreur*, 63.

36. Edgar Quinet, *La révolution* (Paris: Lacroix, 1865), Vol. II, 195.

37. *Le temps*, 6 janvier 1866, reprinted in Furet, *La Gauche et la révolution française . . .* , 200.

38. *Lettre sur la Terreur*, 53.

39. Ibid., 46.

40. Ibid., 51.

41. Ibid., 35.

42. Ibid., 60 [italics in original].

43. Blanc and Carlyle corresponded regularly, especially before 1850 when Carlyle's racist politics no doubt soured their relationship. Carlyle invited Blanc to his house on several occasions. "Can you come and eat a mutton-chop with us, tomorrow at 5 o'clock. There is literally nothing but that, or something equivalent; and the common sight of ourselves; and the uncommon one of that beautiful *Gamin* [Louis Blanc] who is to eat his little dinner with us on that occasion! Come if you have no other engagement"(Carlyle to Richard Monckton Milnes; February 10, 1849; DOI: 10.1215/lt-18490210-TC-RMM-01; *CL* 23: 230) "Robertson who has again appeared on our horizon—is to bring Louis Blanc to tea here on Friday night." (JWC TO JEANNIE WELSH; Louis Blanc January 29, 1849; DOI: 10.1215/lt-18490129-JWC-JW-01; *CL* 23: 209– 13). He also notes having left a card for Louis Blanc on at least one occasion, TC TO LADY ASHBURTON; February 21, 1852; DOI: 10.1215/lt-18520221-TC-LA-01; *CL* 27: 50. He also noted having read his works, "Of late days, I have been reading some of the Books these new Parisian *Kings* had written, which I should not have read otherwise: Louis Blanc, for one, I find to be a truly convinced and sincere man . . ." (TC TO MARGARET A. CARLYLE ; March 22, 1848; DOI: 10.1215/lt-18480322-TC-MAC-01; *CL* 22: 274–76). It should be noted that he is reading Blanc at the same time that he is organizing Emerson's 1848 visit to Paris and London.

I have not found direct evidence that Blanc was citing Emerson by employing the term *representative man*, but indirect evidence suggests that it is highly probable. First, Emerson gave the Representative Men lectures throughout his trip to Europe in 1848 when he visited both Paris and London. In fact, he gave the lectures in Paris while Blanc was still there and then again in London after Blanc's arrival there. Considering that Emerson gave the lectures on a number of occasions and frequented the intellectual circles in which Blanc circulated, it seems highly likely that Blanc heard the lectures, and almost impossible to imagine that he was not aware that they were happening and what they were about. This is even more the case since the lectures generated quite a media stir and Blanc was an avid reader of the press. On Emerson's trip to Europe, see Daniel Koch, *Ralph Waldo Emerson in Europe: Class, Race and Revolution in the Making of an American Thinker* (London: I. B. Tauris, 2012), especially chap. 4, "London and Paris." Finally, Blanc and Carlyle knew each other very well, as their correspondence suggests, and it was Carlyle who organized Emerson's second visit to England in 1848 and helped Emerson find a publisher in England. Carlyle was also responsible for the publication of Emerson's works in England. His first edition of the Essays was published in 1841 with a preface by Carlyle himself. Their correspondence makes clear that Carlyle was actively pushing the ideas of Emerson within the English and European intellectual circles. "My second piece of news, not less interesting I hope, is that Emerson's Essays, the Book so called, is to be reprinted here; . . . 'Write you a Preface,' said he, 'and I will reprint it';—to which, after due delay and meditation; I consented" (LXVI. Carlyle to Emerson Chelsea, London, June 25, 1841). Carlyle also circulated both Blanc's writings and Emerson's writings among his friends. See for example his letters "There is a new small Book of Emerson's, which I meant to send you; but Jane unexpectedly began reading it,—she gets along very slowly. It will keep for your behoof, and be pleasant reading for you some day or other."(TC TO LADY ASHBURTON ; January 18, 1850; DOI: 10.1215/lt-18500118-TC-LA-01; *CL* 25: 3–5). "I send her Louis Blanc's little Book" (TC TO JANE WELSH CARLYLE; April 4, 1849; DOI: 10.1215/lt-18490404-TC-JWC-01; *CL* 24: 11–12). Moreover, it is well known that Emerson developed a fascination with French socialism. And, to conclude this long note, it is worth pointing out that this fascination has been a source of some confusion for some of Emerson's liberal admirers. Sacvan Bercovitch for example suggests that Emerson's interest in French socialism actually marks a turn toward his "conservative" later writings because he interprets this moment necessarily as a turn away from Emerson's radical liberalism. In so doing, he misses the fundamental fact that individualism and socialism were not opposed in most of the writings of the French socialists, especially those of Pierre Leroux and, as we have seen, Louis Blanc, not to mention John S. Mill (see *Rites of Assent*, 318).

44. Thomas Carlyle, *La Révolution Française*, trans. Elias Regnault (Paris: Germer Baillière, 1865). It was later reedited by Alphonse Aulard.

45. Ibid., Vol. I, xv.

46. Ibid., xvi-xvii.

47. "Une histoire de la Révolution du point de vue socialiste, manquait auparavant, et il en rejaillit mille lumières nouvelles." (August 25. 1863), *The Collected Works of John Stuart Mill, Volume XVI—The Later Letters of John Stuart Mill 1849–1873*, ed. Francis E. Mineka and Dwight N. Lindley (Toronto: University of Toronto Press, London: Routledge & Kegan Paul, 1972).

48. T. Carlyle, *On Heroes, Hero-Worship, and the Heroic in History* (New Haven, CT: Yale University Press, 2013), 163.

49. Ralph Waldo Emerson, "Representative Men," in *Essays and Lectures* (New York: Library of America Edition, 1983), 728.

50. Ibid., 729.

51. Shklar suggests that this was the tension at the heart of Emerson's theory. "The great person serves them. And that service is described in the language of democratic politics. The way out of the tension between the sense of the apartness of the great and the claims of humanity was, as in constitutional states, to resort to representation. It is the only way out of the seesaw between anarchy and oppression. Nothing could illustrate more vividly the hold that democratic norms had on Emerson's intellectual imagination." Shklar, "Emerson and the Inhibitions of Democracy," *Political Theory* 18, no. 4: 601–14 (1990): 607.

52. *Lettre sur la Terreur*, 60.

53. Sudhir Hazareesingh has argued that an important part of republicans' apology for Robespierre was their "philo-napoléonisme républicain." (Sudhir Hazareesingh and Karma Nabulsi, *Entre Robespierre et Napoléon: les paradoxes de la mémoire républicaine sous la monarchie de Juillet*. Annales, HSS, septembre-octobre 2010, n 5, 1225–1247.)

54. Leo Loubère, "Louis Blanc's Theory of History," *Journal of the History of Ideas* 17, no. 1 (January 1956): 70–88, 87.

55. Carlyle, *On Heroes, Hero-Worship, and the Heroic in History*, 162.

56. Carlyle writes, "The French Revolution, or third act, we may well call the final one; for lower than that savage Sansculottism men cannot go. They stand there on *the nakedest haggard Fact*, undeniable in all seasons and circumstances; and may and must begin again confidently to build up from that." Carlyle, *On Heroes, Hero-Worship, and the Heroic in History*, 191.

57. Blanc, *L'État et la Commune . . . ,* 7.

58. Blanc, "Préface de 1868," *L'Histoire de la Révolution Française* (Paris: Pagnerre, 1870), xxv.

59. Ibid., xxvi.

60. Bernard Manin, "The Emergency Paradigm and the New Terrorism,", in Sandrine Baume and Biancamaria Fontana, eds., *Les Usages de la Séparation des Pouvoirs–The Uses of the Separation of Powers* (Paris, Michel Houdiard, 2008), 135–71. This quotation is taken from a version available on Manin's website on the internet, 9.

61. *Lettre sur la Terreur*, 51.

62. Manin, "Emergency Paradigm," 11.

63. *Lettre sur la Terreur*, 64.

64. R. W. Kostal, *A Jurisprudence of Power: Victorian Empire and the Rule of Law* (New York: Oxford University Press, 2005), 209.

65. Ibid., 207.

66. John Witt, "Anglo-American Empire . . ." and Kostal, *A Jurisprudence of Power*.

67. Catherine Hall, "The Economy of Intellectual Prestige: Thomas Carlyle, John Stuart Mill and the Case of Governor Eyre," *Cultural Critique*, no. 12, Discursive Strategies and the Economy of Prestige (Spring 1989): 167–96, 168.

68. From Mill to Blanc, Saint Véran, Avignon le 2 Décembre 1865. John Stuart Mill, The Collected Works of John Stuart Mill, Volume XVI—The Later Letters of John Stuart Mill 1849–1873 Part III, ed. Francis E. Mineka and Dwight N. Lindley (Toronto: University of Toronto Press; London: Routledge & Kegan Paul, 1972). June 10, 2017. http://oll.libertyfund.org/titles/253 #Mill_0223-16_560.

69. Blanc, *Histoire de la Révolution Française* (Paris: Librairie Internationale, 1869), vol. 2, 632n5.

70. *Sydney Morning Herald* (NSW: 1842—1954), Thursday, January 25, 1866, 3.

71. Ibid.

72. *Lettre sur la Terreur*, 42.

73. December 2, 1865. *The Complete Correspondence. . . .*

74. Witt, "Anglo-American Empire . . . ," 783.

75. Blanc, *Histoire de la Révolution Française* (Paris: Librairie Internationale, 1869), Vol. 2, 632.

76. Ibid., 632.

77. Louis Fréron along with Paul Barras led the repression and took over in place of the revolutionary tribunal judging those who led the revolt.

78. Blanc, *Histoire de la Révolution Française* (Paris: Librairie Internationale, 1869), 2:633.

79. Indeed, Regnault's translation of Carlyle had also suggested that the fact that the book had described the Terror without prejudice was one of its greatest strengths: "c'est surtout dans cette œuvre que se remarque l'absence de tout préjugé Britannique, nous ajouterons même, de tout préjugé historique."

80. Claude Lefort, "Les droits de l'homme et l'État-providence," *Essais sur le politique, XIXe-XXe siècles* (Paris: Seuil, 1986), 57.

81. *Journal Officiel de la République. Lois et décrets*, March 9, 1871, 1.

82. *Enquête parlementaire sur l'insurrection du 18 mars*, 4–5.

83. Louis Blanc, *Histoire de la constitution du 25 février 1875* (Paris: Charpentier, 1882), 80.

84. Ibid., 81.

85. Ibid., 96.

86. Ibid., 6.

Conclusion

1. Henry Michel, *L'idée de l'État en France*, 663.

2. Alexis de Tocqueville, [Définition de la démocratie], "Écrits et Discours Politiques," *Oeuvres completes*, vol. 3 (Paris: Gallimard, 1990), 196.

3. On these tensions between liberalism and republicanism in late twentieth-century France, see Emile Chabal, *A Divided Republic: Nation, State and Citizenship in Contemporary France* (Cambridge: Cambridge University Press, 2015).

4. On this point, see Andrew Jainchill, *Reimagining Politics after the Terror . . .* , 298.

5. Philip Pettit, *Republicanism: A Theory of Freedom and Government* (Oxford: Oxford University Press, 1999), vii.

6. Pierre Rosanvallon has highlighted this point in his claim that "the classical contrast between the individual and the collective no longer makes sense." In *The New Social Question: Rethinking the Welfare State* (Princeton, NJ: Princeton University Press, 2000), 107.

7. Chantal Mouffe, *Hegemony, Radical Democracy, and the Political*, ed. James Martin (Routledge, 2013), 172.

Index